Daily Offerings

Inspiration for Faith & Life

LEON BLODER

WESTBOW
PRESS®
A DIVISION OF THOMAS NELSON
& ZONDERVAN

WestBow Press books may be ordered through booksellers or by contacting:

WestBow Press
A Division of Thomas Nelson & Zondervan
1663 Liberty Drive
Bloomington, IN 47403
www.westbowpress.com
844-714-3454

ISBN: 978-1-6642-4313-2 (sc)
ISBN: 978-1-6642-4312-5 (e)

Print information available on the last page.

WestBow Press rev. date: 09/23/2021

Contents

Introduction

In the fall of 2015, I finally decided to listen to my wife, who had been exhorting me for some time to begin writing a daily devotional, and I then began emailing roughly a hundred or so subscribers.

What I had thought would be an exercise that would last through Christmas ended up becoming a daily practice that I've maintained for the last five years. So I'll say it here for all of posterity—my wife was right.

The subscriber list grew and grew, and before I knew it there were roughly a thousand or more people reading my devotions each day through email, social media, and my blog.

My wife wasn't the only one who was encouraging me, mind you, but she had the idea first, and it was ultimately at her urging that I decided to undertake it. And then, some years later, she suggested that I might want to put some of these together and create a book.

Writing a daily devotion pretty much every weekday for five years running has not always been easy, but it has been one of the most vital disciplines I've ever embraced.

These inspirational readings are compiled from all of those years of daily offerings. They are reflections on issues of life and faith, and they also contain my opinions, hunches and reflections on the lessons I'm learning on my journey as a pastor and follower of Jesus.

I hope that this devotional guide will inspire you, challenge you and maybe even get you to dig deeper, ask more questions, buy some of the books that are referenced, or simply give you some tools to grow in your faith and discover more about your best and truest self.

Now, may the grace and peace of our Lord Jesus Christ be with you now and always. Amen.

December 28, 2020
Austin, Texas

God Doesn't Waste Anything

The book is called Opportunity it's first chapter is New Year's Day.
—Edith Lovejoy Pierce

Several years ago, I saw a billboard for an attorney's office that extolled the virtues of bankruptcy at the onset of a new year. It displayed a huge photo of a video game console and posed the following question below the photo in large letters: "Don't you wish life had a reset button? It does."

On the surface, it seems like a pretty good idea. What if, when things started to go poorly, you could just push the reset button on life, like on a video game?

What if all of our mistakes, missteps, and misdeeds were actually part of our journey? What if all of the things we wish we could undo, reset, or do over were absolutely essential in making us the people we are today and shaping us into the people who God dreams for us to become?

A very wise pastor once told me something that changed my life. I told him that I wished I hadn't wasted so many years before figuring out what I was supposed to do with my life. "If I'd only got started sooner," I said. "I wasted so much time, so many years doing worthless things."

He laughed and said a knowing smile, "God doesn't waste anything. He knew you weren't ready for what he had in store. He also knew you needed some shaping and molding before you would be." He went on to say that all of the experiences I'd had—even the bad ones—had prepared my heart, my character, and my spirit for the path God had for me.

I think the *idea* of a life-reset button is appealing, but we often mistake the idea of resetting life with the concept of getting a second chance. None of the things that we've done or even the things that have been done to us were wasted. All of life's challenges, triumphs, mistakes, and choices have helped shape us and prepare us for the path ahead.

God can take even the worst things that have happened in our lives and redeem them for his glory. God, as it turns out, is still in the resurrection business—raising to new life what we would consider dead and gone. Life doesn't have a reset button. But we do have a God who loves to dole out second chances to his beloved children.

May you embrace the great opportunity of this new year before you. May you find true joy in the knowledge that God doesn't waste anything in making you into the person you are becoming. May you take your second chance and run with it.

Unconditional Hospitality

I watched from the chancel platform as the visitors to my church made their way into the sanctuary and down the aisle, looking for a pew where they could sit down. The organist was playing a prelude, and I was sitting in my "throne chair," as I not-so-affectionately called it, with the choir to my left as we awaited the start of the service.

It was their first time visiting our small church. They were a young couple, appearing to be barely in their early thirties—a rarity in our aging congregation. They found a pew and sat down. I smiled in their general direction, hoping they could get a glimpse of it.

Just then, I saw one of our long-time members enter the sanctuary. She too began to make her way down the aisle, and I realized in a flash that the pew where our visitors had decided to sit was her regular pew, and they were sitting smack-dab in her regular seat. She realized the same thing in almost the same moment, and her face became wooden.

I wanted to stand up and say something or maybe rush down to intervene. It was like watching a train wreck about to happen and being powerless to stop it. Sure enough, the church member said something to the young couple that I couldn't hear, and their faces flushed with embarrassment. They slid farther down the pew to make room as my church member settled into her regular spot with a slightly triumphant look on her face.

The young couple never came back. I don't blame them. I wouldn't have either. The worst part is, I thought our church had outgrown that kind of behavior, that I had done a better job of teaching our folks to be warm and welcoming, open and flexible. The fact of the matter is, most of us would rather choose our own comfort over hospitality—myself included.

How do we learn, as Christians, to practice what Pastor Joel Osteen calls "unconditional hospitality"? I think we have to look to Jesus's example to see how he handled people outside his circle of friends and family.

Jesus welcomed everyone, in spite of their differences. He didn't care if you were a child, a tax collector, a prostitute, or even a Roman. Jesus's arms were always open. The only harsh words Jesus had were for the people who were overly religious, uptight, and unwelcoming to those who were different from them.

So may you live this day as Jesus would—filled with unconditional hospitality for all those strangers God may send across your path. May your arms be open wide to receive those who may be seeking grace but have no idea where to find it. Show them Jesus, and let them know they are welcome.

Get Up, Tabitha

Do not act out of selfish ambition or conceit, but with humility
think of others as being better than yourselves.
—Philippians 2:3 (NIV)

One of the distinguishing marks of the true church is when followers of Jesus put the needs of others ahead of their own. One act of sacrificial kindness and grace has more power to draw people to Jesus than anything we might say and infinitely more power than any of our doctrines, dogmas, or traditions. I have seen the hardest hearts melt when faced with the humility of a Jesus-follower who simply served and loved with no strings attached.

There is an incredibly endearing story in the ninth chapter of the book of Acts that gets buried in all of the other big, epic accounts of the apostles doing grand things. Peter is traveling to the coastal regions of what is now modern Israel to a town called Joppa. When he gets there, he finds that one of the great saints of the small Christian community there has died—a lady named Tabitha.

The text reads that Tabitha was known for "always doing good and helping the poor" (Acts 9:36 NIV). When Peter arrives at the house where her body has been laid, he finds a bunch of her friends who are mourning her loss. Through their tears, they show him clothes and robes that Tabitha had made for them.

The story ends well, of course. Peter goes in to Tabitha and tells her to get up, as you would if you were an apostle who walked with Jesus and who saw people raised from the dead. (Can I get witness?)

The thing I love about this story (aside from the miracle, of course) is the way the writer of Acts goes on and on about what a selfless, humble person Tabitha was. She was a simple person, living in the background of epic events in those heady days of the early church. But her story was preserved to give hope to countless Christians throughout the centuries.

And what was the central message of this story? What was it that gave those who heard it such incredible joy and hope for the future—despite persecution, despite imprisonment and even death? Simply this: When Christians act with selflessness, sacrificial kindness, and humility, it offers the world a glimpse at what eternal life is like.

Anxiety Is the Dizziness of Freedom

I struggle with acute anxiety occasionally—just enough for me to understand a little of what it's like for people who feel anxious all the time. It's not fun.

If you have never suffered from acute anxiety, you may not know what it feels like. It can take the form of tightness in your chest, accompanied by an overwhelming desire to run, or scream, or both.

Sometimes, it hits you so hard it feels like you can't breathe. Or it will take the form of a sinking feeling of dread that you can't shake, no matter how hard you try. It can also fling you into a rage if you have an aversion to tears, or it can send you on a crying jag if you are afraid of your anger.

The other day, I read the following quote by the philosopher Soren Kierkegaard that helped me reframe my anxiety and begin to think of it differently. He said, "Anxiety is the dizziness of freedom." Kierkegaard believed that life without anxiety was a life without any possibility.

The reason we have anxiety is that we are filled with possibility, imbued with choices. Some of us feel the "dizziness" of that more intensely, but we all share it to some extent.

There's something liberating in embracing this hard and important truth.

What we do with this knowledge, however, is crucial. We can allow anxiety to debilitate us, paralyze us, or drive us to self-destructive action, or we can do something different.

The apostle Paul wrote this to the church at Philippi:

> Be anxious for nothing, but in everything by prayer and supplication, with thanksgiving, let your requests be made known to God; and the peace of God, which surpasses all understanding, will guard your hearts and minds through Christ Jesus. (Philippians 4:6–7 NIV)

This is something more than simply thinking you can pray your worries away. What I'm talking about is a surrendering that comes with truly bringing all your junk and your whole self, anxiety and all, to God.

When you are able to let go of your attachments to the things that bring you anxiety; when you are able to show grace to yourself in the midst of your frailty; when you surrender the outcomes to God, you will begin to know "the peace of God, which surpasses all understanding" (Philippians 4:7 ESV).

Learning to Read the Bible Differently

The other night I taught the first of a seven-week Bible study class that I've been really excited to teach. At one point in the class, I was just reading and teaching from the text, and there was a great energy in the room that you could absolutely feel.

And I thought, *I'm sitting here on a wooden stool in a classroom, teaching from a several-thousand-years-old passage of Hebrew scripture, and everyone is engaged, and the energy is crackling—and I am about to come out of my skin with joy!*

Who knew the Bible could still be so exciting?

Despite all of the energy that we felt in that moment, though, I am constantly reminded of what an uphill climb it is to try to talk about the Bible to people.

And the reason for this is because of the way the Bible is constantly misrepresented by people who claim to hold it in such high esteem.

You see, far too many terrible conversations that exclude, diminish, discriminate, belittle, and shame begin with the words, "The Bible says."

And to people who either don't have any background with the Bible or who have been abused by those who have used the Bible as a weapon, the beauty, energy, and inspiration of the Bible gets lost in a haze of poor impressions, misinformation and, to put it bluntly, "bibliolatry."

We need new ways to read and talk about the Bible. We need to see it in all of its mystery as the unfolding story of God's loving, redeeming relationship with humankind and all of creation.

May you open your Bible today and read it with this in mind. May you find inspiration and joy as you unfold the story of how God is saving the world.

Creation as the First Testament

The great Lebanese poet Khalil Gibran penned a short parable once about two men engaged in a debate over the oneness of things.

In order to make his point that all things in creation are connected, the older and wiser of the two asked his companion to pick up a stone that was at his feet, and then said to him, "All things live and glow in the knowledge of the day and the majesty of the night. You and the stone are one. There is a difference only in heartbeats."

When I read that, it resonated with me so much. The idea of stone having a heartbeat—that there is a mysterious and wonderful kind of energy and life in all of creation—all of it just left me humming with reverence.

And because I'm a nerd about these things, all kinds of Bible passages went through my head.

Like the moment when religious leaders told Jesus to tell his followers to stop praising God on Palm Sunday: "I tell you … if they keep quiet, the stones will cry out" (Luke 19:40 NIV).

Or when the writer of John's Gospel declared that "through [Christ] all things were created … there is nothing created that wasn't created through [Christ]" (John 1:3 NIV). Or when Paul wrote, "He is before all things, and in him, all things hold together" (Colossians 1:17 NIV).

It all makes sense when you pause for a moment and consider not only what you feel and experience in creation but what you also discover in the biblical witness.

The Franciscans refer to creation as the "First Testament" with good reason. And when you begin to read the Bible with that as a lens, it opens up the text in amazing ways.

So go outside today. Breathe in the air, pay attention to your surroundings, and consider the stones at your feet.

Pause and give thanks that you are one with all that you see, united through the power of the Holy Spirit in Christ, who is in all things, and through whom all things are made possible, even your own redemption and rescue.

Learning Humility the (Usual) Hard Way

As the twig is bent, the tree inclines.
—Virgil

One of the most difficult lessons to learn on the Way of Jesus is the lesson of humility. It's difficult most of all because of how most of us are forced to learn it.

Typically, we don't learn humility because of a revelation we have over a cup of coffee on some random Tuesday morning as we are checking email, getting kids ready for school, or planning our days.

It's not like it comes to us like a flash: "Oh! I really could benefit from being more humble!" Unfortunately, almost all of us learn humility by being humbled.

It's the moment when we fall flat on our faces when we were so certain of our footing, so confident in our abilities, so reliant on our talents.

But if we are being honest, the thing that hurts the most about those humbling moments is the fact that we weren't actually all that certain or confident, and we'd buried those feelings deep down inside, afraid to admit the truth.

And we can go in a couple of different directions at that point. We can internalize all of that and begin to believe that we are not capable, are not good enough, and are worthless and weak.

Or we can put up our armor and refuse to admit our part in it. We can shift the blame to others and become angry, belligerent, and recalcitrant. We can pretend.

May you allow yourself to embrace humility, even if it comes in your most broken moments. May you discover a new sense of yourself that is grounded in God's loving way of seeing you.

Into the Flow

Many years ago, I had a conversation with a pastor acquaintance about his personal mission statement. I know—I have riveting conversations.

He told me that he believed his ultimate purpose was "to know and do the will of God." Then he said something like, "It's just that simple."

As I recall, I pointed out that his stated purpose was a lot more complicated than he imagined because it was all predicated on the ludicrous notion that a person would be able to know the mind and will of God.

"The best you can do is guess at it, right?" I asked him. "And what if you guess wrong?" And then—because I've always struggled to understand this—I added, "Or what if you *think* you believe something to be God's will, but it's actually yours?"

The guy had no good answers for me. He grew flustered and blurted out, "If you are maintaining your Christian walk and doing everything to stay in the Word, you'll be able to discern what God's will is!" (*Translation*: If you don't drink, smoke, swear, lust, or become a backslidden Presbyterian—whoops—and you read your Bible every single day, you'll be holy enough to know and do God's will.)

What I've come to understand since that conversation all those years ago is that knowing and doing the will of God is not some sort of puzzle to put together or a mystery to be solved.

The best way I can describe it is this: the "will of God" is a flow. It's like a river, and we are all in it. And if we choose, we can be moved along by the current in this flow, which is gentle enough but firm and purposeful.

Or we can try to fight it by swimming upstream, flailing around, and refusing to drift. Or (and this is the option that most of us take) we can try to change the current through our own efforts because we want the river to flow the way we want it to.

May you find the peace to let go, and let the ever-flowing current of God carry you closer and closer to God's ultimate will. May you discover new levels of trust that God will lead you where God desires for you to go.

Bare Your Soul; Share Your Truth

"My faith is personal. I don't need to talk about it in public."

I've heard that phrase—or something like it—dozens of times over the course of the last twenty years of ministry.

I get it. Sometimes I wish that the judgy, churchy people who are always going on and on about their faith in public would keep their ideas to themselves.

I'm sure that same desire causes a lot of people to decide to keep their life of faith private and girded against critique and controversy. But when we choose the path of least resistance, we often miss out on opportunities to speak grace and peace and life into the universe.

And in case you haven't been paying attention, the universe needs some grace, peace, and life right about now. To put it quite simply, if those of us who have that kind of message to share keep quiet, people will listen to whoever is talking.

And no one wants that. Trust me.

It's hard to put yourself out there. I get that too. It's hard to know exactly what to say and what to share. It's hard to know how it will be received. But if we are going to change the world by speaking life into it, we need to be willing to risk it.

I read an amazing line from poet Billy Collins's poem "Aimless Love" the other day, and I've been thinking about it ever since. It speaks of the feeling that comes when you bare your soul and share your story in spite of your fear:

"But my heart is always propped up in a field on its tripod—ready for the next arrow."

If we are to be true and faithful witnesses to the miracle of Christ that is springing up within us and around us, we can no longer be afraid to share our truth in love.

The world needs to hear that there is a better way. Let's tell them that there is.

I Am Whatever I Believe You to Be

I am whatever I believe you to be.
—Byron Katie

When I read the above quote from Byron Katie, the esteemed author and spiritual director, I didn't know what to make of it at first.

And then, the other day it occurred to me that I knew *exactly* what it meant.

You see, I spent a lot of years in my early days of church ministry worrying over whether I had the right theology and was believing the right things.

My concerns soon extended to the world around me, and I began to view people as either right or wrong, for me or against me, inside or outside.

My worldview became narrowed by this dualistic way of thinking, and I found myself growing arrogant and overconfident in my certainty. And then, my certainty had the rug pulled out from under it.

It took a crisis of faith and a long journey back to myself to discover that my judgments of others, my long diatribes against those who didn't believe the "right" things, were merely projections of my own doubts.

What I've come to understand more fully (though not yet completely) is that when we set aside our need to be right, when we embrace a nondualistic way of seeing the world and others, we open up ourselves to love.

And Christians need to hear this good news now more than ever.

In his most recent book, *Unraptured*, author Zack Hunt writes, "American Christianity doesn't just suffer from bad theology. It's lacking in love."

It doesn't have to be this way. You and I can change this. It begins by simply letting go of our either/or dualistic thinking and the comfort of our certainty as we embrace unknowing and surrender the outcomes to God.

And it also means worrying less about whether someone is getting it right when it comes to faith and worrying more about loving them where they are.

May you discover the peace that grows when you learn to surrender.

Walking Away from a Transactional God

When I was a kid, I heard the same awful sermon virtually every Sunday. I heard it from different preachers in different churches, but it was always the same.

You see, I grew up Fundamentalist Baptist. If you don't know what that means, think about being a Christian but with absolutely 0 percent joy and 175 percent more guilt and shame. Oh, and a constant fear that you might burn in hell for all eternity.

When I was an older teenager, I found myself wondering about the people sitting in pews around me. Some of them seemed like nice people. They were sincere and kind, and a few of them even seemed to be a bit joyful.

And so I would look at them and silently ask, "Why are you here? Why do you sit there and take it while this preacher reduces the Christian faith to a quid pro quo kind of thing, where you have to work your butt off to show that you are worthy of God's love and grace?"

What I didn't realize was the reason I was asking those questions and worrying over the answers so intently was that I was afraid the preachers were right, and I was wrong.

What they preached made a twisted kind of sense, based on the way the world seems to work. They preached that God is a transactional god, and the only way to truly receive God's grace is to do enough to earn it.

I finally decided the only way I was ever going to be free from that transactional god was to give up on Christianity altogether. And so I did—for years. Eventually, I discovered there are other ways to be Christian that are more life-giving and full of meritless grace, and I found my way back to faith.

However, my experiences imbued me with a great deal of empathy for the many people who walk away for the same reasons and never return.

Father Richard Rohr had an amazing insight into why we often chose to believe in a transactional kind of grace/merit when God has simply offered us grace without the merit. He writes:

> The ego clearly prefers an economy of merit, where we can divide the world into winners and losers, to an economy of grace, where merit or worthiness loses all meaning.

As Christians, we need to walk away from a Christianity that divides the world into winners and losers, based on whether they can earn God's favor. We need to share the good news that Jesus is for all of us, not just a few of us.

May you find the joy that comes from living into this kind of eternal life.

Fight Like the Third Monkey

I was really in need of some inspiration this morning.

My headspace wasn't the greatest, mostly filled with thoughts about how I'm not being all that I should be, and my upcoming sermon isn't very good, and I had no idea what to write for today's devo—and I'm wishing I'd done a better job on a handful of tasks.

I do that to myself more often than I'd like to admit. I hide that stuff pretty well, though. Most of us do.

Right about the time when I was about to throw up my hands, I came across a graphic that a friend had posted on social media. It had this quote, which made me chuckle, then grin, then laugh out loud.

It was exactly what I needed to see. And so I'll share it with you: "Fight like you are the third monkey on the ramp to Noah's ark, and brother, it's beginning to rain."

Come on! You know that's fantastic. And now that you have this quote in your arsenal, you will never be the same again. Because *that* is the only way to fight.

All of this got me thinking about an exhortation that the apostle Paul gave to one of the churches he planted, using his own life as an example.

Paul felt less-than. He knew he had a terrible past; he struggled to get along with people sometimes; he second-guessed himself more than once. But then he says this:

I am the least of the messengers, and indeed I do not deserve that title at all, because I persecuted the Church of God. But what I am now I am by the grace of God. The grace he gave me has not proved a barren gift. I have worked harder than any of the others – and yet it was not I but this same grace of God within me. (1 Corinthians 15:9–10 MSG)

Paul knew that what God had called him to do was worth the struggle. It was worth whatever it might cost him. And he fought like that third monkey on the ramp, my friends.

Author and theologian Joan Chittister puts it like this:

When we refuse to give up, when we go on trying—whatever the odds against success—something new is born in us. Instead of a sense of failure, the very matter of trying recreates our sense of purpose, our sense of commitment, the perpetuity of the dream.

May you refuse to give up doing good today and every day. May you defy the odds against you and keep fighting for what matters.

It Takes a Poet

How do you talk about God? Do you ever really think about it?

For most of us, our conversations about God are pretty short and sweet, or they are reserved for the life sphere we've dedicated to church or churchy activities, which is just one among many of our life spheres of influence.

Put all that aside for a moment. If you were to actually talk about God, what kind of language would you use?

Chances are, you'd borrow from the words you've heard or read in scripture. You'd use phrases you'd heard in hymns or praise songs. Or you would come up with something on your own, something that reflects your experience of God in the world or in your life.

We try to capture the essence of God with our words, but our attempts always fall short. Think about it. How do you speak of the unspeakable? How do you describe what is beyond description?

Here is how you will do it:

You'll speak in metaphor. You'll use simile and analogy. You'll personify the Divine. You'll use what is known as *zoomorphism* to describe God as being like certain kinds of animals. It will sound like this:

God is love.

God is like a loving mother/father.

God is all-powerful

God is light.

God is Creator, Sustainer, Redeemer.

God is like a mother hen, a lion, a dove.

And all along, you will use the language of poetry. Because in the end, all of the theological jargon you can come up with to try to explain the event of God will feel flat and jaded.

If we want to feel something when we talk about God—if we want to take our jumbled beliefs and notions about God and imbue them with meaning—we need poets to help us.

Only poetry can give our words about God the wings they need to transcend this mortal coil and soar to heights above. (See what I did there?)

Try this on today. Speak about God using the best words you can think of. Nothing is off limits. Write down every phrase, every image that comes to mind as you try to comprehend God. And let your words lift you up and give you joy.

Lesson Learned from Falling into the Pool

I fell into my pool this morning (Friday) at 4:49.

I'm aware of the exact time because I glanced at the clock on my cable box as I walked, shivering, back into the house afterward, glad that there was no one there to see it. Oh. I bet you want to know *how* I fell in the pool. I just bet you do.

It happened, like a lot of accidents in the home, prior to coffee being consumed. So I was not at my best—mentally or physically, as it turns out.

Both Elway the dog and I were awakened at the same time—around 4:45 a.m.—to the sound of cats screeching at one another. One of the screeching cats was mine, but the other was an interloper.

Elway and I went downstairs and outside to investigate and discovered the strange cat under our patio table. I grabbed a broom to force the new and awful cat out, and it fled, pursued by Elway.

As I stumbled along the side of the pool after the cat and the dog, I slipped and fell in. At 4:49. Prior to coffee. Here ended the story.

The whole thing got me reflecting on the randomness of things and how it's hard to find meaning in the things that happen to us.

I also guess it's because of this line from a poem from the great Irish poet Brendan Kennelly I read recently: "How easy it is to maim the moment with expectation, to force it to define Itself."

The truth is, sometimes things just happen. We slip and fall into the pool at 4:49 a.m.

We lose our job on a Tuesday afternoon in February. A loved one dies suddenly, and we are left breathless and alone. Our children grow up and move away, and we weren't ready to let them go.

And in our efforts to make sense of everything, we maim the moment with our expectations, trying to exact meaning, attempting to rationalize everything.

When maybe what we should do instead is embrace the holiness of it all—of our grief, our surprise, our sorrow, our wonder, and our unknowing. It is all holy, every part of it. Because God is in it.

God is present in all of those moments, and in all things, and in every place. God mourns with us, rejoices with us, weeps with us, and even laughs with us.

I'm pretty sure I could almost hear a chuckle in my head today as I fell into the drink. And it wasn't coming from me. It was holy laughter at a holy moment.

The Most Perfect Prayer

I've been reading the fourteenth-century Christian masterwork, *The Cloud of Unknowing*, and it's been blowing my mind.

There's a lot of archaic language in *Unknowing*, to be sure. Still, it's an odd feeling, at times, to be reading it and to forget that it's seven hundred years old, yet so incredibly relevant.

Take the passage I read today, for example. The anonymous English author of *Unknowing* insists that the most perfect prayer that a person can pray is made up of one simple word: "Help!"

The author wrote this by way of an explanation:

> Why do you suppose this little prayer of one syllable is so powerful enough to pierce the heavens? Well, it is because is the prayer of a person's whole being. A person who prays this does so with all the height and depth and length and breadth of their spirit.

If this sounds overly simplistic, it's because it is. Yet it is also incredibly profound and deep. To coin a phrase from one of my favorite mentors, Rob Bell, it is "the simplicity on the other side of complexity."

The simplicity of this one-word prayer comes from a complex and difficult transformation that results in our being able to finally pray with our whole being.

And the occasions we find ourselves able to pray this prayer typically come when we have exhausted all other means of finding peace, resolution, respite, or restoration. In other words, when we are at the end of our rope.

At that moment, we discover that surrender is the only way forward. We realize that we cannot possibly find our way without help. And so we pray just one word.

If you find yourself at the end of your rope today, discover the simplicity of surrender on the other side of the complexity of your struggle. Pray your one word, and know that help is there—it always has been.

Welcome, Welcome, Welcome

I'm always looking for prayers, poems, quotes, and lines that inspire me and make me think. Or ones that convict me to be a better human. Or give me a platform from which to leap farther into the world, rather than away from it.

And sometimes, the thing I discover is so unbelievably perfect that I can't help but write it down, ponder it, and sometimes share it with you, here in these little reflections I write every day.

I recently discovered a prayer that was adapted by Father Thomas Keating and then adapted again by Father Richard Rohr and adapted by me.

Feel free to shape your own adaption to it—apparently, this is a thing.

> Welcome, welcome, welcome.
> I welcome everything that comes to me today
> because I know it's for my healing and growth.
> I welcome all thoughts, feelings, emotions, persons,
> situations and conditions.
> I let go of my desire for power and control.
> I open myself to the love and presence of God and
> God's actions within me, all around me and through me. Amen.

I've decided to begin each day with this prayer for a while. I want to see how it shapes me. There's so much within this prayer that I long for: freedom from unhealthy attachments, connections with the Divine, peace through surrender.

But the kind of peace and inner joy this prayer describes can only come through intentionality.

I can speak about these things all I want, but if I don't bend my spirit and my will toward God, if I don't lean into surrender, it's a bit like whiling away your life, dreaming of winning the lottery, without ever buying a ticket.

Use this prayer, if you like. Change it to suit you, if you feel the need. But I hope it is a blessing.

Spiritual but Not Religious

In his book *The Integral Vision*, author, philosopher, and teacher Ken Wilber asks an important question:

> Why is it that religion is such a complex, confusing, and polarizing force in the world? How could something that on the one hand teaches so much love and life be, on the other hand, the cause of so much death and destruction?

There were times in my youth when I wanted nothing to do with "organized religion." I preferred to find spirituality everywhere but church because, in my mind, church wasn't exactly the place where you experienced God. What I didn't know then, and what I came to understand much later, is that I was just in the wrong church.

Pastor and author Lillian Daniel reflects on the idea of being spiritual but not religious—being the kind of person who prefers to feel God in a sunset, rather than trying to find God in a pew.

She asks, "Do they think that [those of us who go to church] can't see God in a sunset?"

Obviously, we can. I marvel at the beauty of creation all of the time, and I pretty much spend most of my time at church. The miracle, Daniel writes, is that she can still experience God in church, bumping up against other people who "are just as annoying as I am."

What I've discovered over time is that not all Christian communities, churches, or congregations are created equal. Some are full of vibrancy and life, and others aren't. Some are trapped in the past, and others are hopeful about the future. Some seem full of the presence of God, and others seem completely empty.

But in the end, it's been in the church where I have experienced God more fully, more completely than I ever could have outside of it.

I think what we should start saying to people who tell us, "I am spiritual but not religious," is,

"So am I! I'm not religious at all—I just happen to love gathering, worshipping, and doing life with a bunch of people in my local church who are messy, odd, and stumbling after Jesus as best they can."

So may you discover a community of faith, full of annoying people just like you, and experience God there in ways you could never have imagined. May you fall in love with the notion that religion isn't relationships. May you find a church full of messy people who stumble after Jesus.

I Am No Longer What Happened to Me

There is a thing that happens to us when we experience trauma, or we find ourselves the victims of abuse, violence, or a tragedy.

It's a thing that sometimes finds us sometimes later in life, when repressed memories or feelings come flooding to the surface. Or in many cases, it simply hangs over us like a cloud, always there, never really allowing the sun through.

What am I talking about?

It's the thing that happens when we lose our identities in what happened to us so completely that we believe we are defined by it. It's when we become synonymous with what happened to us, and without that identity, we don't even know who we are.

I know this intimately, as do many of you who are reading this. But we don't have to live this way. The self that has been created when we lose ourselves in what happened to us, is a false self. It is not who we really are.

Who we are, instead, is defined by the great love of God, the One who is constantly speaking into our brokenness and the identity crises we create and says, "Behold, I am making all things new" (Revelation 21:5 NIV).

Imagine what it would be like to live your life free from your past—free from the ways you have defined yourself after past trauma, heartache, and wounding.

I read this wonderful poem today by Tiffany Aurora; say it with me:

> I am no longer,
> what happened,
> to me.
> I am now
> what happened—
> after what happened
> to me—
> Finally. Healed.

Read this poem today, and let yourself hear the words being spoken. Live into the new things that God desires to make in your life. Discover your new identity in Christ, an identity drawn from what is real, good, and true.

But I'm A Good Person!

The other night I heard someone describe a friend of theirs who had experienced a traumatic event as being "mad at God" over it. I understand that feeling. I think that most of us do. But how many of us actually admit to feeling that way when things don't go well for us?

I've had arguments with God in the past about these kinds of things. I will ask God if there is any way God might see the way clear to make things better for me considering all of the work I do on God's behalf.

I know that being a pastor doesn't afford me some sort of privileged status when it comes to hardship, trials, and tribulations. Just because I talk about faith, God, and church-y stuff for a living, doesn't mean that I get a pass on the hard things in life.

But sometimes... I sure wish it did.

In my experience, this is a common response that I've heard from people who have come to me for counsel when they've experienced something hard, a challenge in life, family or relationship troubles, a bad diagnosis...

"I don't know what I'm being punished for. I thought I was a good person."

So there are two things working there that need to be addressed. First, the whole "I'm being punished..." trope is one that far too many of us immediately lift up when we're examining the narrative of our challenges and troubles in life.

Most of us live transactionally, so we assume God does the same. We embrace the harmful theology of that old saying, "One good turn, deserves another," which reduces love and goodness down to a quid pro quo way of being.

As I write this, I am thinking of a song from The Sound of Music called "Something Good:"

> Perhaps I had a wicked childhood
> Perhaps I had a miserable youth
> But somewhere in my wicked, miserable past
> There must have been a moment of truth
> For here you are, standing there, loving me
> Whether or not you should
> So somewhere in my youth or childhood
> I must have done something good...

The singer stands before her Beloved delivering this basic message: "I don't believe I deserve to be in love and be happy, but I suppose somewhere along the way I did something good enough to warrant this feeling."

This isn't how God works. God is not transactional. In fact, (and here's where the "good person" thing comes into play) there is nothing that you and I could do to earn or merit the incredible love and grace that God offers to us every single day of our lives. There is nothing we could do to deserve abundant, eternal life. It's simply given by a God who loves because God is love.

Once when someone came to Jesus for advice, they called him "Good Teacher." Immediately, Jesus responded with a rebuke by saying there was no one who was "good" except God. I've always wondered why Jesus did that. I've come to understand it this way:

God became one of us in Jesus in order to rescue and restore and resurrect all of us, and all of Creation. Through Jesus, God intimately identifies with us and demonstrates just how far God is willing to go in order to connect with us and give us the kind of life God longs for us to live.

So Jesus was constantly reminding his followers that his humanness was a real thing. And that humanness was not meant to be despised because it mattered to God to become matter in order to show God's love and longing for a relationship with us.

It was important to Jesus to be honest about the limitations of humanity not as a means of rubbing our noses in it, but to demonstrate the great love that God has for us not in spite of our frailty, but because of it. God loves us as we are, but also loves us so much that God will never rest until we become our best and truest selves.

And God knows that the journey from where we are to what we will be is a path of enlightenment, fulfillment, true peace, and enduring love.

If you are struggling to understand the complications and uncertainty of the universe right now, rest assured that you are not alone. And know that the God who understands completely what it means to live in that uncertainty is the same God who creates order out of that chaos, life from death and loves you beyond all love.

Fail Better

I'm no stranger to failure. I'm guessing you aren't either. But our familiarity with failure doesn't mean that we enjoy it when it happens. Nor should we, for that matter.

But I've also learned much more from failing than I ever did from any successes I've had. There's a vulnerability that is brought on by failing that breaks down pride and teaches humility.

There are also lessons that we learn from our failures---valuable, lifelong lessons about who we are, how we conduct ourselves when things don't go our way, and how we should act and speak when we lose.

When I was a sophomore in high school I placed first in a speech contest for the state of Florida and was sent triumphantly on to compete in the national competition.

I remember the moment when the winners were being announced at nationals, and I realized that I didn't even place. I was crushed. I just knew that a mistake had been made. But when I received the sheets from the judges, I realized something...

My marks had been high. The comments had been positive and effusive. I ended up finishing in the top ten but I'd been competing in the rarified air of the very best in the entire country, and I'd needed to be nearly perfect in order to win. And I wasn't.

The lesson that I learned is one that I've had the occasion to recall more than once: Do your best and then surrender the outcomes.

Today I was reading Jeff Tweedy's awesome little book How To Write One Song, and he wrote this:

> Failure can be a kind of pain that you shouldn't let go to waste, at least as long as you're in the proper space mentally. It will help you deal with rejection in a lot of other areas of your life.

I've been passed over for promotions, rejected by publishers, denied job interviews, turned down by search committees... I've made mistakes, dropped the ball, missed opportunities... the list goes on and on.

And with each failure, I learned something about myself---lessons that have not been wasted. But I have to say that those failures taught me more about grace, and what it means to keep stumbling after Jesus even when you've fallen flat on your face.

The Apostle Paul reflected on a message he received from the Spirit of Christ concerning his own failures, and shortcomings. He wrote:

But [Christ] said to me, "My grace is sufficient for you, for my power is made perfect in weakness." Therefore I will boast all the more gladly about my weaknesses, so that Christ's power may rest on me. (2 Corinthians 12:9, NIV)

Maybe you have been living with the stigma of past failures, and have had a hard time moving on from them. Perhaps you think they've defined you in some negative way. Nothing could be further from the truth.

I want to encourage you to hold on to the knowledge that none of those failures have been wasted, and neither has the grace afforded to you afterward. The power of resurrection is within you, and you are not done by any stretch of the imagination.

So rejoice in your failures. Learn from them. And know that in your weakness, the power of Christ's resurrection is made evident for all to see.

Is God Hiding, Or Are You?

When I was a kid I remember sitting in Sunday School and being taught the story of Adam and Eve from the book of Genesis in the Bible.

I always felt sorry for them---about the way things turned out for them after everything with the Serpent and all. It felt like an overly harsh judgment considering they were duped.

But the most poignant moment in the story for my young self was when God comes looking for them, and Adam and Eve hide because they are naked and ashamed.

I remember feeling sad as God went about the Garden calling out to Adam and Eve, essentially asking "Where are you?"

I didn't really understand why I felt sad then, but over time I've had some insight. My young self was actually in touch with a universal truth that is embedded in that story from Genesis.

Most of the time when we feel like God is far away, or distant from us... we're the ones who are actually hiding.

Henri Nouwen once wrote this, which speaks right into what I was pondering:

> I am beginning now to see how radically the character of my spiritual journey will change when I no longer think of God as hiding out and making it as difficult as possible for me to find him, but, instead, as the one who is looking for me while I am doing the hiding.

What if all of those moments in our life where we thought that God had abandoned us, left us to twist in the wind, wasn't around, or wasn't paying attention...

What if all of those moments of angst were simply due to the fact that we were doing everything we could to keep from being discovered?

I've written here before about how God is always calling out to us...

I struggle sometimes to hear that Voice, to be honest, but I still trust that it's there speaking over me. I trust that the Voice of God is saying my name, declaring me "Beloved," calling me to Godself... wondering where I went--even though that doesn't seem possible.

Maybe God asks "Where are you?" for our own sake.

Maybe that question is reserved for the deepest part of us that has run away, hidden for shame, and really just wants to be found.

Maybe the act of standing up from behind the bushes we've used to shield us from the Divine gaze, and saying, "Here I am," is what we secretly wish for.

Because then all of the running and hiding can finally end. Then we can finally see where God has been all along and can realize the amount of grace that is available to cover up all of our shame, and that there is more than enough love, acceptance, and mercy.

That's the truest part of the story for me.

The judgment part of the story where God expels Adam and Eve seems like it was added as commentary by someone who viewed God in a clouded and terrible way.

Honestly, that's an important addition to acknowledge. Because the stories that unfold in those first moments of the book of Genesis are not just there to explain away how the world came to be.

They show how the more things change, the more they stay the same. We still fall into the same patterns, we make the same choices, give in to the same foolish pride... and then we hide.

It's almost like we've been projecting our own shame and dread onto God since the beginning of everything.

Maybe it's time to stand up at last, and let the shame fall away. To say "Here I am," and know that the God who calls for you does so out of love, and there is nothing we have done or could do to be separated from that love.

Living Life for a Living

I've had more than a few conversations lately about how short life is and how, the older I get, time seems to fly by more and more quickly.

I was talking to a friend who said it feels like she just woke up one day, and her daughter was grown and in college. "Where did my little girl go?" she told me.

I had to agree. My eldest son and his wife are moving to Chicago this week so he can attend law school. That very sentence makes me shake my head in disbelief.

Where did the time go? How can I have a kid who's married *and* going to law school? And why am I asking myself these things in italics?

The way I see it, you have a couple of choices when it comes to the life you've been given: you can decide to embrace every moment and live it to the fullest, or not. It's kind of that simple.

God knows I've spent my fair share of days not really living life for a living. Those days are easily forgotten, and they all seem to run together.

The days that are memorable are the ones spent doing *eternal* things—laughing, loving, serving, worshipping, restoring, resurrecting, feasting, celebrating, and giving.

And even the days we spend weeping, repenting, praying, and fasting are full of life and are holy in their own right.

In her incredible poem "When Death Comes," Mary Oliver delivers this bit of lasting wisdom:

> When it's over, I want to say: all my life
> I was a bride married to amazement.
> I was the bridegroom, taking the world into my arms.
> When it's over, I don't want to wonder
> if I have made of my life something particular, and real.
> I don't want to find myself sighing and frightened,
> or full of argument.

I don't want to end up simply having visited the world.

For those of us who claim to follow Jesus, we must always embrace the fact that he came to help us understand what it means to live life in abundance. This was Jesus's mission—one that lives on by the power of the Spirit and in the hearts of the faithful. May it be so for you.

Stop Worrying about Going to Heaven When You Die

In his recent book *Unraptured*, author Zach Hunt asserts that one of the worst things to have ever happened to Christianity in America is its obsession with end-times theology and the perpetuation of a faith that isn't grounded in the present.

He describes it like this:

> [A Christianity] focused on the future like a zero-sum game, a faith so over-spiritualized and focused on heaven that it has no practical relevance for the here and now.

This reminded me of the Oliver Wendell Holmes quote: "Some people are so heavenly minded, they are no earthly good."

Jesus wasn't about that. Jesus was firmly planted in the here and now. He spoke more about money than he did about heaven or hell.

He used plain language to tell stories about the expansive nature of the kingdom of God, rather than the overly religious language of the narrow-minded religious elites.

And, as Joan Chittister puts it,

> He cured on the Sabbath, mixed with foreigners, taught theology to women, played with children, questioned every law, chose people over ritual every time, and never made institutional authority a god.

Jesus was earthy. He used illustrations for his stories that were grounded in the everyday lives of the people hearing them. He enjoyed a good meal and a good party. He met people right where they were, as they were.

Sure, I think about what happens to us when we die. I've written and preached on it before, and I believe that it's an amazing gift to be able to think hopeful thoughts about what happens next.

But when we begin to think only about "going to heaven when we die," we also lose the beauty and eternity of the wondrous and naked *now*.

Now is what you have; you only have that. Yesterday is gone. Tomorrow hasn't happened yet. You only have now.

How will you use it? Will you embrace every moment with all your heart, soul, and might? Will you live and love in the now, just as Jesus did? Will you plunge your hands into this earth, this moment, this space, and love it as the Lord does?

To All Those with Checkered Pasts

Years ago, my wife, Merideth, and I were driving away from the parking lot of the church we'd been attending when she said something that was so ridiculous it made me choke with laughter.

I had looked over at Merideth and saw that she was staring at me with a small smile on her face and with her eyes really wide. It was unnerving. "What?" I exclaimed. "What's wrong?"

Then she'd hit me with this: "You would make a great minister."

There was no context for this and no evidence (in my mind) that would lead her to say such a thing. It was ridiculous. It was out of the question. It deserved the derisive, choking laugh of a smoker.

Here's what I was thinking: *Leon, old buddy, your past is more checkered than a pair of classic Vans shoes, or a checkerboard, or a checkered quilt, or a—nope, that's all I got. Plus, there was that period of the last five years or so when you just kind of stopped believing in God—so there's that.*

And because of this, I figured I was disqualified from any kind of Christian service, especially as pastor. So I laughed.

Obviously, despite all of my disqualifications, God seemed to see fit to ruin (transform) my life and send me on a path to being a pastor, despite my objections.

The other day, I read something that made me smile. It came from a fourteenth-century book called *The Great Cloud of Unknowing* that I've been reading, which makes it even cooler:

> I believe, too, that often our Lord deliberately chooses to work in those who have been habitual sinners rather than in those who, by comparison, have never grieved him at all.

How awesome is this? I know, I know, it's not perfect theology. There are all kinds of holes in the argument, to be sure. But still, to those of us who have struggled with doubts, disbelief, and less-than-perfect lives, that is pretty good news.

I'm going to choose to hold on this. You should too, especially if you have felt like God couldn't possibly use you because of the things you've done or the things that have been done to you. If you have felt broken and unusable, rejoice! God deliberately is seeking you out.

May this give you joy and hope.

The Pathway to Hope Begins with Letting Go

It's hard to watch the news on TV. More and more people get their news in snippets from social media, forwarded emails, or from the push notifications on their smartphones.

But any way you look at it, the news we get is usually bad. And most of us have an overwhelming sense that everything is messed up. We live with a steady sense of foreboding almost all of the time.

In recent years, writers like Steven Pinker and Hans Rosling (among others) have been making the case that we are wrong to be so pessimistic about the future and that there is ample evidence to demonstrate that things in the world are the best they've ever been.

The problem is, the statistics on drug addiction, depression, low life satisfaction, and suicide rates in the developed world are not just sobering but alarming.

Author Mark Manson writes:

> Basically, we are the safest and most prosperous humans in the history of the world, yet we are feeling more hopeless than ever before. The better things get, the more we seem to despair.

Manson asserts that it's almost like the better things get, the more we realize what we have to lose, and this has an adverse effect on our ability to hope. Jesus once told his followers,

> Therefore I tell you, do not worry about your life, what you will eat or what you will drink, or about your body, what you will wear. Is not life more than food, and the body more than clothing? (Matthew 6:25 NIV)

You see, Jesus knew that his followers would struggle to truly hope when they were preoccupied with not having enough—enough money, safety, security, and the like.

Jesus teaches us to let go of our attachments to our ideas of what constitutes enough. He teaches us to let go of our attachments to worry, to the fear of lack, the dread of losing what we have.

Instead, Jesus teaches us to focus on what truly matters: things that are good, beautiful, and true. He leads us to focus on bringing God's kingdom to life here and now. His example is one of unconditional and inclusive love.

And this brings hope—for you, for me, and for all of us, and the whole of creation.

May this be so in your life today and every day. And may the grace and peace of our Lord Jesus Christ be with you, now and always. Amen.

Rapha and Yada—"Be Still and Know": Reimagined

One of the most well-used verses in the Bible comes to us from Psalm 46:10, which reads like this:

> Be still, and know that I am God; I will be exalted among the nations, I will be exalted in the earth. (NIV)

That one line—"Be still, and know that I am God"—finds its way into greeting cards, wall art, church signs, and the like. And it sounds so nice, doesn't it? But what does it actually mean?

The Hebrew word that's used here for the phrase "be still" is *rapha*. And get this—it means "to hang limp, sink down, be feeble." That's a lot different from what we usually take the phrase "be still" to mean, right?

I don't know about you, but whenever I heard that verse in the past, I thought it meant to sit perfectly still, to be quiet, to try to meditate—all of which are really good things that we should do from time to time.

But in this context, *rapha* means to let yourself sink, to let go of your rigidity, to allow yourself to be weak, to throw off all of the pretenses of strength and become "feeble." It's more than just being quiet and still. It's complete surrender.

And what happens when we do this? We experience knowledge of God. And by "knowledge," I mean the Hebrew word *yada*, which is the word used here and which means "to have intimate knowledge."

I was journaling about this passage of scripture, and this was what I wrote:

> Allow yourself to become completely weak and feeble, letting go of your need to control and your messed-up ideas about how strong you are, and what you will discover is an intimate, up-close understanding of God that you would have never experienced otherwise.

Let this be your prayer today and every day. You don't have to stop and be quiet to experience God more fully, although there are lots of times in our lives when we probably should.

Instead, we need to simply surrender our need for control, stop trying to be stronger than we are, admit our frailty and our weariness over all of our striving, and simply sink into God's presence.

May this be true for you, and may the grace and peace of our Lord Jesus Christ be with you, now and always. Amen.

Following Jesus Is a Race to the Bottom

When he was teaching his disciples about the importance of letting go of their misguided notions of success and power, Jesus espoused a counterintuitive path to enlightenment that didn't seem to make a whole lot of sense. He told them:

> You know that the rulers of the Gentiles lord it over them, and their great ones are tyrants over them. It will not be so among you; but whoever wishes to be great among you must be your servant, and whoever wishes to be first among you must be your slave; just as the Son of Man came not to be served but to serve, and to give his life a ransom for many. (Matthew 20:25–28 NIV)

Jesus told his disciples that the way to greatness in God's kingdom was a race to the bottom. It was a path marked by servanthood and surrender. He outlined a way that was full of self-sacrifice and self-emptying. To become more, you must become less. To be great, you must become nothing.

Take a moment to think about what that might mean in your own life. What would you have to give up to become less? Does it begin to make you uncomfortable? It does me.

Jesus taught over and over again that the kingdom of God was a counterintuitive proposition for most people. For example, the economy of God's kingdom was based on the kind of generosity that bordered on the ridiculous. It was the kind of generosity that would make someone leave ninety-nine sheep to go search for one lost lamb.

C. S. Lewis wrote about the counterintuitive nature of the new community—the church, the body of Christ—when the followers of Jesus are living into their best selves and truly seeking the kingdom of God over their own needs and wants. He wrote that in the body of Christ, "Obedience is the road to freedom, humility the road to pleasure, unity the road to personality."

The interesting thing is that the church has largely forgotten this, and far too many people who claim to follow Jesus have largely abandoned the counterintuitive nature of the gospel. They've opted instead for a race to the top and don't seem to care all that much about those who are at the bottom.

Some of us have begun to figure this out. We've started seeing how we can no longer be communities that exist for our own sake but rather that we exist for the sake of the world.

You can be a part of this. You can begin to race toward the bottom by letting go of the wrongheaded ideas of power and success that have permeated our culture. You can become more by becoming less. May this be so for you today and every day.

Step Into the Light

I love living in a place where most of the days are sun-drenched. I'd have a hard time trying to make a go of it in a town where most days were cloudy and gray.

Don't get me wrong; I love me a good rainy day or a crisp, foggy fall morning, but if I go too long without seeing the sun, it messes me up.

When I lived in Chicago, I would see billboards pop up during the winter, advertising professional therapy and counseling for people suffering from something called seasonal affective disorder, which is a depressive disorder brought on by the gray skies of winter—months of gray skies, *months*.

The fact that the acronym for this disorder is SAD is not a coincidence, I'm thinking. Because when we are deprived of sunlight, we wither like plants in a dark room.

And we often do destructive things when we begin to wither. Like binge-watch way too much on Netflix and eat more ice cream than we ought. Or we watch too many Scandinavian movies—set in winter, with subtitles, and terribly sad endings.

Interestingly, many of us deprive ourselves of the lightness of life in much the same way. We have lived so long with sadness, grief, loss, bitterness, or regret that they become like old friends we don't know how to live without.

The poet Mary Oliver speaks to this in beautifully crafted words that help us understand how the lightness of life can help us let go of those sad, gray old friends of ours that keep us from being authentically *us*:

> But I also say this: that light
> is an invitation
> to happiness,
> and that happiness,
> when it's done right,
> is a kind of holiness,
> palpable and redemptive.

This ultimately is what God wants for you and me. It's why God became one of us in Jesus—in order to rescue all of us from our false sense of self and our destructive ways of living.

Embrace the lightness of life today and every day. Know that this lightness comes from God—it *is* God. God is our life's light, and this light shines brightest when we seek to be more like Jesus, the light of the world.

Hello Darkness, My Old Friend

The first line of Simon and Garfunkel's classic song, "The Sound of Silence," which was recently redone by one of my favorite bands, Disturbed, goes like this: "Hello darkness, my old friend. I've come to talk with you again."

I've always liked that first line. I've never been afraid of my darkness. It's an essential part of who I am. Sometime—and I almost hesitate to say this—it's a welcome respite from the light.

As I was pondering today's devo, I realized something that I'm sure most of us already know: it's so much easier for us to think and talk about light and lightness than it is to dwell on darkness.

But there are two things I want to point out about darkness that most of us typically gloss over when we're dealing with it in our lives. To begin with, there's no such thing as total darkness. What looks, to the human eye, like pitch-black darkness is actually filled with billions of neutrinos, which are light.

This is wonderful news because it's as if God wanted us to know that no matter how dark we think things might be, there's always light. The darkness cannot overcome it.

This needs to be said. None of us was meant to live trapped in his or her own darkness. We need light so we can not only survive but thrive and grow.

But I also have come to believe that darkness serves a vital purpose to our growth and maturity and flourishing. When we constantly avoid it or seek to dispel it without understanding it, we do ourselves a disservice.

The Jesuit mystic and teacher Anthony de Mello puts it like this:

> The trouble with people is that they're busy fixing things they don't even understand … It never strikes us that things don't need to be fixed … They need to be understood. If you understood them, they'd change.

If you are struggling through a season in your life right now where everything seems dark and oppressive, take heart. There is light there in the midst of it. And there are things that you need to learn and know as you strain to see.

Namely, that you are not alone in this. And the One who spoke light into the darkness is also the One who is with you. You can rest, surrender, and wait patiently for the light to shine upon you. It will come.

Evil Doesn't Get to Win

Some time ago, a friend sent me links to a series of news articles about the horrible atrocities being committed by religious extremists toward Christians living in predominantly Muslim countries.

I have to admit that when I read or hear stories like that, I get angry and wonder whether God might see God's way clear to just rain down some vengeance upon those fanatics, Sodom-and-Gomorrah–style.

I'm not alone in this. None other than King David himself had feelings of vengeance and violence toward evildoers and sick, violent people. In Psalm 58, David prays this:

> Break the teeth in their mouths … Let them vanish like water that flows away … May they be like a slug that melts away as it moves along, like a stillborn child that never sees the sun … The righteous will be glad when they are avenged, when they dip their feet in the blood of the wicked. (Psalm 58:6–10 NIV)

What we need to realize, however, is not once does David say to God, "Just give me a chance. Let me be the one to shoot the arrow. Give me the opportunity to inflict this vengeance." Sure, he's angry, hurt, wounded, fearful, and a host of other things, but he leaves the ultimate justice up to God.

I read a story yesterday about how a bunch of people in Texas armed themselves with various weapons (they have the legal right there to carry them in the open) and staged a protest outside a mosque. I read this story because it was reposted by several of my Christian Facebook friends, including one who is a pastor. And they were posting it because they thought it was awesome.

But is brandishing weapons outside a mosque in a Texas suburb the answer? Do we think that God isn't watching all of this, including our own responses?

I believe that because of the Resurrection of Jesus, the world is filled with a new sense of purpose and a goal that will one day be realized—a new world, a new creation devoid of all this violence and hate.

May you lean into the hope of the risen Christ, despite your fears and even the anger that you might feel at those who do evil in the world. May you guard your heart against becoming too hardened to the gentleness of the Holy Spirit. May you live today, knowing that the God of justice and righteousness will one day set all things to rights in his time and for his glory.

Discovering the Beauty in Hardship

If your life is hunky-dory, you might be prancing through your house this morning with a Danish in one hand and a cup of coffee in the other, without a care in the world.

First, let me tell you that there are a number of us out here in the world who are not morning people, and so if you must prance, do it quietly.

Second, if this is you, then I need to say that today's "Daily Devo" might not apply to you at this particular moment, *but* it most assuredly will apply to you at some point.

You see, today, I'm speaking to all those who are going through a valley of sorts—those who are struggling to put one foot in front of the other; those who are feeling like the weight of the world is pressing down on them.

I'm speaking to all those who are experiencing a difficult season, marked by grief, loss, confusion, pain, suffering, doubt, fear, depression—you know who you are.

Because this is all of us. None of us gets through this thing called life without a nick or two on our chassis. And most of us have some full-on damage to show for our pains.

I've been beating this drum off and on for a bit now, but it's worth repeating: God doesn't waste anything, even our pain.

God may not cause the broken things in our lives, but God definitely causes all the broken things to be renewed, restored, and resurrected, if need be.

And it's in those challenging moments that we grow the most, we learn the most, and—if we are wise—we surrender the most. Maria Goff puts this so beautifully:

> It's as if [God] reminds each of us in our most difficult circumstances that the most beautiful waterfalls only happen in the steepest places in our lives.

Though it may be difficult, do your best today and every day to see the beauty in your struggle. Look for signs of wonder in the middle of your season of hardship. Let yourself be shaped and molded and made new.

The Sin of Certainty

There's a lot of certainty going around right now. Lots of people seem pretty certain about their views on politics. It doesn't seem to matter which end of the political spectrum they happen to inhabit; they are pretty certain that they are right.

And then there are the people who are so very certain about their religious beliefs. I know a lot of these people. Truthfully, some days I'm one of them.

These folks are often more certain about their religious convictions than they are about politics. Sometimes, they are so much the same thing that it's hard to tell their religion from their politics, and vice versa.

But here's where things seem to be unraveling for us. It's not enough that we are so very certain about our beliefs, views, and opinions. It's like we can't stand anyone who holds a different belief, view, or opinion.

I read an amazing poem by the poet Yehuda Amichai yesterday, and it spoke to me so much I had to share it:

> The place where we are right
> is hard and trampled
> like a yard,
> but doubts and loves
> dig up the world
> like a mole, a plow.

Truthfully, there are some people in the world with whom it's nigh impossible to find common ground because they are nigh impossible to deal with.

By contrast, the apostle Paul exhorted his readers, "If it's at all possible, and within your power to do so, do your best to live peaceably with everyone" (Romans 12:8 NIV).

We can begin that process by simply letting go of our need for certainty and our desire to be right. And we can do this in such a way that we exemplify a very important truth: you are able to receive so much more when you live open-handed, no matter what you have to let go of to do so.

Living Your Most Abundant Life Now

I've written more than a few daily devotionals on the topic of the dangers of prioritizing the next life over this one.

And I've also said more than once that theology that purports the chief end of Christianity is simply "to go to heaven when we die" is not only poorly done but dangerous.

But there's more to be said on this, I think. Anthony de Mello spoke into this in one of his teachings on awareness:

> Nobody seems to be grappling with the problem of: Is there a life before death? Yet my experience is that it's precisely the ones who don't know what to do with this life who are all hot and bothered about what they are going to do with another life.

There are more than a few reasons why it is so important for followers of Jesus to not get too "other-worldly" focused. To begin, there is much to be done right here and now to fulfill our calling as kingdom-bearers and -bringers.

And along those lines, as Jesus-followers, we ought to be acutely aware that the incarnation (God in the flesh) of Jesus is a sign and symbol that God not only loves the world (and us) but that God has not given up on here and now.

But there's another reason: Jesus's desire for his followers was that they live their best and most abundant lives, and in order to do that, he knew they would need to be more present—in the present.

In Matthew 5–7, we have the text from Jesus's greatest sermon: the Sermon on the Mount. In this text, Jesus outlines a way of living that is grounded in the now.

And here's the amazing outcome of living the kind of life that Jesus exhorts his followers to live—an outwardly focused life that is justice-oriented and wholly devoted to intimacy with God. When you live that kind of life, you experience heaven, right here, right now. You don't have to wait until you shuffle off this mortal coil, until you trip the light fantastic.

Or to put it less poetically, you don't have to wait until you die.

Take the time today to read Matthew 5–7. Identify two or three ways that you could heed Jesus's teachings and begin living your best, most abundant, and eternal life.

And then put them into practice—experience a bit of heaven on earth, right here, right now as you become more and more fully present in the present.

Further Thoughts on Speaking Life

Yesterday, I preached a sermon on how we desperately need the Spirit of God to help us learn to speak life into the world and not death. I just watched the video of that sermon, as I typically do on Mondays.

Mostly, I watch to see what nervous tics, idiosyncrasies, or other annoying things I did that I need to work on to make me a better preacher. But I evaluate the content and delivery as well.

Our words can heal, but they can also destroy, and it's the latter that seems to be preoccupying our culture and our elected leaders.

The fact of the matter is that our political leaders in the United States need some Jesus. You can quote me on that. And if you are wondering what I'm talking about, stop reading this and go read the Sermon on the Mount from Matthew 5–7, if you hadn't already done so after reading the previous devotional.

In the Sermon on the Mount, Jesus laid down some straight-up truth about living an open-handed, selfless, God-focused, kin-dom-minded, loving, integrity-fueled, generous, courageous, justice-oriented, mercy-filled kind of life.

That's what I mean when I say they need Jesus. And as the words leave my own mouth, they land on me too. Because I need Jesus more than most people.

The fact that some of our elected officials *think* they've got some Jesus is almost always negated by the things that they say about the people who disagree with them on debatable issues. Or the terrible things that they say about their critics.

Or just the terrible things they say, in general.

Here's the thing: those of us who claim to be Christians need the power of the Spirit of God in our lives so that we can speak life into the world more consistently and with greater intentionality.

And then, we need to boldly speak grace, peace, and truth to the principalities and powers of this world. We need to start a revolution of loving, Jesus-flavored speech throughout our public discourse.

Kindness is not weakness. Common ground is possible. Civil discourse, open debate, mutual respect—these are all virtuous ideals that we can achieve if we are courageous enough to try.

The darkness that would seek to divide us, tear us apart, and leave us broken doesn't get to win. You can quote me on that too.

Emunah

What does it mean to say, "I am a person of faith," or "I have faith"? For some people, it means that you have ascribed to a particular set of religious traditions. For others, it means that you put your trust in the Divine.

There are some who believe that to have faith means that you have decided to be faithful to the doctrines and dogmas of your denomination, sect, or religious community. Sadly, for many others, it also means that you have lost your ability to reason.

In his recent book *Days of Awe and Wonder*, Marcus Borg talks about faith from his location as a scholar of the Hebrew scriptures, or, as Christians refer to them, the Old Testament. Borg points out that the Hebrew word for faith in the Old Testament is *emunah*, which has its origins in the sound that a baby donkey makes when it is calling for its mother.

Marcus Borg says that there's almost an element of desperation in that kind of meaning, but there's also an element of confidence that the cry will be heard.

When I read that today, I couldn't stop thinking about it. What a beautiful way of thinking about faith! Desperation mixed with confidence—on the surface, it doesn't seem to make sense. But for most of us, that's what faith is like. We feel as though we are crying out in desperation, longing for all that we hope for in God to be true. We want to believe.

Faith, however, is deeper than belief because it is born of desperation and grounded in paradox. The writer of Hebrews writes of faith that it is the substance of things that are hoped for and the evidence of things that are not seen. Paradox.

Faith is the confidence that comes from knowing that God is there, somewhere within earshot of your *emunah* cries, even though there may not be any clear evidence at the moment that God is listening. It's when we realize that God is truly for us. Marcus Borg puts it like this:

> But to see [the reality of God] as supportive, gracious and nourishing creates the possibility of responding to life in a posture of trust and gratitude.

When we come to this realization, what previously was a paradox, a mystery, or something that defied logic makes perfect sense. It changes the way we see the world. We no longer see it through the lens of dread, fear, or bitter skepticism.

We see the world through the lens of love. And we know that even though things still fall apart, get broken, or become lost; even though we struggle, and find conflict, and often worry; even though we die, when we lift up our *emunah* cry, we are heard, and known, and loved.

The Thin Places

Some years ago, I paid a visit to a homebound church member whom I hadn't seen in a while. We chatted for a bit, but then she suddenly blurted out, "You know I died once." And then she asked, "Do you want to know what I saw?"

The lady told me that a few years earlier, her heart had stopped during the middle of a surgery, and she was technically dead for a few minutes.

She told me that she floated above her body for an instant, and then she found herself standing in front of a long, wooden garden fence. She walked along the fence, and after a few moments, she found a hole in the fence and looked through it.

What she saw defied her imagination. On the other side of the fence was the most beautiful garden she had ever seen. It was filled with colors, beautiful scents, the sounds of birds, and incredible light.

She told me that the light was the most beautiful thing of all. It didn't come from the sun, she said, but it radiated softly over everything. It brought out all of the contrasts in the garden, filling it with a golden glow.

As my church member spoke, my heart began to pound with excitement. I had seen that kind of light before—only I was wide awake.

Years before, I had found myself overwhelmed by the beauty of an incredible garden in Oxford, England. It was during a magical hour of the day, and the light simply seemed to emanate from some supernatural place, filling the garden with a golden glow.

I remembered feeling like the world around me had fallen away, and the air I was breathing was thick with glory and holiness. I found myself wishing with all my heart to be there forever. It felt like God was in that place. Or at the very least, the space between this world and the kingdom of God was so very, very thin.

I'm discovering that, as Christians, we have rich and beautiful ways to talk about those thin spaces and places in our lives when we feel the presence of the Divine so acutely.

And when we begin to take these moments seriously, to feel them deeply, to give them their proper place in our theology, we can also find that we will have new ways to understand God too.

My prayer today is that you and I might have opened eyes and willing hearts. I pray that we might experience more of God in the world. I pray that we might experience glory, beauty, and light.

How Do You Find Your Self?

In her excellent book on the Enneagram, Marilyn Vancil speaks to an aspect of human development that affects every single one of us—the struggle to embrace our authentic selves.

Instead of living into our God-given authenticity, Vancil asserts that most of us settle for an adaptive version of our selves. This version of us is what gets created over time as we deal with wounds, fears, doubts, and the challenges of life.

It's also a shadow of who we are meant to be.

This morning, I happened to be listening to "East," a song by Ryan O'Neal, and I realized that his lyrics painted a vivid portrait of the moment when we realize we've been living as a shadow of our true selves.

In the following stanza, O'Neal writes about a time when he felt authentically himself:

> i set out to rule the world
> with only a paper shield and a wooden sword.
> no mountain dare stand in my way,

And then, he realizes he's been living an adaptive and diminished life:

> now i bear little resemblance to the king i once was.
> i bear little resemblance to the king i could become.
> maybe paper is paper, maybe kids will be kids-
> Lord, i want to remember how to feel like i did.

The prayer that he prays at the end is the secret, longing prayer that we all feel at some point in our lives, even if we can't summon the breath to pray it. It's when we have a come-to-Jesus meeting within ourselves and realize we need to live differently.

The great Christian mystic Thomas Merton once wrote:

> All sin starts from the assumption that my false, the self that exists only in my own egocentric desires, is the fundamental reality of life to which everything else in the universe is ordered.

If you realize today that you have been living a diminished and shadow version of your true self, may you find the strength today to pray this simple prayer:

"Lord, I want to remember how to feel like I did, like I should, like I know I can feel as my true self in you."

What Happens When We Pray?

I've been thinking about prayer lately, and (like I do with most spiritual matters) I've let my thoughts lead me to wonder and my wondering to questions.

For instance, here's a question that I get asked a lot about prayer, and it's one that sometimes keeps me awake at night: why bother praying?

If God is all-knowing and outside of time, then God already knows the outcome to all things. So what's the point of praying about it?

Good question, right? Or how about these—why does it feel like some people's prayers get answered and mine don't? Is it my fault? Did I do something wrong?

The truth is, I don't have a lot of concrete answers on these kinds of questions about prayer. I struggle with them, just like anyone else.

But here's what I do know. When I pray, I feel something. And by *pray*, I mean when I journal because journaling is prayer to me. I have a hard time praying out loud, and I don't kneel beside my bed and fold my hands to pray—I'd just fall asleep.

Journaling is how I pray, but you might pray in other ways—like through music, for example, or art. Or maybe you pray by hiking or walking and letting your thoughts carry you.

Whatever way you pray, this is what happens: you begin to learn more about who you are and who God is to you. Suzanne Henley, who has written some amazing books on prayer and how it works, recently said this:

> [Prayer] reveals who we are to ourselves. And that's where God often seems to set up shop. Each prayer, when genuine, is a birth a labored delivery of twins: both a new self and a new face of God.

May you find moments today to offer your prayers in all of their infinite variety. And as you pray, may you discover the truth about who you truly are in God—a beloved child, loved, cherished, chosen.

May you see God in fresh new ways, all around you, in you, and through you.

Beauty Is in the Eye of the Beholder

The other day, I was driving to the north side of Austin with a friend from out of town. At one point, we drove across the famous 360 Bridge that boasts incredible views of the Texas Hill Country and the Austin city skyline.

My friend exclaimed over the view and then said, "What an awesome place to live!"

I had to admit that the view, the location, the city—all of it is pretty fantastic.

Unfortunately, when you've driven over the bridge a number of times you tend to stop focusing on how beautiful it is, and all you can see is the traffic ahead of you and how long it's going to take you to get to your destination.

And then your friend, who hasn't grown used to it, helps you see the beauty once again.

I feel like the ability to not only see but also appreciate beauty is a skill that we are losing in our current culture.

We lose this skill when our attention is almost always fixed to the small computers we hold six inches or so from our faces. Or when we never pause to look at the world around us because we are too busy rushing from one place to another.

And when we lose this ability, we also lose something even more important: our ability to see Christ in the world.

Simone Weil once wrote "Beauty is the experiential proof that incarnation is in fact possible."

I love that quote because it speaks to the signs and symbols of Christ's incarnation (God becoming what God loves) that are in the world all around us, all of the time.

And all we need to do is stop, breathe, and truly open our eyes to see them/him.

C. S. Lewis wrote of this in his classic work *Mere Christianity*:

> [At] the center of [all of it], there is a something, or a Someone, who against all divergencies of belief, all differences of temperament, all memories of mutual persecution, speaks with the same voice.

May you find moments today to take in the beauty of the world around you and see it more clearly as Christ himself. And may this knowledge give you joy that is indescribable and amazing.

Some Thoughts on Sin

In the churches I attended as a youngster, the idea of sin and what constituted a sin were frequent topics of discussion.

When I was very small, I just knew that sin was bad and that there were a lot of things that were sinful. As I got older, I began to notice a pattern when it came to how sin was defined in my churchy context.

In short, I came to the unshakable realization that everything enjoyable in life was probably a sin. There was even an '80s pop song about defining sin from the Pet Shop Boys that I listened to (which was a sin)—secretly, of course (also a sin).

Here's a bit of the lyrics:

> When I look back upon my life
> It's always with a sense of shame
> I've always been the one to blame
> For everything I long to do
> No matter when or where or who
> Has one thing in common, too
> It's a, it's a, it's a, it's a sin
> It's a sin …

When I first heard that song, I wanted to shout *amen* to it because that's exactly how I felt. Sin is a loaded word. In my opinion, Christians almost always mess up any conversation about sin because most Christians believe that sin is almost always connected to behavior.

In reality, the Greek word for *sin* that is used throughout the New Testament is *hamartia*, which means "missing the true goal and scope of life."

In short, sin is what happens when we live in the confined space of an inauthentic life, as opposed to the expansive freedom that comes from being our authentic true selves—the people God created us to be.

Imagine how our lives would be different if we shook off the shame and guilt of our old definitions of sin.

Such a move would enable us to step away from living in such a way where what is good, beautiful, and true in our lives get twisted into smaller, uglier versions.

And we would then be free to be the people God longs for us to be.

If You Are Looking for a Sign, This Is It

Three years ago, I was at a crossroads. I was facing one of the biggest decisions of my life, and I didn't know which path to choose. I began to pray for a sign from God, mostly out of desperation and without any real hope of finding one.

I got the sign that I was asking for, by the way. It came in a miraculous, can't-be-explained kind of way. But despite the miraculous nature of the sign I'd prayed for, I then found myself struggling to believe it.

This morning, I felt a bit inspired to share the story a bit differently, so here's my attempt at a poem:

> I prayed for a sign to help me decide which way to go.
> And God, in God's infinite capacity for humor
> Painted a really big one, and stuck it in a church
> Six thousand miles from where I first prayed—waiting to be found.
> And I did find it. After boarding a plane, flying for hours
> Booking a cottage, renting a car, traveling for miles,
> and then, after a change of plans, deciding to visit a small town
> in the south of England where I walked into the church
> And saw it there … and doubted.

One of the most important lessons I've learned over the years is that God is constantly doing miraculous things all around us. There are signs and wonders everywhere. God is constantly painting signs.

But at some point, we have to take a step. We have to decide which direction to take and to set out on our journey with faith and (dare I say it) hope.

If you are trying to determine your next steps; if you are standing at a crossroads, wondering which path to take; if you are looking for a sign to show you the way, first, open your eyes. Look around you with the intention of truly seeing. Open your mind and your heart, and let go of all of the distractions and obstacles that have kept you from seeing signs in the past.

And then be prepared to move. You get to decide if you not only will find inspiration in God's ever-present signs but also if you will use that inspiration to get you going where you are meant to go.

When you do move, may you do so with a renewed sense of purpose and confidence that God will go before you and indeed is already there, awaiting you in your future.

There Is No Fear of Bike Riding

Today is the first day of school in our community, and my wife and I just saw our littlest boy off to his first day of third grade. We took the obligatory first-day-of-school photo, and then he mounted his brand-new bike, pulled on his sparkling new bike helmet, and rode off down the street with a friend.

It wasn't that long ago when he was frightened to ride to school on his own. Now he pedals away with the confidence born of repetition and familiarity.

He's learned that his neighborhood is a safe place for him to ride. Neighbors wave at him when he sails past them. The little girl across the street calls him by name.

It's hard to be afraid of what you know.

I read something this morning that got me thinking about how fear affects us. The great Christian mystic Anthony de Mello once said this:

> And there's not a single evil in the world that you cannot trace to fear. Not one. Ignorance and fear, ignorance caused by fear, that's where all the evil comes from, that's where your violence comes from.

We are seeing this play out in our current culture right now. There is so much anger, so much ignorance, and all of it—all of it—is grounded in fear, which is grounded in unknowing.

When you fear the unknown, it's all too easy to decide that it needs a face. And then it is even easier to fall into bigotry, xenophobia, racism, misogyny, homophobia—the list goes on and on. And all of it is grounded in fear.

Two words are spoken by the Divine, over and over again, in both the Old and New Testaments of the Bible. In fact, Jesus spoke them on numerous occasions. Those two words? "Fear not …" (Luke 12:32 KJV).

Those words are spoken by the Divine to us as a way to draw us into intimacy. What God has known since the beginning of all things is that when we allow ourselves to be drawn close so we can know God, we let go of our fear.

Intimacy with God enables us to see the world as familiar, beautiful, and filled with God—God all around us, in us, and through us. This way of seeing changes everything.

May you live your life today and every day in intimacy with God and free from fear. May you come to know this world as God knows it. May you fear not.

Holy Interruptions

When I was a kid, the faith communities that we were a part of were obsessed with end-times theology.

Among the people in the various churches we attended over the years, there was always endless speculation about what was commonly referred to as "the Second Coming of Jesus."

I also remember hearing more than my fair share of sermons about what was going to happen when Jesus "comes back." And brother, it wasn't good. Especially if you're "unsaved."

The preachers in my churches would often quote Jesus from the book of Mark:

> Therefore keep watch because you do not know when the owner of the house will come back--whether in the evening, or at midnight, or when the rooster crows, or at dawn. (Mark 13:35 NIV)

I used to lie awake at night, praying to God not to let Jesus come back. I was terrified that I would be on the outside looking in if he did return. Those verses seemed full of judgment and anger.

But Jesus wasn't threatening his followers when he said those words; he was encouraging them to be awake and aware—because God is always coming, God is always arriving, and God is always returning to us again and again.

Jesus was talking about the holy interruptions that we experience when we finally open our eyes and, in complete readiness, receive the always-arriving, always-unexpected Christ.

Father Richard Rohr puts it like this:

> God is invariably and ironically found in the interruptions, the discontinuities, the exceptions, the surprises—and seldom in the patterns. God has to catch us literally "off guard!"

May you be surprised and interrupted today by the God who shows up in the exceptions. May you be startled by the Christ who appears in the unexpected. And may it fill you with wonder.

And may the grace and peace of our Lord Jesus Christ be with you, now and always. Amen.

Freedom to Live

In Shakespeare's comedy *Twelfth Night*, an exchange takes place between a slightly drunk Sir Toby Belch and the dour character Malvolio that has always made me smile.

Many scholars believe that the character of Malvolio was a not-so-subtle critique by Shakespeare of influential Puritans in Elizabethan England, some of whom were vocally opposed to the theater, which they deemed a vice to be avoided.

Sir Toby dryly says to Malvolio, "Dost thou think, because thou art virtuous, there shall be no more cakes and ale?"

Malvolio had a way of bringing everyone down with his pessimism and piety. But Sir Toby reminds him that despite his best efforts, Malvolio wasn't going to steal his joy and his zest for living.

I've met my fair share of Malvolios in Christian circles over the years.

In fact, there was a time when, as a young man, I came to believe that Christianity was little more than a bunch of Puritans walking around, sucking the life out of life. And so I walked away from it. Eventually, I came to realize that the puritanical version of Christianity I'd fled was not at all representative of the example that Jesus himself set for his followers.

By all accounts, it seems that Jesus enjoyed a good party, loved sitting down to dinner with people, and the only people he really criticized and dressed down were the overly religious Puritans of his day.

The other day, I was reading a poem by the British poet William Blake, "To the Christians," and this line stood out for me:

> I know of no other Christianity and of no other Gospel than of the liberty both of
> body & mind to exercise the Divine Arts of Imagination.

The essence of Christianity is the freedom we have in Christ to live life to the fullest, to enjoy and make the most of every moment we've been given. This doesn't mean that we live irresponsibly, to be sure. Our freedom ends when it impinges on our ability to flourish as human beings.

But it does mean that we occasionally can enjoy a night out with friends, a really great dinner with good wine, laughter, romance, great music, good movies, the occasional party, and even cakes and ale.

And make the most of this precious life we've been given.

Becoming More Yourself

The other day I was reading from Anthony de Mello's excellent book *Awareness*, and I came across a quote that I had to write down. Here it is:

> The three most difficult things for a human being are not physical feats or intellectual achievements. They are, first, returning love for hate; second, including the excluded; third, admitting that you are wrong.

At the time, I wasn't sure what it was saying to me, exactly, but I trusted that it would come to me. Today, as I read it again, I finally saw why it had struck me so strongly.

It comes down to this: if I were able to do these three things well—each and every day of my life—I would actually have a real shot at becoming the person God created me to be.

Jesus taught these three things over and again to his followers.

He took on the worst that the world had to offer and returned love for hate. Even as he was dying on a Roman cross, Jesus prayed, "Father forgive them for they don't know what they are doing" (Luke 23:34 NIV).

Jesus constantly reached out to those on the margins, preferring their company, it seems, over the religious elites and holier-than-thou types. His disciples were from those margins, and they never forgot it.

And Jesus also taught his followers to act humbly, to not think too much of themselves, and to become servants to one another and to their neighbors.

Jesus taught them to admit when they were wrong about all of the preconceived notions about God, faith, religion, and what it meant to be his follower—and it changed them forever.

I'd like to imagine that I can live my life like that—to be shaped by Jesus's example. It's a struggle, to be fair. I want to be my best self, but my lesser self keeps getting in the way.

But in the striving, there is grace and mercy. In the striving, there is hope that I can actually come closer to being the person I'm meant to be. In the striving, I see more clearly how following Jesus changes me, and, in turn, I am able to change the world around me.

So I will keep striving. And so should you. Never give up in your effort to become more like Jesus, which ultimately leads you to become more yourself.

Becoming the Answer to Your Prayers

I get a lot of questions about prayer in my role as a pastor. And almost all of the questions I get are in some way connected to the main question that everyone seems to have about prayer: what difference does prayer really make?

It's a challenging question because we all so desperately want our prayers to be answered. Or at the very least, we want to know that when we pray that we are heard; that somewhere out there, God is paying attention.

The trouble occurs when prayers go unanswered. Or worse, when it seems as though the answer we get is the exact opposite of what we were praying for.

For many people, this is the point when they begin to struggle with praying at all or they begin to wonder if God just might be arbitrary and capricious, favoring some people while seemingly cursing others.

Recently, I was reading from Suzanne Henley's excellent book on prayer, *Bead by Bead: The Ancient Way of Praying*, and I came across this awesome quote:

> I have no idea whether prayer produces any external results. I have come to believe, though, if nothing else, it is where I most squarely meet myself. I think it is the psychic glue between my conscious and shadow self where we all wrestle with Jacob's angel and count our scars later.

I tend to disagree a bit with Henley, in that I do believe that prayer produces external results. I have come to understand that when we pray, we enter into the divine flow between us and everything, which definitely creates action.

But, on the other hand, I agree wholeheartedly that when I pray, I encounter myself more often than not. I quickly discover that almost every obstacle in my life or challenge set before me is either caused by me or has my fingerprints all over it.

It is definitely the Spirit of God that moves me to be better, to do more, to change, to act, to repent. But then, the ball is placed squarely in my court.

It's almost like God is replying to my prayers, "Yes, I agree that would be a great thing. What are you going to do make that happen." Or "The outcome to this might not be what you desire. How are you going to respond?"

As you pray today, may your prayers be pathways of discovery for you as you determine God's desires for your life. May you become the answer to your prayers. May you pray without ceasing. May you feel heard and known and loved.

So How Are You, Really?

Have you ever run into a friend or an acquaintance and asked, "How's it going?" And we typically expect the following kinds of answers: "Good!"; "Great!"; "Never Better!"; "Awesome!"

But how many times have you asked someone that, and then they told you how they really felt? I've actually been that person from time to time.

And what you quickly discover, as you are relating just how awful you might be feeling and how challenging things are in your life, is that the person who inquired after your well-being suddenly no longer wants to hang out with you.

Seriously, you can watch them visibly shrink back and try to find a way to retreat or escape. Which is why most of us don't bother sharing what's really happening with us. We don't want to be a downer. We don't want to be a burden or to let anyone think we can't handle life's twists and turns.

I read a poem by r.h. Sin recently, and it made my heart hurt for all of the times I've felt this way and for all of the times I have made someone feel like they needed to hide.

> it hurts but I find myself
> pretending to be fine
> "I'm OK" has become my favorite lie
> and my smile is usually a mask
> that hides the truth in what I feel

If you have been hiding your pain by wearing a mask and simply saying, "I'm OK," "Never better!" or any number of platitudes designed to hold people at arm's length, I get it, and I'm sorry.

Know this: there are people out there who want to listen. There is a God all around you who wants you to experience the best of life in abundance. There is a Spirit moving through you, connecting you to the world around you. You are not alone.

And when you need something to hold on to, hold on to this prophetic promise from the Hebrew prophet Isaiah, who relates God's ever-present love for God's people: "Don't panic. I'm with you. There's no need to fear for I'm your God. I'll give you strength. I'll help you. I'll hold you steady, keep a firm grip on you" (Isaiah 41:10 MSG).

May it be that you feel the presence of God all around you, in you, and through you today and every day.

When Your Church Service Doesn't Cut It

One of my least favorite passages in the Bible is from the Hebrew prophet Amos, who really let ancient Israel have it when he declared this message from God to them:

> I can't stand your religious meetings. I'm fed up with your conferences and conventions. I want nothing to do with your religion projects, your pretentious slogans and goals I've had all I can take of your noisy ego-music. When was the last time you sang to me Do you know what I want? I want justice—oceans of it. I want fairness—rivers of it. That's what I want. That's all I want. (Amos 5:21–23 MSG)

The reason why this is one of my least favorite passages from the Bible is that it hits me right where I live.

I'm a pastor, you see, and worship gatherings and other assorted churchy stuff are where I spend most of my time and energy. So it's easy to read a passage like that and start to get disillusioned.

But the point of that passage isn't to discourage people from gathering for worship services. It's not to drive people from the church. Quite the contrary.

The point of this passage is that whatever you are doing as a worshipping community needs to be authentic, humble, heartfelt, and true. God wants us to be in community, but God also desires our communities to be focused on the things that matter to God.

So, to put it simply, if the church you attend is all about putting on a show every weekend but lacks substance when it comes to welcoming everyone, it might be missing the point.

If you are part of a faith community where there's a wonderful light show in worship, glitzy kids' programs, and a coffee shop with real, honest-to-goodness lattes, but there are no women in leadership, it might be missing the point.

And individually, God wants us to focus more on becoming more like Christ than "getting our worship on." Anthony de Mello, the late Christian mystic, once wrote this:

> God would be much happier, according to Jesus Christ, if you were transformed than if you worshipped. He would be much more pleased by your loving [others] than by your adoration [in church].

May you be filled with a true sense of worship today and every day—the kind that drives you to be the person God dreams for you to be. May you be filled with holy dissatisfaction for anything that is less than that.

You Need to Be Bonkers to Follow Jesus

I've been thinking a lot lately about what it takes to be a sold-out, bet-the-farm, wild-eyed follower of Jesus.

And by sold-out, bet-the-farm, wild-eyed follower, I don't mean someone who is mean, angry, or belligerent. I also don't mean someone who is off his rocker—at least, not in a bad way. Although I've learned, over the years, that a little bit of "out there" can be a good thing when you want to follow Jesus properly.

What I mean is that it takes passion and desire to be a Jesus-follower. That's the difference in being an admirer of Jesus and a follower. An admirer lacks the passion and desire that permeate a follower. A follower of Jesus gets up, acts, and moves, putting one foot in front of the other as he or she follows (often stumbling) in Jesus's footsteps. An admirer will pretty much stay on the couch where it's safe.

Lots of people merely admire Jesus, even people who claim to be his followers. Admirers of Jesus tend to hold his teachings at arm's length—a safe distance from them, lest they be affected by his teachings completely. The fact is, when you fully embrace the teachings of Jesus, you can't help but become a follower. If you fully follow Jesus, all other relationships, desires, and passions will fall in behind him in the priorities of your life.

Jesus once declared to his followers,

> Whoever loves father and mother more than me is not fit to be my disciple. Anyone who loves son or daughter more than me is not fit to be my disciple. (Matthew 10:37 NIV)

That's a hard thing to hear, to be sure. It's the kind of demand that keeps a lot of people on the couch, admiring Jesus from afar.

If you put Jesus first, you begin to want the same things that Jesus wants. And what Jesus came to do—what Jesus wants more than anything—is for creation to be redeemed and the kingdom of God to be fully realized.

Jesus told his disciples that the answers to all their questions, the fulfillment of all they desired, was right in front of them, if they only had the passion to find them. "Knock," Jesus told his followers, "and the door will be opened unto you. Seek, and you will find" (Matthew 7:7 NIV).

May you discover the passion and desire that it takes to fully follow Jesus. May you become a sold-out, bet-the-farm, wild-eyed follower, who stumbles after him, seeking, knocking, and desiring only what Jesus desires. May the kingdom of God spring up all around you as you go.

Heeding the Warning Signs

Yesterday, I listened to reports on the radio that Washington, DC, was crippled by a light dusting of snow that quickly turned the streets, both inside and outside the Beltway, into a frozen mess. One man declared that it had taken him an hour to drive four miles.

Even the president's motorcade was spinning its wheels during a long commute back to the White House, which I am sure did not sit well with the White House.

People were abandoning their cars on the side of the road because they couldn't move them in the horrific traffic jams caused by the icy streets. The news was made all the more terrible because the city was preparing for a massive snowstorm of historic proportions that is due to hit the eastern United States at any moment.

The mayor of Washington, DC, was blathering on and on that the city was prepared for the coming "Snowpocalypse," despite the fact it hadn't been at all ready for the light dusting the day before. Not surprisingly, most of the people being interviewed for the story were unconvinced by the mayor's declaration.

I felt a bit more charitable. I saw the icy, jammed-up roads and the horrific traffic as a warning sign. It was a wake-up call for the city officials to get themselves ready for the real thing. I wonder what would have happened if the Snowpocalypse had come a day earlier. Can you imagine the carnage that would have ensued?

I see our spiritual well-being in much the same way. From time to time, we receive warning signs that all is not well with our relationship with God and that if something isn't done to correct it, bad things lie ahead for us.

For example, if you find yourself constantly flying into a rage every time something doesn't go exactly as you planned, it's a warning. Or if you become melancholy, full of self-loathing, and beat yourself each time you make a mistake, it's a warning.

One of the great things about a new year is that we get the opportunity to do the kind of self-inventory that we need to start fresh, begin again, and do more and do better in the coming year.

May you discover, this day and every day, the power that comes from starting with God. May you find the strength to let God be your mighty fortress, your shield, and your Rock, as God is described in the Bible. May you be prepared for all of life's storms, ready to stand in courage and great faith.

Letting Go of a Rearview-Mirror Approach to Life

I spent a lot of years wandering, trying to figure out what I was supposed to do with my life.

There have been times when I have looked back on those years and wished I could have them back. I have thought about all the things I would have done differently to expedite my journey and wished that I'd done them.

Over time, though, I've learned to love all of my wanderings and to see them as necessary and vital to the person I've become and to my calling in life. Nothing was wasted, in other words. It was all part of the journey.

I was reading through some of the Proverbs in the Hebrew scriptures this morning and came across this one: "Many are the plans of a person's heart, but it is the Lord's purpose that prevails" (Proverbs 19:21 NIV).

It got me thinking about the fact that once I got my mind around the idea that God has greater purposes for me than I could ever imagine—grand ideas, wonderful things, abundant life—that's when I started to see all of my wanderings differently.

But far too many people never get past their regrets and spend their lives looking constantly in the rearview mirror, neither fully realizing their true purpose nor fully embracing it in joy.

And too many people live without being able to recognize that all of the good things in their lives never would have happened if they hadn't wandered.

I recently read this beautiful poem by Tiffany Aurora that illustrates this so perfectly:

> You do not,
> need to wander aimlessly
> in order to be found—it is just that
> you have not yet made what you hold
> in your hands
> into a true home.

May you embrace all your wandering and learn to love it. May you also realize that in all your wandering, you were carrying your true home with you the entire time and, further, that God was in it all along.

Seeing Yourself as God Sees You

The Christian communities within which I was raised taught me to believe that humanity is essential evil. I remember hearing pastors preach about the inherent wickedness of humankind, going so far to make their point that they would say things like:

"You look at a tiny baby, and you think to yourself, 'There's no way that tiny baby could be evil,' and then you start seeing that tiny baby crying, throwing tantrums, and then you know—that baby has a sinful nature. That baby was born wicked."

This way of interpreting the story of the Garden of Eden from Genesis—where Adam and Eve chose to be like God and eat from the forbidden fruit, thus condemning all of humankind—is widely known as "the fall."

The idea is that after the fall, human beings are born filled with wickedness and are condemned to sweat out their survival through toil, and pain. And then, only an act of divine intervention can save us from our natural, evil state, and this can happen only when we choose to embrace Jesus Christ as Lord of our lives.

The problem with this way of thinking is that it places God in a very unjust light. Why would God punish people for acting according to their nature? If goodness is unnatural and evil is natural, then to act in goodness means that you are living against your nature. That doesn't make any sense.

I believe that people are created inherently good, but I also believe that people have a choice as to whether that inherent goodness will thrive and flourish within them or whither away, fading as they give strength to pride, which ultimately twists what is good.

The story of the Garden of Eden gets played out each and every day. Every day of my life, I have a choice to make about how I want to live. Do I want to live a life in intimate relationship with God, as I am created to live, or do I want to take control and do things my way?

If I choose my own way—if I choose to deny my created, inherent goodness—my very choices will be my punishment. My life will be harder, full of sweat and pain.

But when I choose to follow Jesus and live as he would have me live, I begin to discover my true self. That is essentially what Jesus meant when he told his disciples, "The kingdom of God is within you" (Luke 17:21 KJV).

May you live today and every day to please the Spirit of God in Jesus Christ, who gives us abundant life—life that God intends for us to lead. May you choose today to embrace your created, inherent goodness and to deny the pride that would have you choose otherwise.

Preventive Medicine

I'm still fighting the lingering effects of the wicked cold that I got a couple of weeks ago, the same kind of cold that, apparently, hundreds of thousands, even millions of other people are fighting, too.

I never felt like I was in any real danger when I got sick a couple of weeks ago. It was just annoying. I ate chicken soup, watched a lot of television, snorted nasal spray and waited it out. But there was a very slight chance that whatever I got could have developed into something more serious.

I've heard well-meaning Christians tell their friends or loved ones who are going through tough times, "Well, God won't give you more than you can handle." The truth of the matter is, that's not at all biblically based. God frequently gives us or allows us to take on more than we can handle. The actual verse people are trying to quote when they say those kinds of things reads like this:

> No temptation has overtaken you except what is common to mankind. And God is faithful; he will not let you be tempted beyond what you can bear. But when you are tempted, he will also provide a way out so that you can endure it. (1 Corinthians 10:13 NIV)

To begin, the word that the apostle Paul uses here is *temptation*, which also is translated as "trial" or "test." And further, Paul was speaking of the temptations that many Christians faced in the first century—temptations of idolatry, sexual promiscuity, selfish living, and the like. Honestly, those same temptations still plague Christians today.

I didn't really think about it, but when I got sick a couple of weeks ago, the chance was there that I could have developed a severe sinus infection, which could have led to nasty things, or contracted bronchitis or, worse yet, pneumonia. But because my immune system was fairly strong and I got some rest, fluids, and a few bottles of zinc-laden immune-boosters, I lessened those chances.

Paul indicates that following Jesus isn't going to keep you from being tempted to act against the God-nature within you. But following Jesus and maintaining a strong, intimate relationship with God by following the Way of Jesus will give you a way to get through it.

In other words, the way to beat back the temptations you face is by taking care of your spiritual health before temptation lands on you and then doing what is necessary to fend it off when it does.

Beloved, may you strengthen your spiritual immune system constantly through daily connection with the Spirit of God in Christ. May you find the strength that God has given you to withstand the temptations that come your way—temptations to act in ways that deny the image of God within you.

There's Nothing Wrong with Doubting

I don't always feel close to God. There are days when I wonder what God is up to. Sometimes, I have doubts about my beliefs.

I also understand that for some people, it might seem a bit off-putting to read these sentences and realize they are written by a pastor. After all, pastors are supposed to be professional Christians, right? Except we're not.

We're just like everyone else when it comes to struggles with faith and doubt. But I've discovered a few things over the years. There are basically two ways that people respond when I reveal that I sometimes struggle to have faith: they feel relieved, or they become angry.

People who feel relieved typically respond out of gratitude; they are grateful that they aren't alone in their doubts and even more grateful that a pastor would admit to feeling the same way from time to time. They get that it doesn't give them license to throw Christianity as a whole into question, but it does give them strength to wade through the doubt to the other side.

Bu there are also people who become angry when they hear about my struggles. I've been told more than once that it's "not right" for a pastor to say such things to his congregation, and that I should lead people to faith, not doubt.

When you read the Bible, however, you quickly discover that it's full of doubt-filled songs, poems, prayers, declarations, prophecies, and the like. Take Psalm 44, for example. The singer has some questions for God in the midst of a time of suffering:

> Awake, Lord! Why do you sleep? Rouse yourself! Do not reject us forever. Why do
> you hide your face and forget our misery and oppression? (Psalm 44:23–24 NIV)

There's nothing wrong with doubting. There is nothing wrong with having an off day or two when it comes to your faith that God has a plan for your life. In fact, it's completely natural.

The psalmist who wrote Psalm 44 feels loss and emptiness and struggles with doubt. Yet he doesn't give up completely. There is a shred of faith left in his heart, and it is enough for the Almighty.

"Rise up and help us," the singer proclaims. "Rescue us because of your unfailing love" (Psalm 44:26 NIV).

It is because of God's unfailing, never-ending, unconditional love that even in the worst moments we can hold on and believe.

May you be filled with the knowledge of God's great love for you—love that never fails. May you find, even in your struggles, the ability to cling to that love and know that you are not alone.

Whatever Is Helpful in Building Up

I had a friend on Facebook a few years ago who got an intense amount of joy from ticking off everyone with his controversial Facebook posts. He would argue incessantly with people, saying all kinds of inflammatory things, offending everything, never seeming to really care who he hurt.

And then, I posted something on my Facebook page that he disagreed with. About football.

You see, we had pretty divergent opinions regarding our favorite football teams—as in, he couldn't stand my team, and the feeling was reciprocated on my part toward his. So the guy started attacking me online, and we had a virtual argument right there on my Facebook page for everyone and their brother to see.

Finally, the guy posted the following comment, and it absolutely infuriated me. He wrote, "I can't believe you call yourself a pastor and post things like this."

I thought about all of the mean-spirited and awful things this guy regularly posted online and that he dared to call himself a Christian to boot. So I deleted the post where we were arguing, with all of the comments. Then I unfriended the guy, blocked him from my Facebook page, and generally eradicated him from my online world. It felt awesome—for about a day or two.

It was a passage of scripture that did me in, to be honest: "Do not let any unwholesome talk come out of your mouths, but only what is helpful for building others up according to their needs, that it may benefit those who listen" (Ephesians 4:29 NIV).

It also hit me that I had been judging that guy from afar for a very long time, and then, there I was, acting just like him.

I sent the guy a message after I got convicted over my behavior. I apologized, asked for his forgiveness, and told him that I was going to work hard to be a positive witness on my Facebook page from that day forward.

He never responded. I suppose he just wanted to be angry. I'll never know, I guess.

That verse from Ephesians is one that I am struck by over and again. I want to live into the hope of it. I don't always get it right, but I'm working on it. I think that's all that we can do sometimes.

May you find ways to speak grace and peace into the lives of those around you. May you guard your tongue or your fingers as you type, and consider that what you are saying or writing might be a blessing or a curse, and choose the right one. May your speech reflect the grace of God through Jesus Christ that is yours to have and to hold.

You Are Not Condemned

One of the stories in the Gospels that has always captured my imagination is from John 8:1–11. In the passage, we find that some legalistic religious leaders brought to Jesus a woman who had been caught in the act of adultery. A strict interpretation of Mosaic law meant that the woman should be executed by stoning.

The purpose of these religious leaders was to discredit Jesus as a false teacher who didn't uphold their religious laws. The text later reveals that these guys already had stones in their hands, ready to throw at her. Her verdict, as far as they were concerned, was decided.

But Jesus offers a strange response. He kneels down and begins drawing on the ground in front of these men and then invites any of them who is completely sinless to throw the first stone at her.

John's Gospel reveals that, one at a time, they drop their stones and leave. And then Jesus turns to her and asks, "Who is here to condemn you?" She replies, "No one." Then Jesus says to her, "I don't condemn you either. Now go, and sin no longer" (John 8:11 NIV).

I've always loved this moment in the Gospels, and I've often wondered what it must have been like for this woman as she knelt there on the ground in front of Jesus. He didn't say to her, "You aren't guilty" because her guilt was undisputed. Jesus told her she wasn't condemned.

And then Jesus sends her on her way with an exhortation to live a changed life. To live like she'd been set free. To live like she'd been redeemed, rescued and restored---because she was.

I read something recently that Ann Voskamp wrote in her excellent book *The Broken Way*. She said, "There is always more grace in Christ than there is guilt in us." Come on! How good is that? So why is it that so many Christians don't live like they are redeemed, rescued, and restored people? Why are so many of us who follow Jesus living our lives downcast, filled with remorse, hopeless in our outlooks?

I once read a quote from Thomas Merton that speaks directly into this very thing. He wrote, "There is no way of telling people that they are all walking around shining like the sun If only they could see themselves as they really are."

Remember that you are not condemned and have been set free. Live your life filled with joy, hope, and abundance. Lift up your head and hear the words of our brother, the apostle Paul, who wrote, "The Spirit you received does not make you slaves, so that you live in fear again" (Romans 8:15 NIV).

God Can Handle Your Pain

Many years ago, I was leading a study at my church titled "Experiencing God." There was a moment in the study when I invited the group to talk about times when they struggled to understand why God allowed suffering and pain.

Most of the members shared their own stories—seasons of their lives when they had more questions for God than answers. But one couple seemed perplexed by the exercise. Finally, the man spoke up. "We've never doubted God for a second," he said.

His wife nodded in agreement. "We always just assume that God knows what he's doing," she added.

As we dug deeper, I soon realized that their dogged belief really stemmed from something that they had been taught when they were very young: Never. Question. God.

That sweet couple in my Bible study had a very simple image of God. In their belief system, God's wider view affords God wisdom we'll never attain. God is God; we are not. The sooner you accept this, the better off you'll be.

There's a great deal of truth embedded into this way of thinking about God, but it's an incomplete view of the Almighty.

What we find in the scriptures is a God who doesn't condemn people from asking questions—far from it. Even the name Israel, which was given to God's people in the Hebrew scriptures, means "God-wrestler." As I wrote recently in a sermon on this very topic, God honors our relationship with God by engaging and persisting in the struggle, just so we will know God is with us—truly with us.

I read something today from blogger/author Mark Manson that gave me some additional clarity on this issue. He wrote, "The pain of honest confrontation is what generates the greatest trust and respect in your relationships."

In other words, crying out to God when we are in pain, asking questions when we are struggling to understand, and confronting God about the injustice in the world are all ways that we give pain and suffering meaning when we are willing to be honest with God about how we feel.

Jesus exhorted his followers to engage in an honest, active, and engaging relationship with God. As I previously have related, Jesus taught, "Ask and it will be given to you. Seek and you will find; Knock and the door will be opened to you" (Matthew 7:7 NIV).

Beloved, don't ever be afraid of your questions for God. What God desires is for you to struggle with God, to wrestle with God's will, to ask your questions, to cry out in prayer, and to know, in the struggle, that God is near.

From One Generation to Another

A few years ago, I was driving through the city with my youngest son. I began pointing out landmarks, showing him where his mother and I (along with his oldest brother) had lived downtown.

I showed him the park we used to frequent and where we got our Christmas trees every year, and as we drove, I talked to him about our visits to Grant Park, Navy Pier, Lincoln Park Zoo, and the hospital where his brother, our middle son, was born.

Through the rearview mirror, I could see his face was filled with the most thoughtful expression. I realized he was processing the fact that there was a history of our family that he shared but had not experienced. He didn't know exactly how, but Chicago was a part of him.

As I watched my son, I thought about the way families pass these things down to children and grandchildren. I wondered if, one day, he would drive his own children through the streets of Chicago, telling them about his family and telling them of his own trips there.

That moment with my son got me thinking about how faith is passed down to children and what can be done to ensure the next generations receive it well and (even more importantly) make it their own.

Deuteronomy 6:4–8 contains an exhortation concerning the passing of faith experiences and traditions from one generation to the next. It reads:

> You shall love the Lord your God with all your heart and with all your soul and with all your might. And these words that I command you today shall be on your heart. You shall teach them diligently to your children, and shall talk of them when you sit in your house, and when you walk by the way, and when you lie down, and when you rise. (NIV)

Throughout the passing of faith from one generation to the next, some of the doctrines, dogmas, and pointless traditions, even some of the rules and regulations, often get lost along the way—and that's perfectly all right.

But the experience of God; the milestones of family life lived together in shared faith; the stories of rescue, redemption, love, forgiveness, mercy, and grace—those are the things that *must* be shared, passed down, and retained.

So tell your stories of experiencing God to your children and grandchildren. Tell them that even though they may not have your experiences, they share them, in a way, and one day, they will have their own stories of God to tell.

Stand at the Crossroads and Look

This week I've been traveling some old paths as I have been driving all over the city of Chicago. Essentially, four years of my life were spent here when I was going to seminary and serving as a youth director in Evanston, just north of the city.

It's funny, but it doesn't take long to remember those old paths when you return to a place you knew so well. Without even noticing it, I began driving without my GPS yesterday as I went from one place to the other. I just kind of knew where to go.

I also began remembering little things from the past. A vivid memory of a walk in the park with my oldest son rushed back to me. I saw the neighborhood where we took our kids trick-or-treating on a bitterly cold Halloween and the park where my middle son crawled on a blanket when he was not yet a year old.

Those memories and the places where they were made are all a part of me, but I am different than I was then. I've changed and grown. I have new stories to tell and new experiences that have shaped me.

As I was thinking this morning about all of those memories—the familiar places, paths, and feelings—I had a bit of an epiphany. There was a time in my life when I set aside my faith and walked away from God, the Bible, and church. One of the many things that kept me from returning was a fear that I would never really find my way back.

In Jeremiah 6:16, there is a wonderful exhortation from God, speaking through the prophet. It reads:

> This is what the LORD says: "Stand at the crossroads and look; ask for the ancient paths, ask where the good way is, and walk in it, and you will find rest for your souls." (NIV)

When I returned to faith, I discovered some familiar roads—paths where I had walked before. I was different, I had changed, and I brought new experiences and stories with me, but the essence of those paths were the same. I also learned it doesn't take long before you find yourself walking them with confidence.

If you've struggled to hang on to your faith or feel that you have lost your way a bit, I would urge you to return to your roots, ask for the "ancient paths," and the "good way" because I believe the memories of those paths and ways are within you. Step forward. Your feet will undoubtedly know the way.

Showing Love during Disagreement

The cable news channels I occasionally watch and my social media feeds have had a busy week with the inauguration of a new president and all of the protests and brouhaha that followed.

As I discovered this weekend, I have friends from all over the country who marched in protest on Saturday, but I also have plenty of friends who were not shy about expressing their opposition to the marches.

Some days, it's just too much to process—all of the anger, the outrage, the demonization of the "other." It can wear you down and bring out the worst in you. Try as I might, I often find myself falling into the trap of over-generalizing my view of people who disagree with me. I also have to admit that I'm not all that loving and grace-filled toward them either.

But those of us who call ourselves followers of Jesus are called to a different kind of life. This new life doesn't mean that we can't disagree or protest when we feel that justice demands it. It doesn't mean that we shouldn't vote our conscience either. We should.

However, we are unequivocally called to a higher standard in the way we treat others.

When you read through the Gospels, you find that Jesus spoke truth to power on more than one occasion. But Jesus also ate dinner with people who opposed him and was not above showing God's love to a Roman centurion, a Samaritan woman, and at least two tax-collecting, good-for-nothing imperial collaborators.

The apostle Paul offered this exhortation to the early church: "For you were once darkness, but now you are light in the Lord. Live as children of light" (Ephesians 5:8 NIV).

We need this as a constant reminder to demonstrate the love of Christ to all, regardless of whether they stand in agreement with us.

I think that we are transformed when we live as children of light and learn to love people where they are. Author Ann Voskamp, in a spot-on reflection on this very idea, wrote, "What matters most is not if our love makes other people change, but that in loving, we change."

Even in moments when you are tempted not to be your best self, may you find hidden resources of grace and forgiveness, mercy, and peace.

And may you be transformed forever as you learn to love others, even as Jesus loved and gave himself for you.

Too Busy Not to Pray

It's a busy time in my life right now. So to get an edge today, I set my alarm for four thirty in order to get out of bed a half hour before my usual wake-up time of five o'clock.

And then it all slipped away. A full fifteen minutes of that extra time was spent staring into space and sipping a cup of coffee as I tried to shake the cobwebs from my head.

I don't even know what happened to the other fifteen. I think I might have spent it trying to get my foot working again so I could walk to the other room without falling down.

"There is a time for everything, and a season for every activity under the heavens," as Ecclesiastes 3:1 (NIV) states. Even though "busyness" isn't included in the list that follows after that statement, I think that it sort of falls under the every-activity category.

And when I'm going through a busy season of life, or a trying season of life, or any season of life when things get a bit complicated, I tend to want to get my hands around every little thing, to control the outcomes, to do it all on my own.

It's also easy, in those seasons, to neglect the things that keep me grounded and properly focused. I have to fight the temptation to forgo my usual hour or so of reading, prayer, and reflection in the morning. I have to resist the urge not to walk with my kid to school or not to eat healthier, even when it would be faster to consume junk food.

The great sixteenth-century reformer Martin Luther claimed that he prayed for an hour every day, unless he was too busy. When he was too busy, he prayed for three hours a day.

I think that God finds us in the little things, the details, the small moments when we push back the busyness, the trying times, the out-of-control circumstances, and we simply do life-giving, soul-restoring things that connect us to the Almighty.

Khalil Gibran once wrote, "For in the dew of little things the heart finds it's morning and is refreshed."

In his translation of the Bible, known as The Message, Eugene Peterson interpreted Psalm 46:9 like this: "Step out of the traffic! Take a long, loving look at me, your High God."

I love that so very much. I hope that it speaks to you today as well.

May you find moments to do life-giving things today. May you carve out time in your day for prayer, for silence, and for peace. Breathe in the wonders of creation. Make the time to refresh your heart in the "dew of the little things," where God is waiting to meet you.

The Reason Why Your Heart Breaks

I was watching a video that a friend of mine had shared on her Facebook page yesterday. It was a compilation video of children and teens showing kindness and good sportsmanship to one another on the playing field.

In one memorable moment, a high school softball player, who had been paralyzed from an accident, was carried around the bases by members of an opposing team so she could experience one last home run.

My friend commented that she had tears streaming down her face when she watched the video. I have to admit that I too felt a knot in my own throat as I watched.

I got to thinking about all of the similar feel-good videos I've seen lately on other friends' Facebook pages—quite a lot of them, actually. I've often wondered about the popularity of these videos. What makes us watch them, share them, and cry over them?

In the book of Genesis, the creation account declares that God created humankind (both male and female) in the "image of God." (Genesis1:27 NIV). In brief, this means that all of us are imprinted with the DNA of God. And it is that encoding that draws us to the things that matter to God.

The reason why your heart breaks and overflows with joy when you see people doing things that are beautiful, sacrificial, and life-giving is because that's exactly how it makes God feel.

This world is far from perfect, and it feels like so many of us are more divided than ever over just how to make it right. But in the midst of all of our brokenness, sadness, and outrage, all it takes is one image—one moment of beauty, sacrifice, and goodness—to remind us of who we really are.

Frederick Buechner once wrote:

> To journey for the sake of saving our own lives is little by little to cease to live it is only by journeying for the world's sake--even when the world bores and sickens and scares you half to death—that little by little we start to come alive.

So, beloved child of God, who is created in God's very image, live today for the sake of the world. Share beauty, create beauty, and do what is good, merciful, and life-giving, no matter what it costs you. In other words, live as Jesus lived—he who loved and gave himself for us.

The Real Message of Christianity

This is how much God loved the world: He gave his Son, his one and only Son. And this is why: so that no one need be destroyed; by believing in him, anyone can have a whole and lasting life.
—John 3:16 (MSG)

John 3:16 is probably one of the most famous and well-used verses in the entire New Testament, which is why so many of us miss the intricacies of its message; we've grown too used to it.

Which is why I like to use a literal translation instead of one above that might be a bit more familiar. The Greek word for "world" in John 3:16 is actually "cosmos," which we tend to diminish by translating it into "world. But isn't *cosmos* a whole lot bigger?

And what about the words *so loved*? God so loved the cosmos—the universe, all of creation. When you think of it in those terms, doesn't it expand your view of this God, the kind of God who still loves and still dotes on what God has created?

But the next words truly set the stage for all that comes in the second half of the verse: For God so loved the cosmos as to give

God's unbelievable, never-ending, intimate love for creation (which includes you and me) results in generosity. And this isn't your everyday, run-of-the-mill generosity. This isn't the kind of meager generosity that you and I call generosity.

The kind of generosity, which flows from the loving heart of God, is the kind that offers the greatest gift that could possibly be given—the gift of the Son, the only one.

This incredible gift that was given by God—the gift of the Son—is the only gift that offers the universe (and you and me) the true source of light, through whom all of creation (and us) can experience life to its fullest, both on this side of eternity and the next.

How amazing is the message of this verse—this all-too-familiar verse that contains the entire story of how God is saving not just the world but all of creation? And isn't that the greatest kind of hope imaginable?

That's a story worth sharing.

What Is Your Thread?

One of the many things I love about poetry is the way that it often expands, rather than contracts, the imagination. And the best poems challenge you to enter into the story they are telling, the moment they are describing, and make it your own.

I read the following poem by William Stafford this morning, and I was moved by the imagery it lifted up:

> There's a thread that you follow. It goes among
> things that change. But it doesn't change.
> But it is hard for others to see.
> While you hold it you can't get lost.
> Tragedies happen; people get hurt
> or die; and you suffer and get old.
> Nothing you can do can stop time's unfolding.
> You don't ever let go of the thread.

This poem by Stafford ultimately begs an important question. Did you think of it yet? I had to read through the poem a couple of times before it occurred to me to ask it. Here it is: "What is my thread?"

How would I describe the thread that I follow? How would I describe the thread that I hold on to, no matter what happens all around me? What is that thread that I hang on to for dear life, never letting go?

For me, that thread is the undeserved and abundant grace of God. It is God's grace—as revealed through the captivating love of Jesus—that I have followed and have never let go for my entire life.

Even in moments when I wasn't exactly sure to which thread I was still clinging, it was still God's grace that I was clutching as I felt my way along, hand over hand, inch by inch, stumbling after Jesus, who ultimately shows us all what God is really like.

What is your thread? What has been the constant throughout your life? As you look down at what your hands have been holding, what do you see?

If you feel as though you've been clinging to the thread of bitterness, sorrow, anger, or disappointment, look more closely and deeply. There is a true thread at the heart of it all, something that has been part of your journey from before the beginning of time. And that thread has its origins in the God who created you and loves you and who desires for you to share in the joy of eternal life, both now and forever.

How Like God

I call on you, my God, for you will answer me; turn your ear to me and
hear my prayer. Show me the wonders of your great love.
—Psalm 17:7 (NIV)

There is a moment, early in the Gospel of John, where Jesus meets Nathanael, a young man who would soon become one of his twelve disciples. Nathanael is brought by Philip, who had already been captivated by Jesus and called to follow.

When Philip introduces Nathanael, Jesus declares to all who are gathered, "Here truly is an Israelite in whom there is no deceit." Nathanael asks Jesus, "How do you know me?" Jesus replies, "I saw you while you still under the fig tree when Philip came to get you" (John 1:48 NIV).

Nathanael is amazed because not only has Jesus asserted that he knows who Nathanael really is, but he then goes on to prove it by miraculously revealing his knowledge of something that he could not have known, except through divine sight.

And in that moment, Nathanael pledges his loyalty and love to Jesus by saying, "Teacher, you are the Son of God, you are the king of Israel!" (John 1:49 NIV).

The two greatest longings in every human heart are the longings to know and to be known. We long to know that there is something greater at work around us.

Saint Augustine referred to this as a "God-shaped hole." We also long to be known—by others, of course, but mostly by the "something" or "someone" greater than ourselves.

When that moment comes, when you feel known by God and realize that God not only loves you but has been present in your life, meeting you where you are, it's the most fulfilling feeling you could ever experience.

Poet Lisa Mueller describes it like this: "It's about two seemingly parallel lines suddenly coming together inside us, in some place that is still wilderness."

And how like God to meet us in the wilderness within us, in the places where we feel unknown, lost, and afraid. How like God to find us there and reveal to us the truth about ourselves: that we are loved beyond all love and intimately known.

May you find the very presence of God in your own wilderness spaces today. May you allow yourself to feel the "known-ness" of that presence in your life.

Looking through Busted Glass

A couple of years ago, a random accident cracked the glass on the screen of my laptop and turned half of it into a bunch of pulsating lines that would grow even denser and fuzzier the longer the computer was left on.

When I finally got it fixed, after weeks of only being able to see half of my screen, it was amazing to see the whole display. I finally could see what I was doing when I was editing, writing, and creating.

I started thinking about that many other areas in my life might be just like that—where I wasn't able to see the whole picture. I thought about all of the circumstances, people, situations, and even my own beliefs and convictions, where things were a bit fuzzy and not at all clear.

For most of us, instead of finding new ways to see more clearly in those circumstances, we simply put up with the fuzziness, and before too long, the distortion becomes the norm. We lose our vision for what we could see if we had the right lenses.

The apostle Paul wrote about this in his first letter to the church at Corinth. He writes:

> For now we see only a reflection as in a mirror; then we shall see face to face. Now I know in part; then I shall know fully, even as I am fully known. (1 Corinthians 13:12 NIV)

Paul was writing about a day when all the fuzzy things in his life would become clear to him, a day when all things would be put to rights by the power of the Holy Spirit of God in Jesus. His vision was one for the future, but, as in all of Paul's writings, there was an element of the *now* in the midst of the *not yet*.

Even though we don't have the benefit of God's all-encompassing wisdom and vision, even though we live in a world that has not yet fully realized its full potential, we still have moments when we can glimpse the whole picture.

Maybe it's a moment when you realize that the angry person you can't seem to get along with is dealing with pain, sorrow, or loss, and you see that person differently. Or you realize, in a flash, that there was actually a reason for that one thing that happened to you years ago—the thing that caused you so much pain and that you couldn't figure out why at the time.

Maybe you catch a glimpse of how the world could be through an act of kindness or a story of redemption. Maybe you look in the mirror and finally see that you are so much more than the negative self-talk you've always used to describe yourself. May you find new lenses—new eyes to see the world and everything in it as God sees it.

Missing the Miracle

In the Gospel of John, a passage relates the story of how Jesus healed a man near the Pool of Bethesda in Jerusalem, a spot where a number of sick people would lie.

We learn that the man had been an "invalid" for thirty-eight years, and the moment of his healing is related this way:

> Then Jesus said to him, "Get up! Pick up your mat and walk." At once the man was cured; he picked up his mat and walked. (John 5:8–9a NIV)

So this guy is healed and walks away, carrying his mat—walking upright and well for the first time in thirty-eight years.

But then he encounters the overly religious people in the community, who take offense at the fact that he is "working" on the Sabbath. Here's what they said to him:

> The day on which this took place was a Sabbath, and so the Jewish leaders said to the man who had been healed, "It is the Sabbath; the law forbids you to carry your mat." (John 5:9b–10 NIV)

Don't you just love that?

This guy had been flat on his back for thirty-eight years. Most of these religious types would have visited the Pool of Bethesda repeatedly, and most likely, they would have seen him lying there at one point or another.

And because they are more concerned about the fact that he is breaking some kind of rule, they miss the miracle.

How often do those of us who claim to follow Jesus miss out on his miracles in the world today because we're too busy focusing on our religious checklists?

How often do we not even see what new things Jesus is doing in the world because we're too busy being outraged or boycotting something or another that we don't agree with?

May we all train our eyes to see Jesus at work in the world—healing, restoring, resurrecting, and making all things new. May we lift our heads from our checklists and fix our eyes on Jesus—and Jesus alone.

And may we truly see how, through Jesus, God is drawing all of creation (and all of us) ever closer to God.

If I Could, I Would Come Too

As I write this morning, I am looking out the window of an airplane and marveling at what is shaping up to be a spectacular sunrise.

It's marvelous that I am tens of thousands of feet in the air, gazing out the window at rose-colored clouds and soft orange and yellow beams of sunlight bursting through, and I'm also online, writing this devotion.

What a world—am I right?

While I reflect on all of these marvelous things, I am also listening to one of my favorite albums from 2017—U2's *Songs of Experience*. One of the songs, "Love Is Bigger than Anything in Its Way," is really speaking to me this morning.

> If I could, I would come, too
> But the path is made by you
> As you're walking start singing and stop talking.
> Oh, if I could hear myself when I say
> (Oh love) love is bigger than anything in its way.

For some reason, those words—combined with the sunrise and the overwhelming feeling that I am being drawn into something bigger, something greater than myself, as I'm hurtling along at breakneck speed, high in the air but still tethered to the earth, connected to people who are reading, listening, and wondering, just like me—makes me feel both terrified and hopeful.

I imagine Jesus speaking to the lyrics of the song to his disciples before he disappears from their view. "If I could, I would come too. As you're walking, start singing and stop talking." And then, the realization of the disciples comes after hearing Jesus speak: "Love is bigger than anything in its way."

Whatever is before us, beloved, we can know—without a shadow of a doubt—that because of Jesus, love is bigger. We are making the road before us by walking, stepping forward in faith and trust. And we sing our songs of hope, even as it seems the world has gone mad at times and even when we are afraid.

Because the God who paints the sky with breathtaking artistry is the same God who gave "Godself" sacrificially and with love that is hard to comprehend—love that is bigger than anything in its way.

When All You've Got Is a Glimpse

Over the years, I've been pretty open about my struggles with doubt as it relates to my faith. One of those times came a couple of years ago after the horrific tragedy that occurred at Sandy Hook Elementary School, when a deranged gunman callously executed little children. After that happened, I had a dark moment or two about what God was up to, if God was up to anything at all.

I realized after Sandy Hook that all of the things that Christian culture had programmed me to say were useless and trite. In the end, I had to dive to the bottom of my doubt during that dark time to find some ground to push off in order to return to the surface.

A church member once met with me to share his numerous concerns about some of my recent sermon topics. In particular, he took umbrage over my openness when it comes to my struggles with doubt. "You shouldn't teach people that it's OK to doubt," he chided me. "You should lead people to the truth, not to doubt."

Later, as I had time to reflect on his criticism, I felt sorry for him. I really don't know how to arrive at a real, mature, and vibrant faith without experiencing doubt.

The great Scottish writer George MacDonald (who was a huge influence on C. S. Lewis) once wrote:

> Do you love your faith so little that you have never battled a single fear lest your faith should not be true? Where there are no doubts, no questions, no perplexities, there can be no growth.

I've also come to realize that when I am yearning for meaning and certainty, when I am railing at God to show up and reveal Godself, what I am asking of God is something I ultimately can't handle.

Even Moses wasn't able to handle the full presence and revelation of God when he met God on the mountain. All he caught was a glimpse of God's glory and meaning.

The great preacher Frederick Buechner put it far better than I could:

> Without destroying me in the process, how could God reveal himself in a way that would leave no room for doubt? If there were no room for doubt, there would be no room for me.

May you embrace your doubt not as a curse but as a gift. May you know in your heart of hearts that your doubt is a path to faith, a necessary moment in your journey to wholeness and oneness with God.

Love Is Stronger than Hate

This past weekend, my wife and I spent some time in New York City with a friend who was having surgery there. We also took the time to experience some of the sights of the city.

One of the most meaningful things that we did was to visit the National 9/11 Museum and Memorial on the site of the World Trade Center, which was destroyed in an evil terrorist attack seventeen years ago.

It's hard to fathom the kind of hatred and twisted religious fundamentalism that would cause such death and destruction. As a people, we lost a lot on that day. We lost our innocence, our naive view of the wider world, and our overall sense of safety

I felt old resentments well up inside of me, and hard words began to form on my lips. And then, Merideth said to me, "We have to be better. We have to come from a place of love. We need to speak that into the world."

About that time, we rounded the corner and saw a display in the gift shop of a T-shirt emblazoned with the words, "Love Is Stronger than Hate." I actually had to resist the urge in that moment to kneel down in front of the display (which seemed more like an altar to me) and repent of my anger and bitterness.

When Jesus was asked by his disciples who was the greatest "in the kingdom of the heavens," he called forward and stood a little child in their midst.

> And he said: "Truly I tell you, unless you change and become like little children,
> you will never enter the kingdom of heaven." (Matthew 18:3 NIV)

There have been lots of interpretations of that passage, but I tend to believe that Jesus was calling on his followers to let go of their jaded views of the world and their reliance on themselves.

He was calling on them to innocently, naively, and wholeheartedly embrace the joy of childish trust, faith, and love.

Love is truly stronger than hate. Faith is a gift from God that will carry us through even the darkest moments. And trust is a form of surrender that gives us the freedom to be the people God dreams for us to be.

So become like a child today, and let all your words and deeds come from a place of faith, trust, and love. Speak and live those virtues into the world—an action that brings heaven to earth, right here, right now.

The Surprising Presence of God

Some years ago, I started attending an ecumenical prayer gathering of pastors and church leaders in the small town where I was serving as a pastor.

After a couple of meetings, I began to notice some patterns in the ways some of my colleagues spoke about their decisions and the ways they planned their own lives.

They would say things like, "The Lord spoke to me the other day," or "I knew the Lord wanted us to do this," or "I knew I was being led by God to say this."

All too conveniently, the things my fellow pastors were claiming God was telling them to do seemed to be the very things that they were already sold on as good ideas.

Unfortunately, uncritically claiming one's own ideas and desires as a flash of divine revelation is something that Christian-y people do all the time.

I've seen it taken to the extreme ("God led me to leave my wife"—an actual statement a guy shared with me once), and I've also seen it used to diminish God's work in the world by trivializing it ("God gave me that parking space," or "God just told me to buy that new car"—that the person couldn't afford).

I am sure all of us would love to believe that God wholeheartedly agrees with us on everything we say and do. But none of us can truly claim to have a corner on the market when it comes to God's endorsement.

Instead, we all need to find the humility to surrender our own desires and subjugate our beliefs, plans, and preferred outcomes to the surprising presence of God.

In his excellent book *A Bigger Table,* author John Pavlovitz speaks directly into this when he writes:

> Whatever is real and true about God will be revealed in our midst, and it will testify to itself. We won't need to claim it, or own it, or commandeer it. We'll just be present and be reverent in the face of it.

May you discover where God is at work in the world today and join God in that work. May you be willing to allow God to shape and mold you in God's image. May you be surprised by God's presence today and every day.

Why We Shouldn't Know the Future

A friend of mine recently posted a twenty-seven-year-old photo of us on Facebook from a trip we took to New York City with two other friends, one of whom was my roommate, Greg.

The photo was taken on top of one of the towers of the World Trade Center, marking the beginning of an epic trip to the city, Upstate New York, and eventually Toronto. I was just twenty-two years old in that photo—younger than my oldest son is now.

Just over ten years after this photo was taken, the World Trade Center would be destroyed on September 11. Thirteen years later, at age thirty-nine, my old roommate, Greg, would lose his life in a tragic motorcycle accident, brought on by a drunk driver.

If the passerby who took our photo that day had been from the future and had told me that those things would come to pass, I never would have believed it.

Standing on top of those seemingly indestructible buildings, I never would have imagined that both towers would be gone one day. I also never would have imagined that people could hate so much.

I never could have dreamed that my friend Greg, who was so full of life, energy, and passion, would be gone in just a few short years as well, his life cut short far too soon.

We don't know what the future holds, perhaps blissfully so. Because if we knew the hardships we would face, the losses and the grief, we might choose to never move forward.

Likewise, if we knew how challenging it would be to achieve our dreams—the sacrifices, and the twists and turns that lead to our greatest joys—we might choose to never begin the journey, despite the rewards.

Instead, those of us who choose to follow Jesus need to embrace each moment of the journey as a gift, even the moments that bring us to our knees in grief.

All of our moments are part of our own story, and our story is also part of God's great big story, which is being lovingly and beautifully written in ways that are often hard to comprehend.

And so we trust, and we keep walking. Because even though we don't know what the future holds, we are walking in the footsteps of the One who holds our future.

Doubting Thomas Wasn't Doubting

> Now Thomas (also known as Didymus), one of the Twelve, was not with the
> disciples when Jesus came. So the other disciples told him, "We have seen the
> Lord!" But he said to them, "Unless I see the nail marks in his hands and put my
> finger where the nails were, and put my hand into his side, I will not believe."
> —John 20:24–25 (NIV)

Doubting Thomas.

For centuries, Christians have affixed this ignominious nickname to the one disciple of Jesus who wasn't in the room the first time Jesus appeared to his followers after the Resurrection.

When I was a kid, I was taught this story as a cautionary tale about how I shouldn't doubt when it came to my faith. But now when I read it, I don't see Thomas in that light at all.

When we go back a couple of chapters in the story, we find Jesus telling his followers that he was heading to Jerusalem, even though there were people there who wanted to kill him.

And then Thomas tells the other disciples, "Let us go now to Jerusalem so that we may die with him" (John 11:16 NIV).

I've always believed that what motivated Thomas more than anything, when he declared that he wouldn't believe Jesus was alive, was a broken heart. He was the one disciple who didn't see Jesus at that first appearance, and I am sure he wondered why.

Still, he had hope. It was buried deep inside of him, but he had hope. And what he wanted most of all was to simply touch Jesus and know that everything was OK.

He wanted to know that it was OK to let that buried hope rise. And Jesus met him where he was, and Thomas found himself overwhelmed by hope and faith, so much so that he declared, "My Lord and my God!" (John 20:28 NIV).

His declaration is the most forceful, hope-filled declaration of Jesus's true identity found in the entirety of the Gospels.

Author Juliet Benner once wrote:

> In my groping attempts to hold on to Jesus, I often find that rather than grasping
> him, instead I find myself held, grasped by him and carried by his wounded hands.

May you be filled with the courage to hope today and every day. May you allow yourself to be lifted by Jesus and to have your faith restored, if it's been waning.

You Don't Have It All Together

When I was in seminary, I was required to take class in homiletics. *Homiletics* is a fancy word for the art of preaching or composing sermons. It was a forgettable season in my seminary career, but I still remember something my homiletics professor taught that I chose to ignore.

He told us never to use stories from our own lives as sermon illustrations. He considered this self-indulgent. The reason why I remember this lesson so well is because I decided, there and then, that it was a practice I had no interest in adopting.

And so, whether I am writing or preaching, I talk about my brokenness, as well as the moments when I feel whole. I share the ways I feel the darkness of doubt, and I share the moments when I feel the pleasure of the Lord washing over me like grace-filled rays of sunlight.

One of the passages in the Gospels that means so much to me is the story of the father who begs Jesus to heal his son in Mark 9. Jesus tells him that anything is possible for those who believe.

This man barely had been hanging on when it came to faith because of all he'd been through with his son. He doesn't feel like he has a lot of faith left, but what he has, he gives to Jesus. "Lord, I believe," he exclaims. "Help my unbelief" (Mark 9:24 NIV).

I've said this many times, but that story has always captured my heart because it's what made me decide, long ago, that to withhold my struggles from my preaching, teaching, and writing seemed more self-indulgent than sharing them.

I read this fantastic quote today from French Jesuit philosopher Pierre Teilhard de Chardin:

> Give our Lord the benefit of believing that His hand is leading you, and accept the anxiety of feeling yourself in suspense and incomplete.

What I want most of all is for anyone who hears my voice or reads my words to know that it's OK to feel like you don't have it all together—because you don't. It's perfectly all right to not have all the answers—because you don't. None of us does.

The miracle of the God's great big story of salvation is that despite the fact that none of us has it together, God continues to use broken vessels like us to further God's kingdom and to be the hands and feet of Jesus to the world.

That, my friends, is good news. It's worth stumbling after, giving your life to, and surrendering all your outcomes to, with even the tiniest amount of faith. Because when you do, wholeness happens, eternal life happens, and redemption happens.

God Is Always There First

When I was a kid, I thought God was in the past. Or at the very least, I thought God sort of hung out in the past and was always trying to pull people back into the past where God was.

Most of the Christians I was around in my formative years seemed to be totally fine with this idea. To them, the past was when everything was as it should have been. The present was where the world was headed for destruction.

I think a lot of Christians unwittingly adopt the belief that if we could all just get back to the God of the past, then we would truly be ready to experience whatever God has in store for us in the future.

During the time of Jesus, there was a large movement within first-century Judaism to return to the past, so to speak. The people who advocated for this return were known as Pharisees. The Pharisees saw no hope for a blessed future unless everyone returned to the past. They also perceived that anyone who advocated for a different approach to discovering the blessings of God was a threat to the well-being of society.

Jesus taught that religious laws did little to deepen your relationship with God. It wasn't what you said or who you thought you were that mattered to God; it was what you did right now in the present that mattered—how you lived, how you loved others. He also taught that God was drawing God's people toward a blessed future, where there was an incredible "place" already prepared for them.

For this reason (and many others as well), the Pharisees struggled mightily against Jesus. They were so focused on keeping the letter of the Law that they missed the point of why it was there in the first place. Jesus constantly called them out for their own hypocrisy.

> You Pharisees and teachers of the Law of Moses are in for trouble! You're nothing but show-offs. You lock people out of the kingdom of heaven. You won't go in yourselves, and you keep others from going in. (Matthew 23:13–14 NIV)

It's so easy for us followers of Jesus to get caught up in the same longing for the past that the Pharisees felt. But this subverts the message of Jesus, the good news he came to proclaim. A. W. Tozer once wrote, "God is always previous. God is always there first." I think those of us who call ourselves Christians would do well to remember this.

May you find peace in the realization that God is still speaking, still creating, still acting, still doing, and still redeeming. May you come to know more intimately the God who is already ahead of you, compelling you to move forward in your journey after Jesus to a blessed and hopeful future.

It's the Climb

I rode my bike to work yesterday, fulfilling a vow I made before I moved to Austin, Texas.

So roughly three months after arriving in Austin, and after a ton of research and trolling Craigslist for the right kind of "starter" bike, I pulled the trigger and bought an inexpensive bike to help me fulfill my vow.

Yesterday was the first day I rode it to work. As I pedaled away from my house, I felt incredible. The sun was shining warmly on my face, and a refreshingly cool breeze was blowing behind me, pushing me gently down the road.

A little voice inside my head said, "You did it! You actually pulled this off! You're riding your bike to work, dude. You're saving the earth, doing your part. You, my friend, are an eco-warrior!"

Then I noticed something as I gathered speed out of my neighborhood. The road I was on was mostly downhill.

Then the little voice inside my head chimed in with this little nugget: "Ummm, so this is great right now, but going home is going to be all uphill, bro. Good luck with all that. Oh, and by the way, it kind of feels like your hamstring is about to go out again. Are you sure you're cut out for this?"

When we have to actually work to keep moving forward in our journey with Jesus, the temptation to give up is often powerful and impossible to ignore. More often than we'd like to admit, we give in to that temptation to avoid the possibility of discomfort and pain.

There is a wonderful exhortation from the apostle Paul in 1 Corinthians 9:24–26:

> You've all been to the stadium and seen the athletes race. Everyone runs; one wins. Run to win. All good athletes train hard. They do it for a gold medal that tarnishes and fades. You're after one that's gold eternally. I don't know about you, but I'm running hard for the finish line. I'm giving it everything I've got. (NIV)

Using Paul's analogy, the stakes are high in this race we are running. We need to give it everything we've got because the reward is eternal life, not just in the "ever after" of the future but also right here, right now, in this time and place.

May you find the strength to keep moving forward in your spiritual journey, despite the challenges you might face. May you discover the joy of the downhill moments, and feel a fierce sense of Holy Spirit–fired determination for those uphill climbs.

Making the Dream Come True

Recently, I discovered a great mental exercise that John Maxwell included in his book *Developing the Leaders Around You*.

In this exercise, which is designed to help you identify your dreams, you ask yourself two question: "If I had_____, I would_____."

If you had unlimited time, money, information—anything you asked for—what would you do? Whatever your answer is to the second question is what you're dreaming for your life, Maxwell asserts.

The genius behind this kind of exercise is that once you start thinking about the possibility of your dream, you start to wonder if you might already have all of the resources you need to achieve it or at least a way to acquire them.

I got to thinking about how this applies to our journey with Jesus and the struggles we often have to imagine a world that has not yet been made right.

I'm afraid that more than a few of us Jesus-followers spend a lot of time wondering why things are so bad in the world, and we've got good reasons for doing so. But when we incessantly focus on all the things that are not as they should be, we can easily lose our ability to imagine them any differently.

"That's just the way things are," we might say with an air of resignation. "This is just the new normal. There's nothing I can do to change it."

But following Jesus wholly and completely requires that we exercise some holy imagination. Jesus taught his followers not to accept the world as it is but to imagine what it could be and will be when God gets what God wants.

Jesus also called his followers to be the very agents of change to bring about God's kingdom here on earth. In Matthew 5:14, Jesus said, "You are the light of the world. A town built on a hill cannot be hidden" (Matthew 5:14 NIV).

When we begin to imagine a better world, we also find that we are filled with what has been referred to as "holy discontent." We no longer want to accept the status quo, and we begin looking for ways to use our holy imagination to discover what is needed for transformation.

May you find the spark for a holy imagination today as you dream of a better world. May what you imagine fill you with a holy discontent and a renewed passion to shine your light in the dark corners of the status quo.

Love Is the Hallmark

I went to the H-E-B (our local grocery store, for my non-Texas friends) last evening with my youngest son to pick up some Valentine's Day cards and treats for his class party today.

I was feeling kind of guilty for doing it at the last minute, but I think our family deserves a little grace, considering we're in the process of moving again.

At any rate, as Jacob and I walked in to the store, we realized we were definitely not alone. The place was mobbed with people buying Valentine's Day paraphernalia.

I took a look around at all of the people holding flowers, heart-shaped candy boxes, and the like. I wondered if it was guilt that dragged them out late on a Monday evening to make sure they didn't stiff their significant other on Valentine's Day.

As I looked around at all of the people crowding the H-E-B, my heart broke a little, and then I got self-righteous. *Love shouldn't be commercialized*, I thought. *It shouldn't be something you express out of duty or obligation because some Hallmark holiday demands it.*

This morning, I was reading the parent newsletter that our own Director of Children's Ministries, Chris Gordon, wrote for today. When I read it, I instantly felt convicted about my jaded thoughts.

"Some may call it a 'Hallmark Holiday' in a cynical sense," she wrote, "but I say, as followers of Christ, LOVE is our hallmark."

That is some true stuff, right there. Valentine's Day is the perfect day to consider the nature of true love, and for Christians, true love looks like Jesus. As I was writing this devotion, a Christian song by Clay Crosse came to mind:

> It all comes down to a man dying on a cross
> Saving the world
> Rising from the dead
> Doing what He said He would do
> Loving everyone He saw

May you celebrate this holiday dedicated to Love by drawing closer to the One who "loved us and gave himself for us," sacrificially and unconditionally. May you give of yourself to the world around you as an outpouring of gratitude for that love.

Lessons From a Smoke Alarm

There's a smoke alarm with a dead battery somewhere in my house this morning. Every thirty seconds or so it emits an annoying chirp. I think it's upstairs--at least that's where the chirping seems to be coming from.

Whoever designed the system by which smoke detectors inform you that their batteries are dead was an evil genius--schooled in the art of psychological torture.

I want to go and change it, but I'll need to fetch a ladder, and there will be noise and commotion as a result. At the moment, everyone in the house is sleeping peacefully, and I don't want to awaken them just yet. So, I sit here waiting for the next beep, dreading it until it happens.

In between beeps, a couple of questions that have always plagued me come to mind: I wonder how much of my life I've spent dreading what comes next? And, how many blessings and experiences with God in the present did I miss as a result?

I know that I'm not alone in pondering those questions. In my role as a pastor, I've had more than a few conversations with people who struggle to embrace the joys of the present because they are too busy fretting and dreading what's awaiting them tomorrow.

What's worse is that most of our dread and worry is over an imagined future, not a real one. The Stoic philosopher Seneca once wrote, *"There is nothing so certain in our fears that's not yet more certain in the fact that most of what we dread comes to nothing."*

I have to admit, I've had my fair share of struggles with worry. It has caused me at times to live in dread, rather than embrace the moment, to experience what God is doing right now and find joy in the present.

The words of the Apostle Paul from his letter to the Romans are always a good reminder of why we need not worry or dread tomorrow:

38 For I am convinced that neither death nor life, neither angels nor demons, neither the present nor the future, nor any powers, 39 neither height nor depth, nor anything else in all creation, will be able to separate us from the love of God that is in Christ Jesus our Lord. (Romans 8:38-39 NIV)

May you find courage in the knowledge that there is nothing in this world that can separate you from God's love and presence. May you find the strength to let the cares for tomorrow fall away as you fully embrace what God is doing right here, right now all around you, in you and through you.

The Ordinary Moments

Today, I recalled something I heard a couple of years ago about the busy times when you're parenting (or grandparenting) and hustling through life. It went something like this: "The days are long, but the years are short."

That's one of the truest things I've ever heard, and some days it's truer than truest. Right now, Merideth and I are in the midst of the blur of moving three times in just under a year, kids' school and social activities, work, and everything else in life.

We have gone from one big decision to another more times than I can count this past year. It's easy to look back and wonder where the time went and how we got here and to focus only on those big moments—the huge things that marked our time.

But sometimes, we can miss out on the glory of God, the beauty of God's will, and the joy and peace that come from simply being fully present in the everyday moments, the ordinary times, when we practice being still and know that God is God, and we are not.

Recently, I read something Frederick Buechner wrote about those kinds of ordinary moments of glory when he reflected on the busy years of his life. He said, "It was the unmemorable, the apparently random and everyday ones that turned out to be the key moments."

The other day, right in the middle of the week, we took our entire family to a park near our house where there is a wonderful little creek, just deep enough to wade in, throw rocks into, or fall in fully clothed (which happened to at least one of us).

We sat by the water, talking and laughing, and then stretched out in the sun. Merideth and I happily dozed there to the sound of the water trickling and the two littlest boys splashing and playing, our dog right in the middle of things, and our oldest boy giving warnings and brotherly advice.

It was a random, spur-of-the-moment decision to go there that day, wedging it in between obligations to make it happen. But it was a so blessed and full of glory. It was a moment when we were still, and we allowed God to renew us and draw us together.

May you seek God's glory and beauty in the ordinary moments of your day today. May you push back against the busyness, noise, and distractions, and discover that you have more than enough time to be still and allow God to fill you with God's Spirit.

The Greater Miracle

Today, my littlest boy rode his bike to school for the first time without the benefit of his training wheels.

I thought about how quickly he'd figured everything out, and I was amazed. He'd only learned how to ride his bike with only two wheels last week and was already cruising away as if he'd been doing it for months.

As I reflected on all of this, it occurred to me how—in spite of all of my failings, brokenness, and the stupid things I do as a parent—Jacob is growing up as a confident, fearless little dude, despite the many mistakes I make.

It made me so grateful to God that God allows me to do good in the world in all of the various roles of my life, in spite of myself. Because of the love of God, I am not defined by my past or by bad decisions and the mistakes I've made when I have tried to do life on my own.

I never ceased to be amazed at how, in the words of Philip Yancey, "God wants to share power with the likes of me." God could use hundreds of other ways to do what God needs done in the world but chooses us broken vessels to effect God's will.

Whenever I wish that God would show up in miraculous ways to change and transform the world around me and to demonstrate God's power in clear and direct ways, I am reminded that it's an even greater miracle that God would use me to do it instead.

One of my favorite poets, George Herbert, wrote these wonderful lines nearly five hundred years ago:

> Blessed be the Architect whose art
> Could build so strong in a weak heart.

May you feel the pleasure of the Lord as you stumble forward, seeking to do God's will in your broken and mistake-prone ways. May you know that God delights in your stumbling and relishes the moments when you see God's will being done in the world, in you and through you.

And may the grace and peace of our Lord Jesus Christ be with you, now and always. Amen.

The Allure of Self-Righteousness

Gentle readers, today's "Daily Devo" is coming to you late in the day. I was at the Festival of Homiletics yesterday afternoon and most of today, soaking in some sermons from some of my favorite preachers in the world.

The Festival of Homiletics is a preaching conference, where pastors from all over the country (and the world) gather to listen to sermons and lectures about sermons. Throw in some highbrow worship services, and you have the trifecta of nerdiness when it comes to churchy stuff.

In answer to the question that I get pretty often—"Where do you go to hear sermons and get spiritually fed?"—I would offer events like the Festival of Homiletics as perfect examples.

I heard some things over the course of the last twenty-four hours that shook me up and got me thinking deeply about some of the things I have been struggling with lately.

You see, I suffer from a tinge of self-righteousness when it comes to more than a few aspects of my faith.

It's easy to get self-righteous about our own beliefs. We hold on to some of them tightly, believing them to be precious, and are unwilling to release our grip on them, white-knuckling them almost to death.

And it's easy when we're holding on too tightly to believe that everyone else who isn't doing the same doesn't care about their beliefs in the same way we do. When we start going down that road, it leads directly to self-righteousness, which, in turn, leads to a graceless, imperious kind of faith.

Pastor, author, and speaker Nadia Bolz-Weber offered the following brilliant image for this kind of thing in one of the lectures she gave today: "Self righteousness feels good for a minute," she told us. "It's like how peeing in your pants feels warm for a minute too, but afterward, it just feels cold and wet."

Come on.

That's just the best metaphor for self-righteousness in the history of ever.

May you discover a new capacity for gentleness in the expression of your beliefs. May you find a renewed sense of joy in finding common ground, even with those who hold different beliefs than your own.

Why the Church Is Still Worth It

Over the past couple of days, I've been attending some of the Festival of Homiletics, a preaching conference that is being held in San Antonio this week.

Being in a room full of a couple of thousand pastors and church leaders has been a great experience, but it also has been a sharp reminder of the very real issues facing the church right now. The church is going through a reformation, and reformations are painful.

Not all followers of Jesus who call the church home receive the evidence of that reformation with the same enthusiasm. It's pretty clear that the church is sharply divided over many of the same issues that divide our society.

I read something today by E. Stanley Jones that spoke to me. He wrote, "[The church] must be held together by a single-minded devotion [to Christ]; otherwise we begin to disintegrate."

I've been watching the news lately, and it's disturbing on so many levels. Our society is seemingly being torn apart by constant partisan divisions in politics, a growing economic divide between rich and poor, fierce and destructive debates over social issues, and so much more.

In 1 Peter, we read the following reminder of our identity as the church:

> As you come to him, the living Stone--rejected by human beings, but chosen by God and precious to him--you also, like living stones are being built into a spiritual house to be a holy priesthood, offering spiritual sacrifices acceptable to God through Jesus Christ. (1 Peter 2:4–5 NIV)

I get it. Things haven't been great in the Christian world for some time. The church has taken more than its share of hits. Many of us find ourselves apologizing on behalf of the church and other Christians more than we'd like.

But as Thomas Merton wrote, "No matter how low you may have fallen in our own esteem, bear in mind that if you delve deeply into yourself you will discover holiness there."

May you dedicate yourself to the task of reformation and transformation of the church so that the world may know Jesus in a new light—the light shone by his followers, who are single-minded in their devotion to him.

Learning to Trust the Great Architect

In architectural design, there is a concept known as "denial and reward." Essentially, the idea is to offer users a view of their target, or destination. It could be a staircase, a fountain, a ballroom, or the center of a city park.

But then you divert the path so they can't see it, and reveal it again from a different angle to create intrigue. You continue to reward them with additional experiences and views on their way. According to author Matthew Frederick, "It makes the journey more interesting, the arrival more rewarding."

I talk to a lot of people who struggle in their journeys with Jesus because of their frustration over the unknown. They speak to me about how they have had glimpses of a possible future where they are firmly in the will of God, but then they confess they lose sight of it when circumstances divert their attention.

The psalmist who wrote Psalm 25 offered this prayer: "Show me your ways, Lord, teach me your paths. Guide me in your truth and teach me, for you are God my Savior, and my hope is in you all day long" (Psalm 25:4–5 NIV).

It's humbling to realize that for thousands of years, people have been praying prayers like the one offered up in Psalm 25—prayers that God will show them their destination more clearly and without so many twists and turns.

But it's in the twists and turns that we discover the truth about our relationship with God. As we stumble after Jesus, we often find our faith is tested; our loyalty is strained. At times, we find ourselves wondering if we are on the right path or if the destination we glimpsed in the distance was a mirage.

And all of it—every challenging moment, every curve in the path—makes the journey more interesting and faith-strengthening.

We are wired to feel this. It's like the Great Architect of our lives created us to experience our journey by learning to trust that every turn, every bend will lead us not just closer to our goal but closer to God.

Today, I read this great poem by the seventeenth-century poet George Herbert that I would encourage us all to pray today, keeping all of this in mind:

> Enrich my heart, mouth, hands in me, with faith, with hope, with charity; that I
> may run, rise, rest with thee.

God Is No Fool

In my morning reading today, I read this incredible and uncomfortable quote from Anne Lamott's latest book *Hallelujah Anyway*:

> The world has an awful beauty. This is a chaotic place, humanity is a chaotic place, and I am a chaotic place.

I do feel pretty chaotic most days. Maybe you feel that way too. Much like the particles of the subatomic world that exists below our ordinary vision, we are constantly colliding with one another, exchanging energy, and being transformed (for good or ill) by these constant collisions.

I hold to the belief that God is at work in our lives all of the time, and it is our own limited ability to perceive that keeps us from being aware of God's guiding, loving presence.

Because of this belief, I also hold to the notion that God places people in our paths (and us in theirs) for a reason.

Sometimes, it's easy to see the reasons, when being with a particular person fills us with life, light, and love. But it's more difficult to see the reasons when the person drains us of life and light and is hard to love.

But you can't have it both ways. Either you believe God has a plan, or God doesn't. And we have to hold on in faith that even the most challenging people have something to offer us, something to teach.

Lois Cheney wrote about this very thing in her book *God Is No Fool*:

> I believe in God's master plan in lives. He moves people in and out of each other's lives and each leaves his mark on the other. You find you are made up of bits and pieces of all who ever touched your life, and you are more because of it, and you would be less if they had not touched you.

As you move through your day today, think about the many people whose paths intersect with your own, whose marks are being left on you. Pray prayers of gratitude for them all, especially those who leave marks that feel more like wounds.

It could be that the greatest lesson they might teach you is which relationships to avoid or let go. And you are more because of that lesson.

God's Sneaky Grace

I love being busy. Like a lot of people, I wear it like a badge of honor.

Do you ever find yourself comparing busy schedules with your friends, and suddenly, you feel as though you are in some kind of competition?

"Wow, that seems like you've got a lot going on there, Joe, but *our* schedule is absolutely insane by comparison. When you get to insane-level scheduling, my friend, let's talk then. Until then, don't even think of stepping to me."

It's easy to get addicted to the adrenaline rush of busyness, isn't it? But the problem I face when I am riding the emotional high of busyness is a significant one: it's hard to feel the presence of God when I'm rushing to and fro. It's even more difficult to attune my spiritual hearing to hear God's voice speaking with all of the noise created by my busyness.

When you're trying to hear God in the midst of busyness, it's a lot like trying to have a conversation in a speeding convertible with the top down.

Much like the ancient prophet Elijah, you can't hear God in the rushing wind or the earthquakes around you. You hear God speak in the stillness and the silence and only when you come to a halt and are ready to listen.

And it's in those moments when we slow down and breathe that we begin to see our place and purpose in the world more clearly. Author Anne Lamott describes it like this:

> Being slow and softened, even for a few minutes or seconds, gives sneaky grace the chance to enter.

Jesus modeled this behavior for us by constantly carving out time to slow down, pray, and have some quiet time in which he tended his relationship with the Father.

In Luke 6:12–13, we read about one such instance:

> Jesus went out to a mountain side to pray, and spent the night praying to God. When morning came, he called his disciples to him. (NIV)

Find some time today to slow down and experience God. Push back against the busyness and the rush of wind in your ears. Let yourself feel the slowness and the softening of your spirit that comes from surrender. Listen for God's voice amid the quiet, and let your connection to God be made stronger and deeper in your listening.

Paying Attention to the Moments

This morning I am reflecting on the fragility of my well-thought plans. I had some stuff all worked out, and now, whatever I worked out is kind of falling apart.

Worrying over the outcomes of our planning and arranging can keep us awake at night. It can also steal our joy and rob us of hope when our planning comes to nothing, and we find ourselves where we had no intention of going.

Oswald Chambers has a hard word for that kind of worrying and fretting: "It is not only wrong to worry, it is unbelief; worrying means we do not believe that God can look after the practical details of our lives."

Sometimes, the best way we can renew our belief in God's sovereign love for us is to pay attention to the moments when our worrying and fretting fade away, and we simply rest, connect, renew, and find restoration.

Yesterday, I had some hard things to do—things I worried about; plans I fretted over and generally had a hard time turning over to God.

But then, I also was given the opportunity to see the preschoolers at our preschool celebrate their graduation, which was unbelievable joy. I had an incredible conversation about faith and life with a friend, which turned my mind to things above.

Last night, we gathered with friends for dinner at our house after a long day of work, parenting and "adulting." It was pure grace. We ate, laughed, drank good wine, and played with the kids in the pool until late in the evening.

It's those kinds of moments that can refill you with energy, light, and life. They also can help you put into perspective the events of a challenging day or a difficult season in your life.

Psalm 55:22 offers some incredible encouragement that speaks into this so clearly: "Cast your cares on the LORD and he will sustain you; he will never let the righteous be shaken" (NIV).

May you discover moments of grace, joy, and hope in the midst of your day today. Pay attention to how you feel in those moments, and let yourself be free from worry and anxiety as you allow yourself to be filled with the spirit of peace. Turn over your plans to God, and trust that God has your best interests at heart.

Finding Hope in Community

Anne Lamott writes, "Pope Francis says the name of God is mercy. Our name was mercy, too, until we put it away to become more productive, more admired and less vulnerable."

I feel has happened to what I would best describe as "corporate Christianity" in America. It's lost its way. It's become triumphant and obsessed with bigger and better and forgotten what it means to be merciful.

But I've come to believe there is a "silent majority" of Jesus-followers who have grown weary of the pretenses and posturing of corporate Christianity and are waking up, at last, to pursue their deep longing to simply be more like Christ.

For all of the negative news stories that surface from time to time about a few angry and loud Christians who are boycotting things, banning books, shunning other Christians who don't agree with them, and the like, it's good to be reminded that there are far more Christians simply trying to quietly and earnestly live out their faith, stumbling after Jesus the best they can.

In fact, due in large part to this silent majority, I believe the church is going through a reformation of sorts—a Micah 6:8 reformation:

> He has shown you, O mortal, what is good.
> And what does the Lord require of you?
> To act justly and to love mercy
> and to walk humbly with your God. (Micah 6:8 NIV)

Today, I am so grateful for my church family. As I made my way through my neighborhood this morning, I happened upon some of my church members quietly serving outside the church.

Seriously, though, unexpectedly discovering my church members being the hands and feet of Jesus in the community is something that happens to me on a regular basis.

At the Starbucks where I stopped with my son to get him an iced coffee after a doctor's appointment, I ran into one of my elders, who was mentoring a high school student.

When I dropped my son off at his school, I was greeted by another member, who was volunteering in the school office.

Listen, my church isn't perfect. We give each other bumps and bruises from time to time. We don't always get it right when we're trying to love our neighbor. But every time I turn around, I encounter people who are part of my faith community and are contributing to the Micah 6:8 reformation.

It gives me hope like you wouldn't believe.

Looking through Different Lenses

I've been having a bit of trouble seeing what I'm reading lately. This is a new development in the continuing saga of my getting older. The other day, on a whim, I tried a pair of my wife's reading glasses, and suddenly, as if by magic, I could actually see the words on the page in front of me without any fuzziness.

So I bought my first few pairs of reading glasses, and I've been shuffling back and forth between them and my regular glasses. It's hard to admit that my old way of seeing is no longer adequate, but it's a lot better than not being able to see.

Necessity, as it turns out, often gives birth to flexibility when it comes to these kinds of things. My need to see has caused me to let go of some of my pride and simply carry around an extra pair of glasses.

I believe the same thing might be true for most of us Christians, especially regarding some of our tightly held beliefs. At some point, we come to the realization that the old lenses we were given so long ago just aren't doing the trick any longer. In fact, they might even be keeping us from seeing clearly.

Maybe the reason we came to this conclusion was because of changes in our lives, a tragedy that shook us, an awakening to the suffering and marginalization of others, a new empathy for people who believed differently—a host of reasons may contribute to our necessity for new lenses.

For example, the way I used to view God was through a particular lens that shaped my image of the Almighty into one of a tyrant and a bully. I had my heart broken when I returned to church after a long hiatus and knew that there was more to God than my cracked and dirty lenses were allowing me to see.

In 1 Corinthians 13:10–12, we hear these words from the apostle Paul:

> When I was a child, I spoke like a child, I thought like a child, I reasoned like a child. When I became a man, I gave up childish ways. For now we see in a mirror dimly, but then face to face. Now I know in part; then I shall know fully, even as I have been fully known. (NIV)

May you not be afraid to put on new lenses of faith today and every day. May you discover new ways of viewing God and the world around you that help you grow closer to God and your neighbor. May these Jesus-shaped lenses give you a new perspective on who you are in Christ.

Your Faith Isn't a Checklist

Some years ago, I bought a book called *The Art of Getting Started*. It's an interactive book, designed to help you get your creative juices flowing when you feel stuck.

The book has exercises that are intended to jump-start your creativity and nudge you forward a bit toward something other than staring blankly at your computer screen.

Today, the section of the book I chose was one that didn't seem all that helpful at first. The instructions began like this: "Physically crossing tasks off a list is one of the best ways to create feelings of achievement and motivation." OK, I am on board so far.

Then the instructions took a strange turn: "Cross out each of the tasks below using a different pen. Find your favorite." Below the instructions were the words "Task 1, Task 2, Task 3," and so on. *What?* I figured I might as well give it a try, so I took out a handful of pens and started crossing out the "tasks." When I was done, I looked at them balefully, not really trusting the process.

Suddenly, it occurred to me that while it did feel pretty good to physically cross out tasks on a list and bask in a feeling of accomplishment over getting them done, that feeling was pretty fleeting.

Further, when our lives of faith are nothing but checklists and tasks, it steals our joy and robs us of the unexpectedness of God's grace and love and the surprising hope that we find when we encounter Jesus in the world. Jesus criticized religious people who turned their faith life into checklists—lists that they not only had for themselves but for everyone else as well.

> They tie up heavy, cumbersome loads and put them on other people's shoulders, but they themselves are not willing to lift a finger to move them. (Matthew 23:4 NIV)

It's never enough just to have our own lists, is it? When we start down the path of a checklist-based faith, we not only feverishly work our own lists to death, but we then want to hand everyone else a copy and expect them to do the same.

If your faith has become a series of checklists that you've either created or had handed to you, crumple up those lists, throw them away, and hear these words from Jesus:

> "Come to me, all you who are weary and burdened, and I will give you rest. Take my yoke upon you and learn from me, for I am gentle and humble in heart, and you will find rest for your souls. For my yoke is easy and my burden is light." (Matthew 11:28–30 NIV)

Honoring Our Shared Humanity

Some of the most beautiful and awful aspects of being human are discovered in the frail and finite ways that we interact with one another.

There is beauty to be found in the mystery of another human being—mystery that is contained behind the facade of a smile, an imperceptible nod, or a blush.

We've all had those moments when we think we know someone, but then, they surprise us with their wonderful secrets and closely held bright thoughts and ideas, and we realize (to our delight) we never really knew them at all. But there is something awful in this frailty too. More often than not, we never try to look beyond the surface and tend to believe the worst about a person before getting to know them properly.

We also assume things about one another based on appearance, class, religion, gender, and so many other cultural identifiers without critique, without any thought to how our stereotyping might be dead wrong.

For those of us who follow Jesus, we have an example in him that challenges us to rise above our shallow and two-dimensional visions of one another. Through Jesus, we have the most incredible demonstration of God's great love for human beings—beings who are created (as we read in the creation story) in "God's image."

The apostle Paul wrote that Jesus, "being in very nature God, did not consider equality with God something to be used to his own advantage; rather, he made himself nothing by taking the very nature of a servant, being made in human likeness" (Philippians 2:6–7 NIV).

In other words, God honored humanity by taking on human form in Jesus, who was the physical manifestation of God, the second "person" of the Trinity, God in the flesh, taking up residence among us. In the words of Eugene Peterson, the Creative Word of God (Jesus) took on human form and "moved into the neighborhood" (John 1:14 MSG).

So to those of us who would be followers of Christ, let us celebrate the beautiful aspects of our frail and finite vision when it comes to others who also are created in God's image. Let us look upon all human beings with the joy that comes in uncovering a mystery.

The poet Rumi's words come to mind as a wonderful exhortation:

> Bow to the essence in a human being. Do not be content with judging people good and bad. Grow out of that.

Angels on the Head of a Pin

I was watching a video the other day of three Christian pastors/authors who were arguing about whether God causes all things (both good and bad) to happen to us.

Two of the pastors argued that God does cause all things to happen to us, even the worst things, in order to teach us and shape us. The other pastor argued that God doesn't cause all things, but that God is present in all circumstances and moments, both good and bad.

I get that this is a topic that probably needs to be unpacked. Lots of people have negative opinions about God because they've been taught that God goes around smiting people with awful afflictions and circumstances—for their own good.

For the record, I don't hold that particular notion. But the whole thing made me recall an obscure question that certain medieval Christian scholars debated: How many angels can dance on the head of a pin?

In 1619, theologian William Sclater offered the following criticism of seventeenth-century Christian thinkers and authors.

He wrote that they wasted time and energy debating whether angels "did occupie a place; and so, whether many might be in one place at one time; and how many might sit on a Needles point; and six hundred such like needlesse points."

It comforts me some to know that here was a guy in the 1600s, critiquing the endless debates about Christian doctrine in his own era, and he ended up asking the same question I was asking about the pastors in the video: "Seriously?"

In the first decade of the twentieth century, Oswald Chambers lamented the following:

> Today we have substituted doctrinal belief for personal belief, and that is why so many people are devoted to causes and so few are devoted to Jesus Christ.

As someone who loves to overthink some of these things, I think that those of us who call ourselves Christians are in constant danger of overthinking the Christian faith, to the point where we lose sight of who is at the center of it—Jesus himself.

And when we lose sight of Jesus, we run the risk of completely missing the point about why we do any of the things we do as Christians.

Pursue a real and intimate relationship with Jesus today. Seek to be like Jesus in all that you do and say. Discover ways to be the hands and feet of Jesus to those who desperately need to feel his presence. All the rest—doctrines, questions, debates—will resolve itself.

Facebook Memories, Signposts, and Faith

A little animated video showed up in my Facebook feed this morning, informing me that I have now been on Facebook for ten years. I first joined on June 20, 2007.

Ten years ago, I was not yet forty years old and had just stepped into the role of interim pastor of the church where I had been ordained as an associate.

Merideth and I were praying fervently about whether God was calling us to leave Florida or to stay.

My oldest son, Jay, was in seventh grade at the time, and his brother Jackson had just turned two. My youngest son, Jacob, was not yet a twinkle in anyone's eye.

A lot has happened in those ten years. And as I look back on it all, I am overwhelmed by the unbelievably complicated, intricate way in which God has been at work in my life throughout the last decade.

It's dizzying to think of all of the winding paths I've taken, the circumstances that just fell into place, the too-perfect coincidences that have been a part of my journey in stumbling after Jesus.

It hasn't always been easy, but it has been incredible.

And through it all, I have been so unbelievably blessed to play my small part, working and laboring, so that the kingdom of God can be seen here on earth.

I was reading in Paul's letter to the Ephesians this morning and came across a familiar verse. Paul writes, "God has made us what we are. In Christ Jesus, God made us to do good works, which God planned in advance for us to live our lives doing" (Ephesians 2:10 NIV).

May you find great joy today in the fact that God is at work in your life—moving you, shaping you, and guiding you to the good works that God has planned for you since the beginning of all things.

May you look back on your journey and take courage because the same God who has been with you all along will be with you until your journey's end.

We Don't Have to Guess What God Is Like

Some years ago, I asked the students in a confirmation class I was teaching if they would attempt to draw a picture of what they thought God might look like.

Several of the students sketched a portrait of an old man with a long white beard. Others toyed with the idea of God as a flash of light. A couple of students drew ancient symbols of the Trinity. And a handful of others simply left their pages blank.

What do you picture when you try to conjure up images of God in your imagination?

If you're like most people who believe in God, you probably imagine God much like those students did. And I would also wager that you tend to think of God as being "somewhere else," looking down upon us.

Richard Rohr once wrote, "The belief that God is 'out there' is the basic dualism that is tearing us all apart." The idea that God is somehow above and unconnected to our material reality is a destructive notion. It affects the way we treat the earth, our bodies, and one another.

It's true that the infinite mysteries of God will always be beyond our comprehension, and to even try to imagine or name those mysteries limits the idea of God. In other words, to try to describe God in your own words or images is an exercise in futility.

As Christians, however, we believe that God is not unknown to us. We have a living example of who God is in Jesus himself.

And those of us who claim to follow Jesus are given the task of carrying on the mission that Jesus initiated—to bring the good news that God so loved the world that he has done everything to save it.

E. Stanley Jones put it like this:

> We cannot merely talk about Christ—we must bring him. He must be a living vital reality—closer than breathing and nearer than hands and feet. We must be "God-bearers."

May you be the very hands and feet and breath of Jesus to the world today and every day.

May you show by your words and your deeds that God is here, present, and moving among us. God is not somewhere else—God is right here, right now.

A Lesson on Inclusion from MTV

On March 10, 1983, MTV played the video for Michael Jackson's "Billie Jean" for the first time. Up until that time, MTV executives refused to play the video because they claimed the fledgling music video channel was dedicated to "rock 'n' roll." They only agreed to air the video after the president of CBS Records threatened to pull all of his artists from the channel if they didn't do it.

Before it aired "Billie Jean," MTV was on its way to bankruptcy. It had lost $50 million and was projected to lose even more. Michael Jackson's next three videos from his *Thriller* album saved the channel and helped it turn a profit just a year later.

The problem was, MTV execs had surrounded themselves with people who had the same tastes in music as they did—a move that created an echo chamber, where they were hearing only from people who agreed with them.

Far too many Christians today seem to be doing the very same thing as those MTV execs did. We'll spend our entire existence in an echo chamber of cable news, radio, books, and publications that reinforce our beliefs and tell us what we want to hear.

We'll "shop" for churches until we find one where we'll hear sermons that we agree with and where we can associate with people who share our views.

And then, we'll expend vast amounts of energy in railing against people who disagree with us, engaging in pointless online arguments on Facebook, or training ourselves to defend our faith against anyone who might attack it.

In his recent book *Everybody, Always*, Bob Goff offered the following bit of hard wisdom:

> Am I really so insecure that I surround myself only with people who agree with me? Burning down others opinions doesn't make us right. It makes us arsonists.

If you've discovered that your point of view has become a bit narrowed lately; if you've started to realize that you might be living in a bit of an echo chamber; if you look around and see that the only people you know are people just like you, maybe it's time for a change.

Jesus made a huge effort to reach out to all kinds of people, even those who disagreed with him. If we are to be followers of Jesus, shouldn't we do the same?

Today, make an effort to listen to some new voices. Pray for the courage to not worry so much about hearing what you *want* to hear. Instead, pray that God may allow you to hear what you *need* to hear.

The Strength to Forgive

Years ago, I had a conflict with a church member and youth-group volunteer who was spreading lies about me, both in the church and in our community. When the truth came out, and she knew that she had been exposed, she never returned to the church.

For several months, I did my best to try to arrange meetings—sent her emails, called and left voice messages on her phone, and even sent her a written letter, pleading with her to speak with me so we could be reconciled. She never responded.

I eventually grew angry at her and stayed angry for a long time. She'd done a lot of damage to my ministry and had done her best to divide our church. Further, because of her unwillingness to work it out, the bad feelings between us simply festered.

I don't remember when, exactly, but I eventually found myself feeling sorry for her. Because of her shame over being caught in a lie, she'd lost her church family, her community support, and the ministry she loved.

Bob Goff recently wrote, "Shame does that to us. It makes us leave safe places. It breaks the rhythms we've established with each other."

What I came to learn, through that difficult season, was that even though I wasn't able to be reconciled with my former church member (because reconciliation requires both parties to be all in), I could still forgive her. I read a great essay today by Johann Christoph Arnold, who said of forgiveness:

> Forgiving is not ignoring wrongdoing, but overcoming the evil inside of us and in our world with love Christ wants us to use our hands, wounded as they may be, to extend his forgiveness to the world.

The question that each of us needs to ask ourselves is this: when we extend our own wounded hands, will they be clenched in stubbornness or open in vulnerable love? Will we be able to offer forgiveness, even when that forgiveness doesn't lead to reconciliation?

The apostle Paul answers these questions in his letter to the church at Ephesus when he says, "Be kind and compassionate to one another, forgiving each other as Christ has forgiven you" (Ephesians 4:32 NIV).

May you find the strength to forgive today and every day after. May your hands be open and welcoming to those who are shamed.

Putting Up Unnecessary Walls

I spent the last three days of this week honing my leadership skills and learning some new ones with a group of lead pastors from around the country (and one from Canada). I was the only Presbyterian in a room full of nondenominational, Pentecostal, and Baptist leaders, which was a bit outside of my comfort zone.

Whatever our theological differences might have been, however, we didn't dwell on them. Every single one of us in the room was after the same thing: we wanted to be better pastors and leaders, for the purpose of sharing the good news with a world that needs to hear a word of hope.

Every so often, I find myself grieving over the seemingly hopeless divisions between Christian groups, churches, and denominations. And sometimes, my grief turns to anger, and my anger leads me to create barriers.

The walls that have been up between Christians have done very little to advance the kingdom of God, which was the focus of Jesus's life and ministry and the task he gave to his followers. Yet we continue to put up walls with little thought of how they hurt those who should be our sisters and brothers.

It reminds me of the lines from Robert Frost's wonderful poem "Mending Wall:"

> Before I build a wall I'd ask to know
> What I was walling in or walling out,
> And to whom I was like to give offense.

I have grown tired of being part of the problem. That's why I sought out a cohort group that was outside of my tribe.

Was it difficult sometimes to listen when the conversations turned toward things that stirred up my feelings of grief and anger? Sure, but if I am not willing to offer the gift of listening, how can I expect to be heard when I choose to speak?

If we are going to be Resurrection People, we need to live as though Jesus has risen. And I'm guessing that Jesus wouldn't be all that thrilled about the petty squabbles or the walls between his followers.

Starting today, allow yourself to be taught by someone who doesn't share your ideas on faith. Find friends who are outside of your Christian tribe, and listen to their stories. Through kindness and gentleness, earn the right to be heard in your own right.

And in so doing, begin tearing down the walls that obscure the light of Christ.

Get Close Enough to See the Real

Sometimes, things look a lot more put together and beautiful from farther away.

From a distance, the basket of flowers on my front porch looks dazzling and perfect, but when I move in and inspect it from a few inches away, I can see the blemishes on the petals and that the individual flowers have begun to brown.

The closer I get, the more I am able to see the flowers as they really are.

It's then that I have a choice to make: I can choose to remain close and aware of their blemishes and find beauty in them anyway, or I can keep my distance and maintain an unmarred (and incomplete) view of them.

The poet Mary Oliver wrote about this choice in her poem "The Ponds." She acknowledges that close proximity brings a more intimate relationship, but it's sometimes tempting to simply hold the world at arm's length.

Still, what I want in my life is to be willing to be dazzled—to cast aside the weight of facts and maybe even to float a little above this difficult world.

I think that many of us struggle with this very thing when it comes to our faith. We worry that if others get too close to us, they will see our flaws and will realize that we're not always as we appear to be.

And as a result, we lose sight of the beauty in our struggle. We forget how important it has been for us to not always know what we believe but to keep following anyway. We begin to think that the only thing that matters is how we look from a distance.

Bob Goff recently wrote, "When what our faith looks like becomes more important than what it is, it's evidence we've forgotten who we really are."

If you've been holding the world at arm's length in order to avoid the vulnerability that comes with intimacy, practice letting down your guard today. Worry less about the appearances of your faith, and focus more on the substance. See the beauty in your struggle.

Apprehend God in All Things

This morning, my wife and I were sitting outside, enjoying the crisp spring air, at the outset of what is shaping up to be a beautiful day here in the Hill Country of Texas.

We have a variety of birdhouses and bird feeders in our backyard, scattered among terraced flower beds and rose bushes. One of those houses has become the home for a family of sparrows.

While we sat and watched this morning, the mother sparrow would fly from the birdhouse and then return minutes later to feed her babies. As soon as she would perch on the outside of the house, we could hear the little sparrows begin to cheep in unison.

The mother went back and forth, tirelessly. Never stopping. It was a beautiful rhythm. I felt like I could sit and watch her forever.

As I sat there, I couldn't help but recall Jesus's words of comfort to his disciples when he said, "Are not two sparrows sold for a penny? Yet not one of them will fall to the ground outside your Father's care" (Matthew 10:29 NIV).

We get so caught up in the tyranny of the urgent sometimes. We worry needlessly about things we cannot change. We try so terribly hard to solve our problems, all on our own. We often wonder if God cares about our struggles.

But watching the sparrow, I was overwhelmed by a sense of God's timelessness and wisdom. I saw, in her rhythms, the gentle pace of God's peace. I glimpsed holiness in her service and a simple joy in her duty.

The great Christian mystic Meister Eckhart once wrote:

> Apprehend God in all things, for God is in all things. Every single creature is full of God and is a book about God. Every creature is a word of God. If I spent enough time with the tiniest creature—even a caterpillar—I would never have to prepare a sermon. So full of God is every creature.

Look around you today, and diligently read the holy scriptures that are being written in God's good creation. Find your place in the peaceful rhythms of grace that are embedded in our world—a world saturated in God's glory and love.

The Comfort of God's Silence

I'm having one of those days when it feels like I have a lot more questions than answers when it comes to God.

My training and education tell me that I am processing loss—struggling through it, searching for answers. I've read the books and taken the classes on all of this—six years' worth of higher-level learning. But then again, nothing teaches like experience.

I've had my fair share of shouting matches with God over the years. In a strange way, I feel like God likes it when we get angry and mix it up with God. Maybe it's just me, but I've always felt heard after one of my angry tirades with the Almighty.

Over the past few months, however, I have found that I can't seem to summon the energy to be truly angry or to lament to God about my struggles. I started to feel like the answers weren't going to come—at least, not in the way I wanted them.

I felt like God had gone silent on the topic of my grief and sadness. I felt like God wasn't speaking in response to my questions. And then I read the following amazing words from the late philosopher Alan Watts:

> If I just yell a monotone yell with no rhythm to it at all, it won't be long until you tell me to cut it out. It's annoying—nobody wants to hear that What we long to hear is the gap, the break. Those silences create the rhythm, and more complex patterns of silences create even more interesting rhythms.

It occurs to me that as frustrating as God's silences might seem, they may be the very thing that we need. A rhythm is created in the silences, a rhythm that invites us to enter into the music that is playing and let ourselves be carried along by the song being sung.

And it is in the silences that we often hear what the old prophet Elijah might have known as the "still, small voice of God." The ancient Hebrew words would describe it as a "sound of sheer silence" (1 Kings 19:13 NIV, NRSV).

When Elijah experienced that silence, he knew instinctively that God was in it. And it was only when Elijah acknowledged the God-rhythms created by the silence that he was finally able to truly hear the voice of God, speaking, singing, and carrying him along.

May you find solace in the silences today. May you rest in the quiet when it feels as though there are no answers to your questions and no words to comfort your spirit.

And may you finally feel the rhythms of the song that is being sung over you by the Creator and Sustainer of your life, both now and forever.

God's Persistent Loving Presence

Yesterday, I wrote about silences and the rhythms they create in the song that is being sung over us by God. I felt like I had stumbled upon an important and life-giving truth.

And then today, the majority of my devotional and scripture readings, the music I'm listening to, and the poems I've read all speak of God's presence and the depth of meaning behind God's silence.

I suppose you could call it a coincidence, but I'm going to choose not to dishonor the beauty of this feeling by relegating it to the realms of chance.

Instead, I prefer to think of it as God's sly and loving way of telling me I am known.

I also prefer to see this as a grace-filled invitation for me to embrace my uncertainty with confidence—the kind of confidence that comes when I surrender all my outcomes to the One who is the center of all things.

Bob Goff writes, "What a shame it would be if we were waiting for God to say something while He's been waiting on us to do something."

For me, *doing something* means actively listening and choosing to trust what I'm hearing and feeling, and what I am feeling is the realization that I am never far from God.

As Richard Rohr once said, "You cannot *not* live in the presence of God." I love that so much. Despite all of our efforts to distance ourselves from God, we can never escape God's loving presence, which is all around us, in us, and through us.

I was listening to a song today by Sleeping At Last (songwriter Ryan O'Neal), titled "Bad Blood." The lyrics stirred something deep in my heart, and I thought I'd share them:

> You fixed your eyes on us,
> Your flesh and blood,
> A sculpture of water
> And unsettled dust.
> So we wrestle with it all—The concept of grace
> And the faithful concrete
> As it breaks our fall.

It is a jarring and unsettling moment when we come up against the solid, unmoving persistence of God's loving presence. But we need to know that whatever is shattered at that moment will be put together, stronger than ever before.

Work in the Name of Jesus

Many people have a strange notion when it comes to what they consider "spiritual" activities as opposed to "nonspiritual." This contrast also has been described as the difference between what is "secular" and what is "sacred."

For example, going to church has often been classified as a spiritual or sacred activity, whereas meeting friends for dinner at the pub is described as secular.

Some people might take this further and extend the descriptions to vocation. Being a pastor, for instance, is considered by many people to be a sacred vocation, whereas being a businessperson is considered a secular one.

I can't tell you how many times I've had conversations with people about their lives of faith, and they will say things to me like, "Well, I'm just a banker, not a pastor," or "I'm only a stay-at-home mom, not a minister."

The great Christian mystic Thomas Merton once wrote, "You can tell more about a monk by the way he uses a broom than by anything he says."

The sixteenth-century reformer Martin Luther summed it like this: "Even dirty and unpleasant work is pure and holy work if it comes from a pure heart."

For Luther and for Merton, even the most mundane of tasks was made holy by the intent and heart of the doer. We should embrace this idea wholeheartedly in all aspects of our lives of following Jesus. No matter what we do, we should do it with the notion that we are doing it for the glory of God.

The apostle Paul wrote to the church at Colossae about this very idea:

> And whatever you do, whether in word or deed, do it all in the name of the Lord
> Jesus, giving thanks to God the Father through him. (Colossians 3:17 NIV)

Today, as you work, whatever your work might be, do it in the name of Jesus. Whether you are cleaning your house, caring for an elderly parent, changing diapers, doing home repairs, going to a meeting, selling real estate, or driving the kids to school or to dance class or to summer camp, it is all holy work when you do it with what the apostle Paul called "the mind of Christ."

May you find ways today to see all your work, your vocation, your calling in life as holy and worthy of being done in the name of Jesus to the glory of God the Father. May you discover worth and purpose you have never experienced in the mundane and even the exasperating aspects of the ordinary.

Give of Yourself with No Expectations

As part of my daily reading this morning, I happened upon a short testimonial by a pastor who declared that Mondays "were the worst."

This pastor confessed that on Mondays, he would wonder how his sermon had been received, what he could have done better, how the worship service could have been improved, etc. Then he would move on to whether anything he had done had made any difference at all.

"The tricky part," he declared, "is that more often than not, the results of our efforts are not visible."

I have to admit that there are *some* Mondays when I find myself wondering the same things as that pastor. And while most of it is a desire on my part to develop better skills, sometimes self-doubt creeps its way into the mix.

But then again, pastors haven't cornered the market on wondering whether their efforts to do good and change lives have an effect or not. All of us deal with this, to some extent.

Let's face it; much of the good that we do in the world goes unnoticed by human eyes, and if our only motivation for doing good is the affirmation of others, we'll soon find ourselves frustrated, then discouraged and, ultimately, fatigued.

In his letter to the Galatians, the apostle Paul spoke encouragement to first-century Christians who struggled with the same issue. He wrote:

> Let us not become weary in doing good, for at the proper time we will reap a harvest
> if we do not give up. (Galatians 6:9 NIV)

There's a beautiful poem by Wendell Berry titled "Sabbaths" that echoes Paul's admonition:

> Whatever is foreseen in joy
> Must be lived out from day to day.
> Vision held open in the dark
> By our ten thousand days of work.
> And yet no leaf or grain is filled
> By work of ours; the field is tilled
> And left to grace. That we may reap,
> Great work is done while we're asleep.

May you surrender the outcomes of the good you do today. May you give freely of yourself and your gifts, without expectations of return. May you trust that the Lord of the harvest will cover your efforts with his glory and goodness.

Shine Your Light Today

The struggle to extract meaning from the challenges and obstacles in life is perhaps the most difficult struggle that we face as human beings.

And sometimes, that search for meaning can feel like a search for light in the darkness. We look for any break in the shadows, any illumination at all that can help us see more clearly.

I recently rediscovered a musical artist I've been loosely following for several years—Ryan O'Neal, otherwise known by his recordings as Sleeping At Last.

(If you've never heard Sleeping At Last, I highly recommend you rectify that immediately, and visit the website at www.sleepingatlast.com.)

I was listening to one of Ryan's songs yesterday, and the lyrics seemed to speak directly to that idea I mentioned—the idea of our desperate search for meaning in the darkness of all life's challenges and trials.

> But the sweetest thing I've ever heard
> Is that I don't have to have the answers,
> Just a little light to call my own.
> Though it pales in comparison
> To the overarching shadows,
> A speck of light can reignite the sun
> And swallow darkness whole.

Doesn't that just make your heart ache and then soar?

We spend so much time trying to figure all of this out—trying to find the right theological statements and explanations to dumb down the experiences of the Divine that all of us feel deep within us.

We offer up Hallmark-card platitudes of sympathy and half-hearted encouragement in our feeble attempts to mitigate sorrow, cover up grief, and push down doubt. And in the end, we have to admit that we don't have all the answers.

But we can take incredible comfort in the knowledge that we do have a little bit of light. And the light that has been passed to us comes to us from the Source of all light, who tells us that *we* are the light in the darkness.

Shine your little light today. Shine it in the dark corners where light never seems to reach. Shine it, and know that you are the light of the world. And the darkness cannot overcome you.

Allow Yourself to Feel God's Love

When Bishop Michael Curry delivered his sixteen-minute sermon at the royal wedding of Prince Harry and Meghan Markle, he didn't hold back. His sermon, which was unabashedly Jesus-centered and love-focused, quickly became the most memorable moment of the ceremony.

He preached with a passion and power that had hitherto been unseen or unheard in the hallowed halls of Saint George's chapel. Millions upon millions of people heard his stirring and inspiring words on the power of love to overcome injustice and heal all wounds.

The British newspaper the *Guardian* put it like this: "The American bishop did it black. And he shocked the congregation by refusing to tone down his passionate message on power and love."

I've been thinking a great deal about why Curry's sermon caused such a stir. Those words written in the *Guardian* speak volumes. People were shocked that he didn't tone down "his passionate message on power and love." Shocked. They were shocked to hear a message of love from a Christian preacher.

The reaction to Curry's sermon reveals that those of us who claim to follow Jesus have been working too hard to answer questions that almost no one is really asking. Our hearts have become hardened to our culture. We've become focused on defining ourselves by what we are not.

It's time we chipped away at our hardened hearts and allow them to become soft again for the center and true foundation of our faith: the great love, grace, and inclusive embrace of God expressed through Jesus.

The thirteenth century poet Rumi wrote:

> but come! Take a pick-axe
> and break apart
> your stony self
> the heart's matrix
> is glutted with rubies
> springs of laughter
> are buried in your breast.

Today, instead of working so hard to try to prove your love for God, why not simply be still and allow yourself to feel the love of God for you? Don't be afraid to let the hard shell around your heart begin to break. And learn to live in such a way that no one is shocked to hear that the love you feel from God is the kind of love that is freely offered to all.

Pray with Your Legs

I prayed for freedom twenty years, but received no answer until I prayed with my legs.
—Frederick Douglass

"Prayer changes things."
"I'm sure they felt the prayers."
"They could really use our prayers right now."
"Our thoughts and prayers are with you."
"We all need to say a prayer right about now."

People of faith have all kinds of ideas about prayer and all manner of platitudes to describe them. The above list includes just a few of the platitudes that I've used on occasion when I'm responding to a need or a tragedy or simply to comfort and encourage someone.

I think, if we're being truly honest with ourselves, there have been more than a few times when we have simply said that we would be "praying" for someone or something, when we didn't really know what else to say.

For the record, I *do* believe that prayer changes things and that it makes a difference—just not in the same way I once believed. In fact, my entire attitude toward prayer has shifted over the years in ways that have transformed and enlivened my prayer life.

Rather than approaching prayer as a way to beseech the Divine for some request or another, I've come to view prayer as a way of keeping company and connection with God. And I also have come to see that the "thing" that prayer changes is actually me.

When we pray, we open up the possibility of a deeper connection with an understanding of the energizing and convicting Spirit of God all around us, in us, and through us. We have the potential to be more aware of God's will and desires for us.

And we also can begin to realize that nine out of ten times, we are the answers to our own prayers. When this happens, we soon discover new ways to approach problems, new perspectives to our struggles, and a new way forward when the path seems unclear.

This kind of approach to prayer frees us from seeing prayer as if we are constantly asking God for favors that God may or may not grant. Instead, it allows us to find ways to align our will with God's and to let ourselves be transformed and made new.

May you pray today with a renewed sense of optimism and hope. May you discover that your relationship with God deepens through your prayers.

Receiving a New Heart

Today, I find myself reflecting on how you don't have to be a genius to know that the world is not as it should be. But you do have to be a genius to skillfully avoid seeing or hearing about all the ways things are messed up and broken.

These days, the constant stream of bad news seems to find us, no matter what barriers we erect to shield ourselves from it.

And it can make you feel sick inside—weary and overwhelmed. If you are not careful (and even when you are), you can quickly and easily begin to see the world solely through the distorted lens of a half-empty glass.

This morning, I got to thinking about all the ways I've allowed myself to define my view of the world (and some of the people in it) in negative terms.

I also felt a surge of passion and desire for something better—for the world and for myself. It filled me like a huge, deep breath—the kind you take when you're about to jump off a high dive.

Today in my morning reading, I was struck by a wonderful poem by Ryan O'Neal titled "Taste."

> I wanna feel, tectonic shifts;
> I wanna be, I wanna be, astonished.
> I wanna be astonished.
> So I propose a toast:
> To fists unraveling, to glass unshattering.
> To breaking all the rules, to breaking bread again.
> We're swallowing light, we're swallowing our pride.
> We're raising our glass, 'til we're fixed from the inside.

As I read O'Neal's poem, I recalled another poetic verse that was uttered by an ancient Hebrew prophet by the name of Ezekiel. Ezekiel delivers the words of God to God's people—an assurance of God's desire for them to live bigger, to be alive with possibility.

> I will give you a new heart and put a new spirit in you; I will remove from you your heart of stone and give you a heart of flesh. (Ezekiel 36:26 NIV)

May you be filled today with a new spirit, the kind that opens up your whole life to the positive possibilities of this beautiful and divinely loved world. May the stony walls you've erected to guard your heart be cracked and fall away to reveal your true self.

Jesus Takes Out the Guesswork

Just giving people commandments on tablets and stone doesn't change the heart. It may steel the will, but it doesn't soften the heart like a personal encounter can.
—Richard Rohr

Some years ago, when I was working on my master's degree at Florida State University, I was walking with some fellow students through one of the many common areas on campus when we encountered a street evangelist who had attracted a crowd.

The evangelist's name was Brother Jed, a loud and obnoxious self-appointed preacher, who makes a career out of protesting on college campuses all over the United States.

Jed's modus operandi is to say as many offensive, bigoted, and hateful things as possible in order to start arguments with people, which he then records on video to post on his website.

In short, Brother Jed is not a nice guy. On this particular day, Brother Jed had a huge sign that used the word *gay* as an acronym to spell this unbelievably horrible sentence: "Got Aids Yet?"

My companions began spouting angrily about how narrow-minded, hateful, and awful Christians were. They said a lot of really hard things, using some choice language. They forgot, momentarily, that I was a Christian, even though all of them knew it.

When it dawned on them that their choice words might have wounded me, they told me they were sorry, but I responded by telling them they had no reason to apologize. I told them quietly, "You have to know that most Christians are not like that guy."

I then went on to explain that for people like Brother Jed, you can't gloss over their bad behavior by saying, "Well, his heart is in the right place," because his heart was obviously filled with hatred and anger.

I then let my friends know that Jesus wants no part of that, period.

I was able to share with them that because of Jesus, we don't have to guess what God wants (for us to have abundant life), what God desires (God's *shalom* in the world), the things God would say, who God loves (everyone), and how far God is willing to go to rescue us.

Richard Rohr once wrote, "In Jesus, God was given a face and a heart."

We need to find ways, every single day, to help people connect with the face and heart of God—to help people see Jesus in our words and deeds. There are far too many people out there claiming to speak for Jesus, and though their voices might be loud, we will speak louder with our love.

And what we have to say is worth hearing.

Being Intentional about Spiritual Growth

Recently my wife and I made a decision to stop griping about a particular situation that we were dealing with and to start praying about it instead.

What precipitated this decision was an even more important decision that we made together: the decision to begin our day with some Bible study and prayer time, just the two of us.

And if I want to be inclusive, what started the whole thing was a piece of word art on the wall in my home office—a quote from Johnny Cash, which I thought was awesome and spoke of Cash's great love for his wife, June Carter Cash.

Here's the quote:

"This morning with her, having coffee."—Johnny Cash, when asked for his definition of paradise.

My wife found that piece of word art offensive because I rarely, if ever, had coffee with her in the morning. Instead, I guarded my morning devotion time against interruptions like a junkyard dog.

So we started having coffee (she drinks tea, though) every morning we are together. And we started reading the Bible together and talking about what we read. And we started praying together about all of the things that were on our minds.

Which led to us deciding to stop griping about a thing that was causing us anxiety and anger and to start praying about it instead. Now you're all caught up.

Here's what we discovered when we did this: our thoughts and feelings about that situation changed. We softened. We became more open to feelings of forgiveness and hope. And as a result, the situation changed too.

I'm discovering even now, in my fiftieth year, that one of the many keys to a deeper relationship with God, a deeper spirituality, is to simply be intentional.

I am certain that if we had not agreed to be intentional about carving out time together to study and to pray that my wife and I probably would probably missed an opportunity to grow in our faith and to find peace over a stressful situation.

If you are not intentionally making time to be inspired by sacred texts, to spend time talking with God, and to create spiritual connections with loved ones or trusted friends, you may be missing out on some valuable learning.

Create space in your life for intentional study and prayer. You won't regret it.

Living Peaceably with Everyone

I've been watching with interest this week the unfolding story of a viral video that created a firestorm of controversy.

The initial video of a confrontation between high school students and a First Nation protestor ended up making the rounds on all of the cable news networks and all over the internet, where it caused so much outrage that some of the students in the video received death threats.

It is clear that there is definitely more to the story than what was portrayed in the original video released from what has been characterized as a "fraudulent" Twitter account (the account subsequently was suspended).

And proponents of each side of this story all claim their side of the story is the truth. What can't be disputed, however, is what the entire story reveals about us as people.

The incident was charged with anger, resentment, prejudice, lack of understanding, fear, and hatred. It highlighted how we are still so very divided—some might say, hopelessly so. For me, it also highlighted something troubling about how Christians present themselves in these divided days.

As I watched all of this unfold, I thought about what my responsibilities are as a Christian in moments of tension and division. I thought about this because it was widely reported that the students who were part of the incident claimed to be Christians.

The apostle Paul once wrote the following exhortation: "Do all that you can to live at peace with everyone" (Romans 12:8 NIV).

Perhaps if those of us who say that we follow Jesus actually did all that we could to live at peace with everyone, moments like the one in question wouldn't happen with such frequency—or maybe not at all. Perhaps we wouldn't provoke others into arguments. Perhaps we wouldn't put ourselves in situations where we have to try to explain away what is perceived, at first blush, as bigotry and hatred.

The philosopher Ludwig Wittgenstein once said, "If you want to know if a man is religious, don't ask him, observe him."

I think this is a moment when followers of Jesus need to preach louder with their actions than with their words. We need to be called to faithfulness when it comes to the way we present ourselves. Because if our actions cause others to stumble, it doesn't matter one whit what we say.

Your Words Matter

Words matter.

Sometimes when people take umbrage over the ways that words are often used to marginalize, dismiss, or gloss over the voice, ideas, or even the true humanity of others, there are those who collectively roll their eyes and chalk up such notions as simply hypersensitivity to politically incorrect speech.

And truth be told, I've been one of those people. I've rolled my eyes when someone parsed my words and took offense to something I said or wrote. I've even ranted about it.

"I never wore a seat belt growing up," I'd say. "And I never wore a bicycle helmet either. I also didn't get a trophy just for participating on the Little League team. People just need to grow a thicker skin."

But our words matter. It's a pesky truism that can't be shaken or diminished, no matter how uncomfortable it makes us or how inconvenient it is for us to confront.

The great British theologian G. K. Chesterton once wrote:

> Why shouldn't we quarrel about a word? What is the good of words if they aren't important enough to quarrel over? Why do we choose one word more than another if there isn't any difference between them?

Our words matter—which is why we should pay close attention to how we use them.

Our choice of words can mean the difference between healing and wounding, between love and indifference, between life and death.

And here's something else: our lack of words matters too. Sometimes, what we *don't* say can have an even more profound effect on others than what we do say. There are times to speak, for sure, but there are also times to be silent.

But sometimes, our silence can be wounding. We need to use our words to speak life and hope into the world around us, to not withhold the blessings of words that are good, true, and beautiful.

So make your words matter today. Speak life. Speak hope. Speak faith. Speak love.

Unruly, Holy Curiosity

I once read a parable about two rabbis who spent years arguing with one another over the meaning of a particular passage in the Torah. They grew old together in their argument, as their disagreement went on for decades.

At last, God decided enough was enough and appeared to the two old men when they were in the middle of one of their debates.

"I'm tired of listening to you two argue," God told them. "I'm going to tell you the meaning of the Torah passage, and maybe it will shut you both up at last."

Both men looked at one another, and then one of them burst out to God, "How dare you! We don't want you to tell us what this means. We've only started to figure it out ourselves, and we are doing just fine, thank you!"

I've always loved that parable. It speaks to me on so many levels.

On the one hand, it reveals just how stubborn we are as human beings and so over-confident in our own abilities to figure out the mind of God.

But there's another way this parable speaks. It also speaks to the beauty of the struggle and the lengths to which our own curiosity keeps urging us forward as we gain snippets of knowledge, glimpses of God's glory.

I read the following wonderful quote this week by British author Ian Leslie:

> Curiosity is unruly. It doesn't like rules, or, at least, it assumes that all rules are provisional, subject to the laceration of a smart question nobody has yet thought to ask. It disdains the approved pathways, preferring diversions, unplanned excursions, impulsive left turns. In short, curiosity is deviant.

My prayer for you today is that your unruly curiosity will lead you to sacred moments of revelation and wonder. I pray that you will never stop seeking knowledge and glimpses of God's glory in the world around you.

Feeling the Kavod

When I was a kid, summer was like magic. During those summers long ago, I would wake up in the morning with a rush of possibility. There would be a fierce sense of joy that would fill my chest as I contemplated the day to come.

And those days would last so long, wouldn't they? When I was young, I wanted to wring every bit of adventure from those summer days and nights. I would stay outside as long as I could, until it was almost too dark to see.

One memory seems to stand out for me today; it's one that I've brought to mind over and again throughout my life.

In my mind's eye, I can see myself at age ten, catching fireflies with my cousins in the gathering South Carolina dusk. My parents are young—younger than I am now. My grandmother, four uncles, and my aunt are alive and laughing.

It was a holy moment, and it is a gift to be able to recall it with such vivid detail.

In the New Testament, a Greek word is used to describe holy time: *kairos*. This word speaks of what the apostle Paul called the "fullness of time" (Galatians 4:4 ESV) or a moment when the space between this world and the next becomes thin enough to actually *feel* the presence of God.

There's a heaviness that comes with that feeling. The air is thicker. Time seems too slow. You feel a rush of possibility—a fierce sense of joy. The ancient Hebrew people described this as the *kavod*, or the "heaviness" of God's glory.

Frederick Buechner spoke of this once when he wrote of a similar experience:

> It was not much and lasted only for a moment before it was gone. But it happened-- this glimpse of something dimly seen, dimly heard, this sense of something deeply hidden.

May you approach this, the longest day of the year, with a sense of joy and possibility. May you find the thin places where you feel God's glory. May you have glorious moments of *kairos* time with friends and loved ones.

If You Ain't First, You're First

I am about to share something with you that is deeply personal and vulnerable. Once I share this, many of you may find that you have something new and wonderful in common with me.

Here goes: one of my favorite movies is Will Ferrell's *Talladega Nights: The Ballad of Ricky Bobby*. Don't judge. Remember what Jesus said about judging others—you get judged by the same measure. I bet you've got a movie or two that you just love (like *Ernest Goes to Camp*, for example) that would make the rest of us go, "Huh?"

In *Talladega Nights*, Will Ferrell's character, Ricky Bobby, is a NASCAR driver who falls on hard times. For his entire life, he's held to a motto he heard from his ne'er-do-well father, Reese Bobby, when he was a child: "If you ain't first, you're last."

When he's finally reunited with his father, Ricky Bobby has the following exchange with him about that life motto:

> Ricky Bobby: Wait, Dad. Don't you remember the time you told me, "If you ain't first, you're last"?
> Reese Bobby: Huh? What are you talking about, son?
> Ricky Bobby: That day at school.
> Reese Bobby: Oh—son, I was high that day. That doesn't make any sense at all, you can be second, third, fourth—you can even be fifth.
> Ricky Bobby: What? I've lived my whole life by that!

I know, I know—this isn't the classiest devotional I've written, but hang in there.

This conversation with his dad was a turning point in the movie. When Ricky Bobby starts to fail, when he is no longer winning races, he doesn't know how to handle it because he'd structured his whole life around the idea of a certain kind of success and winning above all else.

But as the movie progresses, he begins to learn more from his failures than he ever learned from his successes.

Jesus constantly taught that humility and becoming less-than leads to true success. "If you want to save your life," he taught, "you have to lose it." In the kingdom of God, Jesus proclaimed, "the first will be last, and the last will first" (Matthew 20:16 NIV).

May you learn true spirituality and intimacy with Christ from your low moments, your stumbles, and your foibles. May you give up your need to be successful in the eyes of our culture, and strive instead for the humility and lowliness that Christ himself took on willingly to his ultimate glory.

Total Submission and Then Joy

In 1654, the famed mathematician Blaise Pascal had a profoundly mystical and spiritually uplifting experience one night from 10:30 until 12:30. How do we know this? He wrote it down on a piece of paper that he later sewed into the lining of his coat.

We can only surmise that the reason he did this was to preserve it and keep it somewhere close to his heart. It was only after his death that the paper with his words from that night were discovered.

His note began: "The Year of grace 1654 … From about ten-thirty in the evening to about half an hour after Midnight … Fire."

Pascal continued his note by writing: "I separated myself from [Jesus]; I fled him, renounced him, Crucified him. May I never be separated from him!"

And then, finally, this: "Total submission to Jesus Christ and to my director. Eternally in joy for a day of trial on earth."

I imagine Pascal sitting at a small seventeenth-century wooden desk, feverishly writing this all down with his quill pen, his fingers stained with ink. On his face is a broad smile, a joyful expression—the kind that can only come through the peace of complete and total surrender.

I have had my fair share of dark nights of the soul. I am sure you have as well. It's something we all share. But there are other moments too. There are moments when the presence of God surrounds me, and my heart feels as though it might burst through my chest with gratitude and wonder.

Lois Cheney wrote a poem in the 1960s that captures the essence of such a moment. She claims she is "looking for a word" to best describe those kinds of heart-through-your-chest moments, and she thinks the word she is looking for is "joy."

And then she writes, "Or maybe it's 'God.' Then again, maybe they're the same word."

My prayer for you today is that you will have more and more moments in your life where you experience the indescribably joy of the Lord. I pray that you will be consumed by the fire of the Holy Spirit in your heart.

I pray the very prayer that the apostle Paul prayed for the church at Rome:

> May the God of hope fill you with all joy and peace as you trust in him, so that you may overflow with hope by the power of the Holy Spirit. (Romans 15:13 NIV)

Following Jesus Breaks You, Then Makes You

The other day, I had a conversation with a church member who told me that she had become hopelessly convicted to do something to help refugees.

She told me that she had begun to feel "uncomfortable" about her feelings and that she couldn't shake them.

She said, "I really feel like this is something that Jesus wants me to do."

I replied, "That pesky Jesus—always showing up and wrecking our lives."

We laughed but not the kind of laugh that you would laugh at a joke or a video of someone falling into a pool. It was a knowing laugh, tinged with a bit of trepidation.

It was the kind of laugh that you laugh when you are about to jump off the side of a cliff into a lake or a river. Even if you are scared out of your mind, you can hear yourself giggling madly in those moments, right before you step off the edge.

So my church member and I laughed together about how Jesus was messing with her, and I think we both knew that things were probably going to change for her in the near future if she made the choice to respond to the call she was hearing.

You probably have heard the old adage that accepting a challenge will either "make or break you." I think following Jesus is a challenge all unto itself. Following Jesus first breaks you, then makes you.

If your journey with Jesus seems kind of boring, placid, and full of ease and contentment, you're probably doing it wrong.

Seriously, you could attend church regularly, drop checks in the offering plate, go to Bible studies, and volunteer here and there when you have the time and still be missing the point.

I was reading a devotion by Father Richard Rohr this morning; he wrote the following: "If your spiritual practice doesn't lead you to some acts of concrete caring or service, then you have every reason not to trust it."

Rohr goes on to say that Saint John Cassian (c. 360–435) called the feeling that my church member is feeling the *pax perniciosa*, or "dangerous peace."

Know this: whatever it's called, you can't shake it when you feel it.

May the grace and peace of our Lord Jesus Christ be with you, now and always.

Stepping Fully into the Ordinary

I am late getting my devotion done today.

My wife and I got up early and took our youngest son and his friend to camp, all the way on the north side of Austin.

Then we had a coffee meeting with some potential ministry partners, followed by an impromptu meeting to talk and dream about improvements to our church campus—improvements that would expand our ability to do ministry and help people grow in faith.

It was a busy morning.

I wondered what I would write about today, considering I was feeling a bit guilty for putting all those other things ahead of my regular schedule of thinking and writing early in the morning.

And then it occurred to me that I was beating myself up for not completing an important task. The reason I hadn't completed it, however, was because I was doing equally if not more important tasks instead.

But here was the problem: I was diminishing the value and importance of those tasks because they somehow didn't seem to measure up to the "special-ness" of writing the daily devotion for today.

Completing the daily devotion is a vital part of my weekday routines. Lots of people tell me they enjoy them. Some people have shared that they use them as part of their own daily routine.

And when I feel like I am letting people down, an internal struggle takes place, where I start to feel like I am not good enough, like I am somehow not measuring up.

Earlier this morning, I read this great quote from author Lois Cheney:

> I can't wipe out the doubts and fears in my self-knowledge of not measuring up, but I can walk each day seeking to fulfill what [God] wants in me. I may not achieve hours of grace, but I can achieve the moments of gentle approval.

Most of the time it's the ordinary things that we do (things like caring for our families, connecting with friends, finding ways to be generous with our time, having coffee with someone, doing life with others) that make all the difference to God.

May you find ways to embrace the moments of gentle approval from a God who loves it when you step more fully into life—all of life, especially the ordinary moments.

A Little Bit about Circumcision

Today's Daily Devo is going to take a sharp left turn right out of the gate. Buckle up.

> For in Christ Jesus neither circumcision nor uncircumcision has any value. (Galatians 5:6a NIV)

Nothing like starting your day off with an awesome and inspiring verse about circumcision; am I right? This verse was part of a letter sent to a first-century church in Galatia (in modern-day Turkey) by the apostle Paul.

Paul was responding to some critics of his who had showed up at the Galatian church and began telling them that everything Paul had taught them about what it meant to be a follower of Jesus was wrong.

These critics taught that the only true way to be a follower of Jesus was to convert to Judaism, which meant that you had to keep the 613 laws that are found in the Torah (the first five books of the Hebrew scriptures), and you had to be circumcised.

Paul believed that keeping laws and being circumcised didn't make you a follower of Jesus. If that was your thing (if you were already Jewish), he was fine with that, but if you were a Gentile, it wasn't necessary.

But his critics kept coming back again and again to the whole circumcision issue. It was the thing they insisted was the most important. We can assume that they thought if you were really serious about following Jesus, you would take care of it.

Paul, on the other hand, had a different way of seeing the whole issue. In the second part of that verse shared at the beginning, Paul tips his hand on what he believes it really takes to follow Jesus: "The only thing that counts is faith expressing itself through love" (Galatians 5:6b NIV).

Paul called out his critics by saying they'd become distracted from the main point of what it meant to be a follower of Jesus—o love.

If your faith has become about checklists and rules and guidelines for behavior, if following Jesus means that you spend most of your energy calling out other people for the ways they aren't making the grade, then maybe it's time to refocus on the only thing that counts: faith in Jesus that expresses itself in love—love for God and for others.

Your Best-Laid Plans

The other day, I was trying to leave the parking lot of a shopping center during rush hour and to get turned around in the right direction for home.

This meant that I would have to navigate my way to a narrow median and then wait for a break in traffic before flooring it to get into the desired lane. Suddenly, I saw my moment—things were going to work out perfectly, with the oncoming cars moving just in the right sequence.

Everything was perfect until one of the drivers decided to make a turn, and the whole sequence fell apart.

"Aaaaghhh!" I exclaimed.

My wife, Merideth, sat quietly for a second and then asked, "Did you seriously just get mad at the person for making a turn?"

"Yes!" I exclaimed, "they messed up my whole plan!"

"You're ridiculous," she told me.

I knew she was right, but I didn't admit it.

Until now, that is.

In one of my readings this morning for my own daily devotions, I ran across a quote from the Roman emperor and Stoic Marcus Aurelius that spoke right into my angst over the driver who turned and messed up my plans.

Aurelius writes, "While it's true that someone can impede our actions, they can't impede our intentions or our attitudes, which have the power of being conditional and adaptable."

In other words, almost on a daily basis, other people are going to do things that will thwart your plans, foil your best-laid schedules, and otherwise mess you up. You can't control those kinds of things, but you *can* control how you react to them.

In Romans 8:6, the apostle Paul wrote these words:

> But to set the mind on the flesh is death, but to set the mind on the Spirit is life and peace. (NIV)

Paul, who was almost definitely influenced by the Stoic thinkers of his day, appropriates Aurelius's advice but sees it as a practical way for Christians to follow Jesus more fully.

Essentially, when we are focused on following Jesus and are being led by his Spirit (which means being fully surrendered to God), we find that no one (or no thing) can steal our peace.

May you see all the moments when your plans are thwarted today as opportunities to learn, to grow, and to draw closer to Jesus. May you surrender the outcomes of those moments and embrace the peace of Christ—the peace that "passes all understanding."

You Were Made for This

I believe that the Spirit of God within us creates a longing to connect, not just with other people but with God, who knows us better than we know ourselves.

We long to know and to be known. We long to truly feel, to not give in to the despair that comes from the resignation that this is all there is, and there is no Creator or Designer, no plan or purpose. Because when we resign ourselves to this—even slightly—we end up trying to fulfill our longings with other things, other feelings, or even what some might call other "gods."

But when those longings are met for real, we know it. When we realize (sometimes surprisingly) that there really is a God and that God is actually connected to us, it draws out emotions—feelings we didn't know we had.

And when we respond to these emotions, we often sing or pray or weep or stand up and dance, or we fall down to our knees or on our faces This is called *worship* by some people—a full-on, emotionally charged, hard-to-explain feeling that can't be shaken and can't be faked.

Here's an awesome thought: you were made for this. That stardust inside of you contains not just your DNA for this moment but the very DNA of the One who spoke all of this into existence in the first place.

Which is why, when we see others going through the motions of worship or we find ourselves doing the same, we know that it's not real. We feel stuck in a rut. It might feel comforting for a bit, but the energy isn't quite right. It doesn't feel the same. It's not authentic.

It doesn't make you want to dance. It's not true worship. True worship doesn't just go through the motions.

True worship is the response to an authentic encounter with the God who imprinted us with his DNA, who loves us more than we can ever know, and who also desires to be connected with us by any means necessary.

I would encourage you to experiment with something today: when you experience joy, when you feel a moment of a connection with someone, when you feel peace wash over you, when you have a feeling of gratitude, when you are angry over injustice, when you mourn with someone who is mourning, stop and silently acknowledge these feelings as a movement of the Spirit of God within you.

Pray a prayer of thanksgiving that the wind of the Spirit is blowing in your life. Then celebrate—however you feel you can in the moment.

It's in You

The first time I heard a sermon on grace was when I was twenty-four years old in a Presbyterian church in Ocoee, Florida. I can't remember exactly what the pastor preached, but I couldn't stop crying. I'd been an agnostic for some time. I was bitter. I had spent years trying to fulfill the longings of my heart by appeasing one god or another.

And I thought that the God I had learned about in Sunday school was angry and required negotiations. There wasn't anything imminent about that God—and by *imminent*, I mean up close, personal, and real.

But then, there I was, hearing how much God loved me, and for some strange reason, I had to bite my hand to keep from sobbing out loud. I was experiencing true worship because the Holy Spirit of God was all around me and in me—and I was finally in a space in my life where I was open to responding to the urging of the Spirit.

True worship is a response to God's Spirit, but before it can be a response, it has to be a recognition. When you are truly worshipping, you recognize that you are connected to something or someone that is outside of you; that there is something deep inside of you that is humming with reverence.

You suddenly realize that despite all of the ways you may be tempted to think otherwise, there really is too much good in the world for your feelings not to be true. And then it hits you.

You are feeling connected because you have been called. Someone outside of that deepest part inside of you—the part that is humming reverence and seeing beauty—is calling you. The Spirit of God is calling you.

And by the time you realize that you are being called, you are contacted. And then your life is never the same again. Because those atoms that make you *you*—the same ones that were pigeons and Oprah and stars—share the same DNA as the One who made them, who made you.

The reason you feel something when you begin to understand the unbelievable love of God, or marvel at the beauty of a sunset, or laugh with friends over dinner is because all of this wonder, joy, hope, and beauty is in you.

The Spirit of God is in you.

May you spend today marveling at all the ways you are called and contacted by the Spirit of God. Decide that, today, you are going to be open to the recognition of God's Spirit at work in the world and in you. Determine that when you recognize the Spirit's work that you will respond in acts of worship, wherever you happen to be.

The Spirit Sings Karaoke

I went on a cruise to Alaska a few years ago. While on the cruise, my wife and I joined some new friends for an evening of karaoke and drinks. Actually, drinks and then karaoke. Trust me; the order is important.

For the final number, my friend Stuart was asked by the deejay to come up and sing Gloria Gaynor's "I Will Survive." As the first strains of the song played over the speakers, every woman in the crowd, it seemed, was on her feet, singing along: "At first I was afraid, I was petrified."

And then they came to the dance floor. Young women in their twenties. Teenagers. Single moms. Middle-aged women in super-high heels. An elegant woman in her mid-seventies. Two lesbian couples. A couple of old ladies who couldn't walk very well. And Stuart.

They sang at the top of their lungs. In unison. Triumphant, proud, hopeful, and full of unbelievable joy. It was one of the most beautiful things I had ever seen.

There is something about that song that speaks to so many women, isn't there? A universal tug on their collective spirit. And their infectious joy landed on us all. At one point, I found myself dancing like John Travolta—literally.

The Spirit moves among us collectively sometimes, joining our hearts together as we share all of the things we have in common and let all the things that divide us fall by the wayside.

And in those moments, the Spirit reveals something true and real about God and God's relationship with us. God is not angry. You don't have to work so hard to please God and get in God's good graces.

What God wants is simply for you to be who you are created to be and to be aware of the Spirit of God in, through, and all around you. The Spirit urges you to worship with all that you are. To respond in joy to God's grace and goodness.

True worship is an authentic response to a loving God who, through Jesus, has already saved the world. You can analyze faith; you can debate it; you can spend all of your time studying it so you can defend it

Or you can learn to dance when the Spirit is blowing, singing, and moving you to channel your inner John Travolta and belt your life song at the top of your lungs.

May you listen for the music of the Spirit today. Let it wash over you and move you to dance, to be filled with joy and hope. May your encounter with the Spirit connect you with others, as you experience the Spirit moving within them.

Prayer Is Openness

As you recall from earlier this week, we are constantly exchanging the atoms that make us *us*, with one another and everything else. Energy flows around us, in us, and through us all of the time. And to think that we aren't affected by this billions-of-atoms-a-second energy exchange is ludicrous.

So there's all of this energy flowing back and forth between us—energy that bears the very DNA of a God who is not far away in his holy temple, tuning in occasionally to hear our puny prayers. This God is here, present, flowing through us in what Christians call the Holy Spirit. And I believe this God is speaking, laughing, guiding, whispering, and creating in the midst of all of it.

When we read about the way Jesus always seemed to be speaking to God, sharing something special with God, maintaining an open channel, so to speak, with God, it makes you wonder if this was exactly what Jesus was trying to demonstrate.

Which makes me wonder if maybe prayer is simply a way to be open to the God-energy, the Holy Spirit, the presence of Jesus all around us.

When you are open-minded and open-hearted to God, you have a tendency to be more aware of what God is doing, saying, and creating. And prayer is a huge part of that openness.

So how do we remain open in our prayer life? How do we pray incessantly (as the apostle Paul exhorted)? I think it begins with honesty, which, as it turns out, is actually the best policy when it comes to prayer. Being honest with the ones we love ultimately draws us closer to them.

In the same way, when you are honest, when you tell the truth, you are close to God. Honesty might sound simply like, "I'm tired"; "I'm exhausted"; "I'm afraid"; "I don't know"; "I feel joy"; "I'm in love." Honesty might even sound like, "I hate you"; "You abandoned me"; "Where are you?"; "I don't know if I believe in you."

Here's a secret: God can handle your honesty. God invites your honesty because God wants to be close to you.

Practice honesty with God today. Speak out loud how you are feeling (don't scare your coworkers by doing this in your cubicle), and let yourself hear it. Ask yourself afterward if you feel closer to God or farther away. Chances are, your honesty will draw you closer, even if you are struggling to be in relationship with God right now.

May you find a new way to experience God and to be enlivened by the Holy Spirit through your raw and open faith.

Prayer in the Privy

In the Jewish tradition, there are prayers for literally all aspects of life because, according to the ancient rabbis, being open to God requires a shift in your understanding about what is sacred and what is "profane"—another word for what is seemingly earthly and not holy.

In fact, there is a very old "privy" prayer that is meant to be prayed after you have finished doing your business in the privy, which is the old English word for bathroom.

Consider this from Rabbi Abayei:

> Abayei said, when one comes out of a privy he should say: Blessed is He who has formed man in wisdom and created in him many orifices and many cavities. It is obvious and known before Your throne of glory that if one of them were to be ruptured or one of them blocked, it would be impossible for a man to survive and stand before You. Blessed are You that heals all flesh and does wonders.

If you think that was a prayer of thanksgiving for your being able to go potty, you are correct.

This kind of prayer life gives new meaning to the word *incessantly*. A person who is praying incessantly is so open to the incredible, joyous energy of the Holy Spirit that they actually pay attention to the wonders of their own body and how it works.

There's nothing more honest than saying to God, "Thank you that my body works like it's supposed to. Oh, and thank you for air freshener as well." By now, I hope I have your attention. Stop giggling.

So what happens when you are honest and open in your prayer life? Does anything really happen when we pray?

We already know that there is a massive, largely invisible energy exchange going on between us and the world around us, all of the time. And we have given the source of that energy a name—the Holy Spirit of God.

What I think is also happening is this: The Holy Spirit of God is flowing all around us, in us, and through us, and when we incessantly pray with openness and honesty, we find we are close to God and are "tapped in" to that energy. We are more able to hear the voice of God speaking, to notice the way God is revealing Godself all around us.

May you spend today in continuous prayer, tapping into the Holy Spirit energy in you, through you, and around you all day. May you find yourself filled with a new sense of openness to the movement of the Spirit and the voice of God, and may this fill you with unbelievable joy.

Prayer Is Taking a Chance

Why do we pray? What happens when we pray? Does prayer really work? These are questions that most people have asked or will ask at least one time or another over the course of their lives.

The ancient mystic of the church Teresa of Avila said that "prayer is nothing else than being on terms of friendship with God."

English poet George Herbert described prayer as "reversed thunder" and "church bells beyond the stars." Almost as if he believed that when a person prayed to the God of the universe, something actually happened.

Not everyone, however, embraces the mystical when it comes to prayer.

Practical theologian Tony Jones doesn't see prayer as a therapeutic exercise and doesn't buy into the notion that if enough people pray for something to happen, God will listen and share his power to answer those prayers. But, he admits, "I need to pray. I now pray out of obedience because Jesus tells us to pray."

I have to admit that it feels a lot better to think that my prayers actually make a difference in the world, rather than being a rote act of obedience.

This is where lots of people want to chime in with all kinds of thoughts on the best kinds of prayers, which books to use, what formulas to employ and such.

All of us are different, and it's not always helpful to try to prescribe the "correct" ways to pray, when what is correct for some is actually downright joy-stealing for others.

One of my favorite authors Anne Lamott writes this about prayer:

> Prayer is taking a chance that against all odds and past history, we are loved and chosen and do not have to get it together before we show up.

I rather like her definition of prayer, to be honest. There's an openness and vulnerability to it that speaks to me—and honestly should speak to all of us.

But I do feel that something happens when we pray, both to us and to the universe we are connected to through the God who made us.

The apostle Paul wrote that we should "pray in the Spirit on all occasions with all kinds of prayers and requests" (Ephesians 6:18 MSG). Try that on today—offer your prayers to God about everything that comes to mind. Stay in conversation with God about your day, the people you meet, the joys and challenges you face.

Prayer Changes Us

Years ago, someone gave me a little plaque that is on the mantel in my office. It reads, "Prayer Changes Things." Maybe you've seen this little aphorism before. This is an excellent little phrase, but I think it needs to be nuanced just a bit.

I would say the following is more accurate: "Praying changes things; prayer changes us."

As I pray—when I am open to the power of the Holy Spirit and to hearing the voice of God in all of the infinite variety in which God speaks—I can easily be transformed by the very act of praying itself. My heart can be moved; my thoughts transformed; my very being realigned with God's purposes.

Listen—every single one of us has had prayers go unanswered. We've prayed and prayed, and all we hear is silence. I've had more than my share of conversations with wounded and broken people who have said to me, "God didn't answer my prayer."

Maybe you were the answer to your own prayer.

There's a popular Christian song on the radio in which the singer asks why God won't do anything about world hunger, human trafficking, and poverty, and God replies, "I did—I made you."

At this point, someone might be thinking, "But what about that time I prayed for God to heal my loved one—and they died? What about the time I prayed that God would heal my marriage—but it ended? Are you saying that I was the answer to that prayer? That it was my fault or something for not seeing it?"

No, I don't know why bad things happen. I have said repeatedly that I don't think God causes all things to happen. But maybe God wanted to be close to you when things went south. Or maybe there's more going on than you can see right here and right now.

Listen—if you can't see the energy exchange that is happening right now between you and your chair, chances are you aren't aware of everything that's going on in the universe.

And you probably aren't aware of all that God might be up to in, around, and through you. I've learned over the years that when it comes to God's plans for my life, I'm playing checkers and God is playing chess. I think I've got it all figured out, but God is so many moves ahead of me, not to mention that God's not even playing the same "game."

Practice trusting God today by prayerfully surrendering the outcomes of some difficult moments. Pray the prayer that Jesus prayed when he was facing his worst moment and completely surrendered his will to God: "Father not my will, but yours be done" (Luke 22:42 NIV).

Continuous Prayer Keeps Us Connected

When I was a little kid, we went to a tiny Baptist church that had Wednesday-night prayer meetings every week. At the end of these informal church services, all of the males in the church would leave their pews and head to the front of the sanctuary, where they would kneel on the steps leading up to the chancel, while all the women would stay in their pews.

What can I say? It was an old-school, hard-shell Baptist church, with all kinds of patriarchal hang-ups.

Once all the guys had gathered, however, a good old-fashioned pray-off would begin. The object was to pray out loud for as many things as you could think of, throw in as many *thees* and *thous* as you could, say *Father* a hundred times a second, and keep going until you ran out of things to say.

And there were always these two guys who would be the last two dudes praying. By the time they were the last two guys, they were basically praying nonsense: "Father, I thank thee for this floor that is beneath my knees and for the godly people who tithed so many years ago to build this floor, and I thank thee that thou made the wood for that floor and gave someone the skill to turn a tree into the wood for that floor."

Finally, one of them would give in, and the other would pray a bit longer, just to show that he had something left in the tank. It was a silly tradition.

But here's what I remember, more than those two pompous nonsense-praying dudes: I remember kneeling in my church, with my dad next to me, and I could hear him praying in a deep voice. I remember trying to think of all the people in my life I could pray for—my parents, my grandparents, my aunts, uncles, cousins. I prayed for my dog. I prayed for the sun to shine the next day.

I remember thinking that many of those family members were in the room, and that felt pretty good too. I loved the way things smelled—all churchy and awesome. I also decided that God was somewhere in the room too. Or if God wasn't exactly in the room, God was close. And I had the funny feeling that somehow, despite all of the people praying in the moment, God had heard me.

And the act of praying changed me. I never forgot those moments—ever, not even when I tried to laugh at them and poke holes in the memory because it was a silly tradition. When I would close my eyes, I'd be right there—feeling warm, surrounded by something or someone far bigger than me.

Continuous prayer keeps us tapped in to the Holy Spirit energy that is between us and all around us—energy that connects us to one another and to the Divine. Because continuous prayer keeps us connected to God.

The Dignity of Notice

Dr. Jill Bolte Taylor is a neuroanatomist from Harvard.

She studies the brain. I had no idea what *neuroanatomist* meant either

Taylor suffered a stroke, and in the midst of that stroke, she was able to study her left-brain and right-brain functioning. When the left side of her brain started shutting down, she started losing the ability to comprehend numbers, analyze, and verbalize.

But here's where this gets odd.

As the right hemisphere of her brain began to grow stronger, Taylor discovered that her sense of individualism decreased, and her relational connection to the world around her increased. She also began to experience a sense of joyous well-being, shared reality, and peace.

Taylor concluded that what's happened in our culture is that we've been trained through our industrial-era educational systems to approach the world with left-brain angles. And this one-sided approach can diminish our ability to care for others and feel connected to the world around us.

My wife has a beautiful way of engaging everyone she meets. When we visit a restaurant, stay at hotels, or go on cruises, she easily becomes the most popular guest. All of the stewards, concierges, and wait staff love her and bend over backward to joyfully serve her.

I asked her recently about this incredible trait that she possesses. She told me that she actively thinks about it every day, wherever she goes. She said to me that what people are responding to is what she calls the "dignity of notice."

The dignity of notice.

Here's what I think. At the very core of our being—where those trillions of atoms that make us *us* are exchanging energy with other things and other people, to the tune of billions a second—we are imprinted with God's DNA

Something happens when we actually see other people, truly see them. I think the God DNA inside of us sings for joy; it hums with happiness. I believe that the God-energy between us, the Holy Spirit of God in Jesus, thrives on the moments where we exercise the dignity of notice.

Practice the dignity of notice today. As you travel through your day, find people to share this wonderful gift with, and see what happens.

Where We Begin Our Journey Matters

Yesterday, I returned home after spending a week in Guatemala with the various mission teams sent by my church in Austin, Texas.

I had the unique privilege to move from team to team over the course of the week, staying in different parts of Guatemala and seeing how all of our mission teams work together to create unique, sustained partnerships with ministries and organizations within Guatemala.

And it also happened to be the first foreign mission trip for my son Jackson. I will be forever grateful to the adult leaders of his mission site (an orphanage where some seventy or eighty children live) for all they did to care for and encourage him while I was moving from site to site.

The trip had a profound effect on him. I can tell he's still trying to figure out how he feels, now that he's back home.

One of the adults on the trip told me that the bed Jackson had selected for the week was pretty terrible. At one point, they told him he needed to move to one of the empty bunk beds, which was more comfortable. Jackson declined and went on to say that many of the children in the orphanage had to sleep on far worse.

Bear in mind that this is the same kid who complained last night about having to walk the dog because he couldn't wait to play video games—so there's work yet to be done. But still, he'll never forget his experience, and neither will I.

Being in community with people who love to do life, mission, and ministry together; a family of faith where Jesus is the center and the kingdom of God is proclaimed—this is what the church is truly all about.

And it's one of the many reasons I continue to labor and serve within the church. God has not given up on the church (in spite of her many problems), and neither have I.

Philosopher and theologian Peter Rollins told this story recently:

> A woman visiting Ireland was trying to reach Tipperary and got lost. She asked an old man for directions, and he told her to take out a pen and paper to write them down. "First of all," he told her, "I wouldn't start here."

Where we begin our journeys in life truly matters. If you don't have a community of faith, find one. You need it. We all do. It matters to have a good place to start when we launch out into the world. And it matters to know that place is there when you return.

Real in Relationship

Most of us learn in elementary school that electrons are one of the "building blocks" of the subatomic world. We even learn to draw various atoms with electrons in orbit.

But did you know that the relationships that exist in our crude grade-school drawings can also tell the story of a relational God, who created all things to be connected to God and to one another?

In 1925, Werner Heisenberg devised a new theory about electrons that set the scientific community on its ear. First, Heisenberg theorized that there is no way to predict where an electron will appear and reappear. Scientists can only calculate the probability of where it will pop up.

About this unpredictable nature of the subatomic world, physicist Carlo Rovelli wrote, "It's as if God had not designed reality with a line that was heavily scored, but just dotted it with a faint outline."

But back to Heisenberg, who further theorized that an electron is essentially a set of observed jumps from one interaction to another and that electrons only exist when they are interacting with something else.

Think about it for a moment. At the most fundamental level of creation, things are real only when they are in relationship.

Over 2,500 years ago, the ancient Jewish prophet Isaiah conveyed God's words on this subject to the people of God this way:

> "I have put my words in your mouth and covered you with the shadow of my hand—I who set the heavens in place, who laid the foundations of the earth and who say to Zion, 'You are my people.'" (Isaiah 51:16 NIV)

We become the people we are meant to be when we are in relationship as God intended—connected to others and to God through the Spirit for the purpose of creating shalom, or peace, of God on earth.

As you journey through your day today, think about how you are created for connection to those around you, and find ways to draw closer to them in real relationship. Give thanks to God that you are "fearfully and wonderfully made," created to long for what's real and true (Psalm 139:14 NIV).

Look for Beauty and Goodness

I was listening to NPR this morning and heard a story about an Uber driver in St. Petersburg, Florida, who saved a suicidal man's life.

Chad Farley, an Uber driver from Gulfport, Florida, was about to call it a night when he felt a strong urge to accept one more fare. He became alarmed when he realized the passenger had asked to be driven to the highest point of the Sunshine Skyway Bridge, which is one of the top spots in Florida where people commit suicide.

According to the *Tampa Bay Times*, "Farley chatted up the passenger, learned he had brain cancer, prayed with the man, held his hand—even snapped a photo of them smiling together before dropping him off at the rest stop to the north of the bridge."

Farley immediately called 911. Florida Highway Patrol officers responded and ended up rescuing the man from drowning himself in the Gulf.

When asked about the incident, Farley reported that it was by "divine appointment" that he encountered the young man that night. He essentially surrendered to what he felt God might be doing in the moment, and because of his surrender, he saved a life.

I needed this story today.

I needed to be reminded that there are lots of people out there in the world who are trying to listen to God, trying to do what is pure, good, lovely, and beautiful.

I needed to be reminded that, inch by inch, God is reconciling creation to himself through the risen Christ.

I also needed to be reminded that those inches add up, and in spite of all evidence to the contrary, God is getting what God wants—one inch, one moment, one life at a time.

So go out into the world today, and look for the beauty and the goodness. Join God in what God is doing in the world to make this world right. Be a force for positive change, radical kindness, and unconditional love.

God Is with Us in Loss

Today I'll be attending the funeral of my wife, Merideth's, uncle, Senator Richard Langley. Senator Langley was a larger-than-life figure in his beloved Lake County, Florida, but he made an indelible imprint on the entire state of Florida during his years of service in the Florida House of Representatives and the Senate.

He lived his entire life to the fullest, wringing the most out of every single day and leaving an incredible legacy to his children and grandchildren.

He was also a man of faith, who spent a lifetime wrestling with scripture, examining his beliefs, and fully and completely placing his trust in God, as he did his best to follow Jesus.

Although he and I approached our faith from different perspectives, I know for a fact that he prayed for me and my ministry, and I will always be grateful for the gift of his prayers.

The role that Senator Langley played in Merideth's life, however, is the one that was most dear to me. To her, he was "Uncle Dick," and for the past several years, he worked alongside her as an attorney in her firm, which now bears his name next to hers.

Merideth's Uncle Dick is the reason she became an attorney, having grown up interning in his office, listening to his stories, and being inspired by his love of the law. She also was a witness to his quiet generosity, the kindness and charity work that he did without fanfare, away from the limelight.

Senator Langley was proud of Merideth for her success as a lawyer but more importantly because she is a great woman of faith, character, and goodness. I am certain it gave him great joy to know he was an integral part of her growth, both in business and in life.

While I know that Merideth is feeling the loss of her uncle deeply, I also know that we can take great comfort in the knowledge that he is at peace because he is now one with God, where there is no more pain, suffering, sickness, or death.

I've always loved the following verse from the book of Revelation, which offers us these incredible words of comfort during times of loss:

> Then I heard a voice from heaven say, "Write this: Blessed are the dead who die in the Lord from now on." "Yes," says the Spirit, "they will rest from their labor, for their deeds will follow them." (Revelation 14:13 NIV)

If you are feeling the loss of someone close to you today, take comfort in the hope of the Resurrection. God is with you in your loss and offers an incredible vision of a future filled with newness and life.

Hold Your Beliefs Lightly

I am sitting in a pediatric dentist's office in Florida this morning. My littlest boy had a dental emergency, and they were able to squeeze him in for an appointment.

I actually wish I could go to this dentist. The waiting room is decorated like a theme park and is loaded with video games. There's also a Disney movie playing on a big-screen TV in front of all these comfy seats.

The group who works here knows what they are doing with kids. They use the most state-of-the-art equipment and have obviously studied how to minimize the negative feelings children have with going to the dentist's office.

When I was a kid, my dentist was a no-nonsense guy with a sterile office and a waiting room stocked with decades-old *National Geographic* and *Reader's Digest* magazines.

Once, the guy went against what nurse told him and brusquely injected the wrong side of my mouth with Novocain. He eventually admitted his mistake, thankfully, but I walked out of there over an hour, unable to feel anything in any part of my head.

I am glad, for my son's sake, that there are dentists out there who have advanced in their understanding of dentistry and who are doing everything in their power to make it a positive experience.

I wish that the majority of Christians approached their faith the same way.

Unfortunately, far too many of us are afraid to grow and expand our understanding of God. We take the interpretations, traditions, and expectations that we were handed, and we assume that if they were good enough for us, then they should be good enough for everyone.

But there is a world full of people who long for a better story. And if we want to be the kind of Jesus-followers who actually attract others to join with us in our journey, we're going to have to allow the gospel to transform us, mold us, and shape us.

Jesus told his followers that they should be "salt" and "light" to other people. In other words, people who don't really get the whole God thing should see God better when we're around. And they should taste the God-flavors in the world better when they are with us.

May you learn what it means to be salt and light today as you seek to know more about God and what it means to truly follow Jesus.

Allow yourself to hold on to your beliefs tightly enough that they are not wrenched from you by force but loosely enough that they can be open to transformation.

Created for Community

This morning, Merideth and I got our two youngest boys out the door for the first day of school. Our first-grader rode his bike to school this morning with two of his buddies (and a couple of dads, including yours truly). Our eighth-grader (all dressed up) walked to school with two of his friends who live on our street.

At our littlest boy's school, we ran into church members, preschool staff, friends from our neighborhood, and teachers we have come to love. I'm sitting in a Starbucks now, while Merideth visits with moms from our church—a drop-in event organized by one of our awesome church staffers.

Later this morning, we are driving to San Antonio to attend the swearing-in ceremony of one of our church members who is becoming a US citizen. I'm excited to see this ceremony, and I am super-excited for our friend and to be able to share this incredible milestone with her and her family.

This is what it means for me to be a part of a church—to do life with other people. To raise kids in a wide village that includes but is not limited to Sunday morning gatherings. To know that we are part of an extended community that touches people beyond the four walls of our church building.

Sometimes people who aren't part of a church will tell me, "I'm pretty good with Jesus, but the whole church thing really isn't for me."

I get it. The church has its problems. It can be exclusionist, corrupt, and misguided. Some churchy people can be downright mean, narrow-minded, and awful. And that's why we all need Jesus.

I've come to believe, however, that the benefits of being part of a faith community are worth the risk of being wounded now and again. And further, living your life in community with others who share your story is one of the most energizing, generative things you can do as a human being.

God created us to be in community. Through Jesus, we are drawn together in a loving, hospitable unity that transcends and includes our diversity. If you aren't part of a faith community—part of something that is bigger than you—maybe you should give it a try.

It very well could be the most life-giving thing you will ever do.

Don't Sweat the Small Stuff

Each day, my wife, Merideth, and I plot out our day, planning how we are going to devote our time and energy. It never ceases to amaze us how few hours there are in a day as we plan how we will spend them.

One of the things that we work hard to do, each and every day, is to ensure that we spend time doing the most important things, like spending time with family, eating together, doing life with friends, and pouring ourselves into the good work that God has given us to do.

Are we awesome at this? Nope. We trip and fall on a regular basis, and there are plenty of days when we get hijacked by the "tyranny of the urgent," and we find ourselves struggling to be at peace. But we've discovered that when our intentions are to focus on the things that matter, more often than not, we do.

Several years ago, therapist Richard Carlson wrote the bestselling book *Don't Sweat the Small Stuff.* In the book, Carlson essentially argues that most of us spend almost all of our time and energy focused on things that don't really matter. And as a result, we have little time and energy to devote to the most important things in life: family, friends, faith, service, etc.

The second-century Roman emperor Marcus Aurelius once wrote:

> It is essential for you to remember that the attention you give to any action should be in due proportion to its worth, for then you won't tire and give up.

Nearly a hundred years before Marcus Aurelius, the apostle Paul wrote this to the church at Philippi:

> Whoever sows to please their flesh, from the flesh will reap destruction; whoever sows to please the Spirit, from the Spirit will reap eternal life. Let us not become weary in doing good, for at the proper time we will reap a harvest if we do not give up. (Galatians 6:8 NIV)

May you find ways today to do good, and may it give you life as you do it. Focus on the most important things today, and don't let the little things steal all your time and energy. Turn your day into a constant prayer that God will order your steps, guard your calendar, and fill you with peace.

Go to Your Room

Over the past twenty years or so of ministry, I have fielded a lot of questions about prayer. These questions have ranged from the simple ("How do I pray?") to the complex ("Why did God ignore my prayers?").

For the next couple of days, I am going to address a couple of the most frequent questions that I've received over the years: "How do I pray more effectively?" and "How do I know my prayers are appropriate?"

First, let's address the notion of effective praying. Jesus told his disciples the most effective way to pray was to do this:

> When you pray, go into your room and when you have shut the door, pray to your
> Father who is in the secret place; and your Father who sees in secret will reward
> you openly. (Matthew 6:6 NIV)

I've heard lots of teachings on this passage, and the interpretations of "go into your room" are wide and varied.

Some people have said that what Jesus meant was to draw your prayer shawl over your head and create a "room" wherever you are, as in the Jewish tradition. Others have said it means to go into a literal room in your house designated for prayer.

One of the best ones I've heard comes from Oswald Chambers, who speaks of "shutting the door of your mind" and closing out all of the distractions of life so you can hear the Holy Spirit.

The point is, each day we should find a space (either physical or spiritual) to close ourselves off from the things that keep us from sharing intimacy with God.

For some of us, our "room" is the outdoors—hiking, walking, biking, kayaking and the like. For others, our secret place is a nook in our house where we find peace and quiet.

Still others of us can create quiet in our thoughts, as we steal away for a cup of coffee at our favorite coffee shop or our favorite bench in a park.

May you find your prayer "room" today, and take the time to simply be with God. Create the space in your life for you to have a conversation with the One who longs to be in relationship with you and who desires your company.

God Wants a Relationship With Us

Today we're going to be continuing our conversation on prayer—the second of two questions on prayer that I feel are very important for those of us who struggle sometimes to understand prayer, how it works, and whether it makes any difference.

The question for today is, "How do I know if my prayers are appropriate?"

At the heart of this question is an observation that is fairly obvious: there is a difference between prayers for healing, or for spiritual direction, or for peace in the world, and prayers for a prime parking spot at the mall.

I've heard the following statement more than a few times in my life: "All your requests matter to God, no matter how small or insignificant they might seem to you."

Honestly, I don't think God cares in the same way about all of the requests we might bring to God. There's no way that a first-world problem like a parking space is on the same level as peace in the Middle East.

The fact of the matter, however, is that God cares about us. God wants to be in a relationship with us. And all of our prayers, both great and small, are part of being in relationship with God.

In his excellent book *Prayer: Does It Make Any Difference?*, Philip Yancey writes:

> If God counts on prayer as a primary way to relate to me, I may block potential intimacy by devising a test for appropriateness and filtering out prayers that many not meet the criteria.

Jesus told his followers to bring all of their cares and concerns to God because God wanted to hear them share—much like a parent who wants to hear about their child's day at school.

> Which of you, if your son asks for bread, will give him a stone? Or if he asks for a fish, will give him a snake? If you, then, though you are evil, know how to give good gifts to your children, how much more will your Father in heaven give good gifts to those who ask him! (Matthew 7:9–11 NIV)

Stay in conversation with God today. Talk to God about what is happening with you; share your deep fears and doubts, your cares and concerns; and share the little things as well. Keep the conversation going all day long as you seek good things from a good God who loves you.

God Loves Us So We Can Change

The past couple of days, my wife, Merideth, and I have been doing some pretty intense walking as part of an exercise regimen we're trying that fits our busy schedule.

My oldest son has enjoyed making fun of the whole intense-walking thing. I get it. I always made fun of people I saw who were power-walking through the neighborhood. But now that I am one of them, I repent of everything I said.

Merideth and I ended our thirty minutes and three miles of walking/jogging today covered in sweat, out of breath, and feeling pretty righteous. Plus, we did it together. We're working to change some of our old, unhelpful habits and replace them with new ones.

Changing old habits is hard.

Inertia is a powerful demotivator when it comes to getting healthy—physically, emotionally, and spiritually. Once you find yourself in a rut, it's hard to come up with the energy or imagination to get out of it.

Since most of my days are spent helping people figure out the spiritual side of their lives, I can say, with a great deal of conviction, that breaking free from a spiritual rut is at least as difficult, if not more so, than breaking free from emotional and physical ones.

And the reason for this difficulty is often centered around our lack of belief in God's great love for us. We might say that we believe that God is a loving God, but most of us don't really internalize what that means for us.

I was rereading Richard Rohr's amazing book *Breathing Underwater* today and came across this profound thought: "God does not love us if we change, God loves us so that we can change."

The love of God enables me to see myself differently. I am not a poor sap, stuck in a rut, unable to imagine a way out of it. I am a child of God, loved and cared for—uniquely created to fulfill God's purposes. It is God's never-ending, never-failing love that gives me the strength to change.

If you find yourself in a spiritual rut today, remind yourself that you have nothing to prove to God. All your efforts to change in order to make God love you more will just wear you out. God loves you just as you are but loves you far too much to let you stay that way.

You Are Not Alone

This morning, as I was reading through my devotional books, I read from Psalm 93, which contains these words:

> The seas have lifted up, Lord, the seas have lifted up their voice; the seas have lifted up their pounding waves. (Psalm 93:3 NIV)

As I read those words, I glanced down at the newspaper on my desk, which had a photo of a woman being carried to safety through the floodwaters that had overwhelmed her home in Houston. Hurricane Harvey did a number on my new home state this week.

Thousands of people who live on Texas's coast are homeless today; millions are without power. In some areas of Houston, there will be over four feet of rain by the time the storm finally moves northward.

This week, we have seen the waters of the sea lift up their pounding waves, the rivers overflow, and the rain fall in historic amounts. I am sure it feels like it will never stop for those who have been in the midst of it for these past several days.

Some of you may not be facing a physical storm with wind and rain right now, but you feel like the storms are never going to stop. It might even feel like you are chest-deep in water with no end in sight.

I want to encourage you with the words that I continued to read from Psalm 93 that came right after the verse about the pounding waves of the sea. The psalmist writes:

> Mightier than the thunder of the great waters, mightier than the breakers of the sea—the Lord on high is mighty. (Psalm 93:4 NIV)

The rain might be falling, the waters might be rising, but the Lord of the storm, the Commander of the waves, is near. Do not be afraid; whatever storm you are facing will not last forever.

The sun will rise, and the waters will subside, and peace will land upon you like a dove.

Because the Lord on high is mighty.

And you are not alone.

Know That You Are Forgiven

In his excellent book *Breathing Under Water,* author Richard Rohr speaks of our need to ask God to help us overcome our shortcomings. The asking often comes at the end of a hard realization of what we've become and who we have hurt.

Rohr writes, "If you go after [sinfulness] with an angry stick, you will soon be left with just an angry stick—and the same faults at a deeper level of disguise and denial."

I was listening to some music this morning, and one of the songs that came across my playlist was "Forgiven" by David Crowder. (If you have never heard of David Crowder, you should look him up. And then you should buy some of his music—you'll thank me later.)

The song this morning really resonated with me because of something I have been reading—more on that in a moment. The words of the first verse felt incredibly powerful:

> God, I fall down to my knees
> with a hammer in my hand
> You look at me, arms open
> Forgiven! Forgiven!
> Child there is freedom from all of it
> Say goodbye to every sin
> You are forgiven!

Crowder is using a familiar bit of imagery here, placing himself symbolically at the crucifixion of Jesus and in the garden of Gethsemane, betraying him. The artist confesses that his pride, his sinfulness, denies and crucifies Jesus anew.

And just when we are overwhelmed by the weight of what he's done, he hears the voice of God speaking comfort to him: "Forgiven! Forgiven!"

The words of this song are beautiful. But I wonder how many of us truly hear those words when we are struggling with our own darkness.

May you hear God's words of forgiveness today and every day. May you stop chasing your shortcomings with angry sticks and simply fall to your knees and let God's grace fall upon you like a song from above. Know that you are forgiven, and be at peace.

The Temptation of Egypt

There is a moment in the book of Exodus from the Hebrew scriptures when the Hebrew people have only just escaped slavery in Egypt, and they discover, to their utter dismay, that they are being pursued.

The story tells us that after allowing the Israelites to leave Egypt, Pharaoh (king of Egypt) repents of his decision to let his slave workforce escape and heads after them with his army.

Immediately, the Hebrew people start lamenting their circumstances:

> As Pharaoh approached, the Israelites looked up, and there were the Egyptians, marching after them. They were terrified and cried out to the Lord. They said to Moses, "Was it because there were no graves in Egypt that you brought us to the desert to die? What have you done to us by bringing us out of Egypt? Didn't we say to you in Egypt, 'Leave us alone; let us serve the Egyptians'? It would have been better for us to serve the Egyptians than to die in the desert!" (Exodus 14:10–12 NIV)

All the Hebrew people could see right then was their present difficult circumstance, which caused them to say, "It would have been better for us to serve the Egyptians than to die in the desert."

The uncertainty of the moment clouded their memories of lives lived in constant bondage, never-ceasing work, dehumanizing conditions, and generations of servitude

In that moment, they forgot their cries for deliverance from God, which were answered. They forgot the miraculous way that God had caused Pharaoh to release them from bondage.

How many of us do this very thing in our own lives? We try to leave behind the bondage and slavery of our bad habits, sinfulness, and pride

We try to leave behind our slavery to busyness and success, and as soon as things start to get difficult, we long to return to Egypt.

If you are struggling to trust God to lead your path away from the things that have held you captive, let go, and surrender the outcomes. Trust that the God who led you out of bondage will part the seas and make your way clear.

God Is Not Angry with You

On July 8, 1741, Jonathan Edwards preached what would become his most famous sermon, "Sinners in the Hands of an Angry God."

Edwards must have had a particularly bad week leading up to that sermon because this is what he told his congregants:

> The God that holds you over the pit of Hell, much as one holds a spider, or some loathsome insect, over the fire, abhors you, and is dreadfully provoked; his wrath toward you burns like fire; he looks upon you as worthy of nothing else, but to be cast into the fire.

This image of God that Edwards painted would become, perhaps, the dominant image lifted up by Christians in America for centuries—one that still persists today.

In fact, I have had more than a few difficult and painful conversations over the years with disillusioned Christians who can't get beyond the images of a seemingly angry, vengeful God that appear throughout the Bible.

Sadly, far too many Christians who lift up the image of an angry God also seem to be pretty angry too. It doesn't have to be this way, though.

Author Brian Zahnd recently wrote:

> However else we address the problem of proof-texting an angry God, we must always remember that any depiction of God, from whatever source, is subordinate to the revelation of God seen in Jesus.

He adds, "As it turns out, God is neither menacing nor faceless, Jesus Christ is the face of the Father."

In other words, as Jesus himself said, "If you have seen me, you have seen the Father," or "I and my Father are one" (John 14:9; 10:30 NIV).

I don't know about you, but this is truly good news to me—the kind of news that I think our world needs to know right about now. God is not angry at you. God loves you more than you will ever know. And Jesus is proof of that love and of how far God is willing to go to draw you closer.

May you find ways to embrace the loving images of God that you see in Jesus. May you seek to know him more and to follow him more fully.

Aggressively Listening to God

I've been thinking a lot lately about transitions. Check that. I've been thinking a lot about transitions because I've been immersed in one transition or another for almost six months.

When you're in the middle of a transition, it's hard to put your finger on exactly how it feels or how it's going to look on the other side of it.

I used to wonder if people who lived through the great moments in history paused to reflect and say things like, "This Great Depression sure is something!"; or "How about this World War II?"; or even further back, "Man, this Protestant Reformation thing seems to be really changing some stuff."

It's only when you look back that you can see all the changes and transformations a bit more clearly. It's only with hindsight that you can see how it all fit together to get you where you were going, even though you had no idea exactly how it would turn out.

And when we look back, we also can see more clearly how God was at work in the midst of our transitions all along.

Even though we don't have the benefit of hindsight in the middle of our transitional moments, we can clearly feel the presence of God in them. That's what I long for the most when I'm going through changes. I want to feel God's presence. I want to experience God in very real and personal ways.

And I think it's a deep desire for God that gives us better vision and better hearing. Jesus often exhorted those who listened to him teach to have "eyes to see and ears to hear." In other words, he wanted them to be alert, to be waiting and watching for the moments where God's glory was revealed.

My wife, Merideth, often prays a prayer that inspires me: "God, I am aggressively listening to you."

This prayer has helped her to focus more intently on her awareness of God and to discover God's ever-presence, even in the middle of the most challenging times of change.

As you go through the many transitions in your life, remember that it's not just hindsight that offers 20/20 vision.

May you not only see where God has been at work in your life but also see clearly where God is at work even now. May you actively listen for God's voice, speaking words of hope, love, and purpose.

Feeling the Intimacy of God

As I write this, sixteen years ago today, on September 11, 2001, the world was forever changed by an unspeakable act of terrorism and violence.

I remember parts of that day clearly, but most of my memories are less about the details of the day and more about how I felt in the moment. The feelings of disbelief and horror, the sorrow and loss—it was all overwhelming.

At some point during that morning, my wife, Merideth, and I decided that we needed to get my son from school. He was six years old at the time, a first-grader. I don't really remember how we decided it, but it felt right to get him out of class and take him home with us.

When the world feels like it's falling apart, you want your loved ones close to you, particularly your children, no matter how old they are.

When the winds of Hurricane Harvey began to howl through Texas, I took a lot of comfort in knowing that all my boys were under one roof, together with us. My greatest desire was to have them close when the storm came.

That same night, I saw so many of my friends in Florida posting Facebook posts and texts of their children and families gathered together to ride out Hurricane Irma.

One friend posted a photo of her son, sleeping peacefully in a pile of blankets in the kitchen pantry. She'd had a sleepless night from the howling winds, but her child rested, oblivious to the storm.

I was reading today in the second chapter of Hebrews, where the writer speaks of how, through Jesus, God became like us "in every way."

Like a loving parent, God desired intimacy and closeness with us so much that he took on flesh and walked among us, moved into our neighborhood, and drew us closer than ever before in order to demonstrate God's great love for us.

May you feel the intimacy and love of God today and every day. May you know that even during the worst moments of your life, God's desire is to draw you close and be with you in the midst of it.

Let this knowledge give you hope and peace.

God's Way of Discipline

It takes discipline to achieve the things we long for in life—to be the people we want to be. And discipline is nothing more than developing the right kind of habits.

This is the point where some of us check out. We hear the word *discipline*, and we think all kinds of things, most of them bad.

When I was in second grade, I got paddled in school just about every day for a period of a month or so. It seems I couldn't remember to pick up the proper folder from my cubby when we changed subjects in the classroom.

When you forgot your folder, you got a mark on the board. After a few marks on the board, you got a paddling. When I think of discipline, that's what I tend to think about, so I get it.

We might believe that we aren't disciplined enough to effect transformation in our lives, but we always do what is important to us. We will develop habits around these values, and we become what we repeatedly do.

But true discipline—the kind that matters, the kind that can truly change your life for the better—is something a bit different. As Pastor Craig Groeschel once said, "Discipline is choosing between what you want now and what you want most."

Most of us struggle with this choice. The apostle Paul spoke of his own struggle to make the right choice in his letter to the Romans:

> I don't really understand myself, for I want to do what is right, but I don't do it. Instead, I do what I hate … I want to do what is right, but I can't. I want to do what is good, but I don't. I don't want to do what is wrong, but I do it anyway. But if I do what I don't want to do, I am not really the one doing wrong; it is sin living in me that does it … Oh, what a miserable person I am! Who will free me from this life that is dominated by sin and death? Thank God! The answer is in Jesus Christ our Lord. (Romans 7:15, 18–20, 24–25 NIV)

When all is said and done, what we need to know is that our way through this struggle, our guide to the right decision, is none other than Jesus. We don't have to walk around in guilt because we miss the mark.

We simply keep stumbling after Jesus, who is ultimately leading us to a fuller, more abundant life.

May you embrace this truth today and every day.

God's Incredible Hesed

Yesterday, I was listening to a news story about an American couple who were vacationing on the island of St. Maarten when Hurricane Irma made landfall. They spoke of their harrowing ordeal, the destruction of their hotel, and, eventually, their rescue.

Think about what it means to be rescued. Here—maybe this will help; think about the greatest rescue movies of all time. What would be on your list? Here's a short list of mine:

1. *Schindler's List*—I mean, come on; this has to be number one.
2. *Black Hawk Down*—more than just a guy flick.
3. *The Last of the Mohicans*—"Whatever shall occur, I will find you!"
4. *The Searchers*—classic John Wayne movie.
5. *Taken*—Liam Neeson comes for his daughter and kills everyone else.
6. *Cast Away*—Tom Hanks and Wilson traverse the ocean.
7. *Rambo*—I, II, III, IV, whatever.

Every one of these movies taps into something that is at the heart of each of us—when we are in trouble, when the way forward isn't clear, we want to know that Liam Neeson is going to wreck Paris to find us. Or Daniel Day Lewis is going to don his leather leggings, prime his musket, and run up an impossibly tall mountain to save us.

We want to know that when we need help that help is on the way.

Oswald Chambers once wrote, "Simplicity is the secret to seeing things clearly." And the simple truth about God is that God is faithful and ever-loving. The Hebrew word for this kind of rescuing love is *hesed*, which can be translated as "never-ending, never-failing, always-present, loving-kindness."

Our doubts and fears often complicate and cloud our vision and can leave us despairing in the middle of what we perceive as dire circumstances.

But when we simply surrender ourselves to the ever-present, never-ending *hesed* of God, we often find the clarity that we need in order to see our dire circumstances as opportunities to trust in God, who is never far away.

If you are in despair today, do not fear, beloved. Help is near. Trust in hope that flickers in your spirit. It's evidence of God's incredible *hesed*.

Don't Be Afraid of Taking a Fall

My littlest boy just turned seven and received a "big boy" bike for his birthday.

His new bike sits a little higher, brakes differently, and is a bit harder for him to handle than his old bike. Still, every day he rides, he gains more skills and becomes more and more confident.

But I have noticed that when he encounters atypical circumstances—a hard turn, a sudden drop, a steep hill—he tends to lose that confidence and overcompensates by sticking his leg out to stop, turning too hard, or any number of things that result in a spill—and occasionally some frustrated tears.

What I know that he doesn't is that at some point, he'll become adept enough at riding that he won't be moving out in front of his skill.

This realization got me thinking that so many of us often find ourselves in circumstances that invite us to move ahead in our faith into unfamiliar territories and new paths, sometimes beyond our comfortable beliefs and traditions.

Oswald Chambers once wrote:

> Many people have turned back because they are afraid to look at things from God's perspective. The greatest spiritual crisis comes when a person has to move a little farther on in his faith than the beliefs he has already accepted.

And because we fear "taking a fall" when it comes to our faith, we are often tempted to avoid anything but the easiest, most familiar ways of thinking and believing, even as God may be leading us forward into more challenging roads.

Maybe today you feel as though you are asked to step out in faith ahead of what you have come to believe. Maybe you feel a bit wobbly, like you're losing control and about to take a spill.

To you, I offer these beautiful words from the prophet Isaiah:

> "I shall hear a word behind me, saying, 'This is the way, walk in it,' whenever I turn to the right or the left." (Psalm 16:11 NIV)

Keep going. God is with you, ready to pick you up if you fall.
Live into this hope.

God Doesn't Hold a Grudge

Almost every day of my life, I do things that make me dissatisfied in myself. I yell at my kids. I get impatient when I am driving around slow people, when I'm waiting in line at Chipotle, when I can't do all of the things I need to do in a day—the list is pretty long.

If we are being honest, most of us struggle to be the people we know that we should be.

And what we tend to hear, most of the time, from other Christians is that we can get it all together; we can overcome our feelings of inadequacy by reading that next Christian self-help book about thirteen ways to be a better parent/wife/husband/child/church member/American or by going to church more often, being more religious, trying harder, keeping more rules.

But as Craig Groeschel writes, "Religious behavior can make you nice, but it won't make you new."

As Christians, we say we believe that following Jesus makes you new. You can be a new creation. Like the apostle Paul said, "The old has gone, the new has come."

But what does that even mean? Do we really stop to think about it? And do we really believe it—I mean, deep down inside?

Paul wrote further about this in his letter to the church at Corinth:

> At one time we thought of Christ merely from a human point of view. How differently we know him now! This means that anyone who belongs to Christ has become a new person. The old life is gone; a new life has begun!" (2 Corinthians 5:16–17 NIV)

The "one" time that Paul is referring to is a place in the past before the Resurrection. Nothing about that time matters, except to contrast with now. Now, Paul says, we experience the risen Jesus. The Resurrection changed everything.

So what does this mean for you and me?

It means that God doesn't hold our pasts against us, and neither should we.

It also means that because of Jesus, we have the choice to live differently. Because we aren't defined by our pasts, we can look to the future with incredible hope.

May you live into the hope of this Resurrection future—a future not defined by what you've done or who you've been.

Don't Just Say You're a Christian—Be One

The Greek word *christianos*, which means "follower of Christ," comes from the word *christos*, which means "anointed one."

But the ending to the Greek word *christianos* is borrowed from the Latin to denote belonging to, as in property.

So to say that you are a Christian is so much more than saying that you are a follower of Jesus Christ. When you say you are a Christian, you are essentially saying that you "belong to Jesus" or, as Paul puts it, you are "in Christ."

When we say that we follow or belong to Jesus, we identify ourselves as part of something that is far greater than we are; we declare that we are set apart from the ordinary. We have no fear of the future because we are filled with unbelievable, childlike hope.

As I mentioned yesterday, we have been emancipated from our pasts and from the things that used to define us. And we declare unequivocally that we are no longer owned by the things of this world. Our allegiance is with Jesus and Jesus alone.

When you choose to follow Jesus, to call yourself a Christian, you belong to him, you are defined by him, and you are called to stumble after him the best you can—striving to be like him with all your strength. Because of Jesus, you aren't defined by who you were; you don't have to be that person any longer; you have been transformed.

Live today as someone who has been transformed. Evaluate every conversation, every thought, every action in light of the newness of life you have because you belong to Jesus.

Don't just *say* you're a Christian—*be* one.

Living a Congruent Life

When I say that faith is a "heart" rather than a "head" thing, what does that mean to you? Which one sounds better than the other, just off the top of your head? What's the difference between the two?

Here's the thing: what you tell yourself about yourself matters far less than how you act. You can tell yourself (and others) that you are a "good person," but if you live unethically and selfishly and exhibit hatred, judgment, prejudice, and anger throughout your life, your actions speak much louder than anything you might say.

Lots of people call themselves Christians and claim to have experienced transformation—the kind of transformation that we've been discussing this week. But their lives, their actions, the way they conduct themselves show very little evidence that anything about them has changed.

I know I struggle with this, too. I have really good intentions to live congruently—to make my outside match my inside—but I often find myself living in ways that don't line up with what I say I believe.

I quoted another preacher in a recent devotion when I said that being religious might make you nice, but it won't make you new.

But more often than not, being religious doesn't make you nice either. Some of the angriest, most combative, rigid, and selfish people I have ever known are religious.

Jesus rebuked the religious people of his day with these words:

> Woe to you, teachers of the law and Pharisees, you hypocrites! You clean the outside of the cup and dish, but inside they are full of greed and self-indulgence. Blind Pharisee! First clean the inside of the cup and dish, and then the outside also will be clean. (Matthew 23:25–26 NIV)

May you strive today to live a congruent faith, a faith balanced between head and heart—this is a faith worth having. May you find moments today to live out this congruent, balanced faith, where your inside matches your outside.

You Belong in the Game

When it comes to a life of faith, there is a difference between being in the game and being on the bench. When you're not in the game, it's easy to keep a "bench" mindset. You can find a comfortable routine, stay in the same sort of ruts, so to speak, and just be content to watch other people play.

We've all been in bench mode at one point or another in our faith journeys. Maybe some of us are in bench mode right now. We're bored with church and with religion. We're too busy to really commit. We're too distracted by other things in our lives, or maybe we're too disillusioned by religion itself to stand up and get in the game.

Some of us have been on the bench for so long that we don't even know how to play. Some of us don't even know if we're on the team.

And most of us feel like there is no way that God would ever want us to do big, important things, like telling his story. We never would suspect that God would actually want us to get in the game.

But what I've come to understand is something that is incredibly true and empowering: God uses unexpected people to tell his story. Think about it.

Jesus's twelve disciples were a mishmash of guys who would have never been picked to play by anyone in their right mind. Jesus hung out with sinners and tax collectors, prostitutes, overly religious people—it's almost like he wanted to demonstrate that the story he was telling was so good that it didn't matter who helped him tell it.

So if you're feeling like you don't belong in the game today, think again. It's time to leave your comfortable seat and find out how God is going to use you to change the world.

Choosing Relationships Over Comfort

In a former church, I helped launch ministries and worship that were designed to attract unchurched and dechurched people.

Most of the newcomers were young, and some were covered in tattoos and piercings. There were a couple of single moms, a young man who had just come out as gay to his family, more than a few skeptics, and a smattering of recovering alcoholics.

It didn't take long for some of the existing church members to begin complaining about the kinds of people who were showing up on our church campus. Finally, after a few weeks of listening to their various gripes, I told them that they needed to get over themselves and that the church was a hospital, not a country club.

They got offended. Some of them wrote me nasty emails. One of them came to my office to harangue me about how our ministries and worship were "ruining the church." I was angry; I felt they should have been offended by the way they said one thing and did another—how they claimed to be followers of Jesus but actually kept others from really seeing him.

The truth is, I do the same kind of thing all of the time. It's hard to be in a relationship with people who are different, who challenge our status quo. Just like most churchgoing, Christian-y folks, I often prefer my comfort over the challenging relationships Jesus is leading me to build.

In his book *Ragamuffin Gospel*, Brennan Manning tells this parable:

It seems there was a young man who had sinned so much that the church excommunicated him and cast him out. He was told that he was never welcome there again. He wanted to return and repented of what he'd done but could find no healing.

> So he finally found his way to Jesus. "Lord," he told Jesus, "they won't let me in because I am a sinner." To which Jesus replied, "What are you complaining about? They won't let me in either."

We all need to own this: the church has not been the most hospitable place for broken and hurting people.

However, if those of us who make up the church are going to be the kinds of people Jesus dreams for us to be, we are going to have to change. We will never be a safe place for the hurting if what we do is different from what we say we believe.

Practice being a safe place for someone to land today. Make yourself available to share someone's journey—someone who might challenge your status quo. Open yourself to the possibility that you might very well be the way for someone to find the courage to begin stumbling after Jesus with you.

God Doesn't Want You to Be Happy;
God Wants You to Be Holy

The other day, I was running late, and my day was shaping up to be tougher than it needed to be. On my way out the door, I grumpily said to my kid, "Ninety percent of life is having to do things that you don't want to do. You'd better get used to it."

He just nodded and went back to playing video games.

It's easy to equate all of the things that are inconvenient to us—that thwart our plans and make our days stressful or mundane—as somehow outside of God's will. Because God just wants me to be happy, right?

The problem with this kind of thinking is that it reduces God to a happiness slot machine. We throw enough effort into our faith to consider whatever we've done for God as an investment—coins that we've dropped into the machine.

And then, when we pull the lever on this happiness slot machine and it doesn't work out for us, we not only feel like we might be outside of God's will, but we also are tempted to wonder what the in the world God is doing.

Would it shock you to know that God doesn't want us to be happy? It's true. God doesn't want us to be happy. He wants us to be holy.

In his first epistle, the apostle Peter wrote to the early Christians, "But just as he who called you is holy, so be holy in all you do" (1 Peter 1:15 NIV).

But what does it look like when I am really striving for holiness? What does it look like if I am following Peter's advice to be holy like Jesus? Does it look boring? Does it look prudish? Not fun? No!

Jesus told his disciples what it means to pursue holiness—true holiness that leads to true happiness. He told them, "These things I have spoken to you so that my joy may be in you, and that your joy may be made full" (John 15:11 NIV).

God doesn't want us to pursue happiness; he wants us to pursue him. And the most excellent way we can pursue God is by following in the footsteps of his Son, Jesus, who shows us what God is like.

May you push back today against the notion that your purpose is to pursue your own happiness, and instead, run with wild abandon after Jesus as you pursue holiness that leads to abundant life.

Sabbath Intentionality

I've been thinking about the idea of Sabbath rest lately and how it's so difficult to carve out Sabbath time in our increasingly busy and over-connected lives.

Saint Augustine once wrote, "You have made us for yourself, O Lord, and our soul is restless until it finds rest in you."

In the book of Hebrews, we have this bit of wisdom:

> There remains, then, a Sabbath-rest for the people of God; for anyone who enters God's rest also rests from their works, just as God did from his. (Hebrews 4:9–10 NIV)

So how do we find rest in a world where it's becoming increasingly difficult to carve out space for quiet and rest, a world that is shaped by our constant reliance on social media and technology?

There is actually a recognized phobia that has now become widespread and totally associated with smartphone technology. It's called *nomophobia*—the fear of being away from your phone.

For many of us, our phones are the last things we check before we go to bed at night, just to see if we missed any texts, emails, or Facebook status changes. And they are the first things we reach for in the morning.

I used to smoke cigarettes, two packs a day. I would often have a cigarette close to bedtime, out walking the dog and whatnot. And my cigarette pack was the first thing I reached for in the morning.

For most of us, our phones have become as addicting as cigarettes.

The writer of Hebrews declares to us that God has a special rest in Christ for those who are willing to embrace it.

This is more than just keeping rules and regulations. It's a lifestyle, a way of life, a mindset. The special Sabbath we find as followers of Christ frees us from the tyranny of the urgent, the slavery to our schedules, and allows us to find newness of life, rest, regeneration.

What will you do after reading this? Will you immediately check your phone to see if someone texted you? Or if you got a comment on your last Facebook post? Will you keep scrolling for the next email? Or will you simply take a few moments to be still and find quiet in the moment?

Be intentional today about taking Sabbath moments to be still and seek God's presence. Find space to be quiet and rest as you pray for the ability to enter more completely into a Sabbath lifestyle.

Turning Regret into Redemption

For the next couple of days, I'm going to write about how we can be set free from some of the things that might haunt us and keep us from living an abundant life in Jesus.

Today, we're going to spend some time talking about regret, so I thought I would share a few of my own regrets.

I regret not buying Microsoft stock before the '90s. I also regret not buying Apple stock before the 2000s.

I also regret kissing this one girl when I was fifteen—she was missing a couple of teeth, a fact I didn't really notice until it was too late.

I seriously regret my hairstyles in the '80s—sort of parted down the middle and feathered on both sides. I could go on, but I won't. I regret saying too much already.

There is a good side to regret, according to *Psychology Today* magazine. Regret can help us make sense of the world when we see both the positive and negative implications of our actions.

The same study, however, also studied the effects of long-term regret and found that they were devastating.

People who are obsessed with regret suffer from higher rates of depression, chronic stress, weakened immune systems, depleted hormones, and a variety of mental, emotional, and physical maladies. All of this contributes to a shortened lifespan.

As it turns out, one of the slowest ways to die is to live in regret.

This isn't something new. The apostle Paul wrote about this very thing when he said, "Godly sorrow brings repentance that leads to salvation and leaves no regret, but worldly sorrow brings death" (2 Corinthians 7:10 NIV).

This is the choice that we have—to live in hopeless regret or hope-filled life. We can choose godly sorrow when we make a mistake, suffer loss, or choose poorly, and let God redeem the whole mess. Or we can choose worldly sorrow and begin to wither away and die, both inside and out.

May you choose to cover your regrets in godly sorrow and turn them over to God to be redeemed, restored, and made whole. May you be filled with hope and abundant life as you let them go and are set free.

If You're Hurt, Take Heart

There is a fantastically melancholy song by the band R.E.M. called "Everybody Hurts," and the lyrics go something like this:

> If you're on your own in this life
> The days and nights are long
> When you think you've had too much of this life to hang on
> Well, everybody hurts sometimes
> Everybody cries
> Everybody hurts sometimes
> And everybody hurts sometimes.

It's actually a pretty uplifting song, just melancholy. And it highlights something that is true for each and every one of us. Everybody hurts. Every person has experienced hurt in his or her life. We've been wounded, let down, disappointed, betrayed, or worse.

One of the many things we learn in the Bible is that the things of earth will one day pass away, but those things that are of God's kingdom will last forever.

The hurts that we've experienced will not be present in the kingdom of God. There will come a day when all things will be made right, when God will wipe away all tears, when there will be no more sorrow, pain, or haunted feelings—period.

But as those who follow Jesus, we are called to live like that day is already here. Which means seeing things as they are. Naming them for what they are. The things of this world are temporary, not meant to last, not eternal.

Hurt has no place in God's kingdom. Nothing on this earth lasts forever, even our pain.

Psalm 30:5 contains these beautiful words that offer us incredible inspiration in those moments when we are tempted to think that our hurts are never going to fade: "weeping may stay for the night, but rejoicing comes in the morning" (NIV).

If you are experiencing hurt today, if you feel as though your pain will never fade, never go away, take heart.

You are a Resurrection child of God. Sunday's coming, beloved. The dawn is going to break, and God is still in the business of breathing new life into the world, and that includes you.

Stumbling after Jesus

When I was a kid, I was asked to ponder a question that was frequently posed in sermons, youth meetings, Sunday school, and a host of other church environments. The question went something like this:

"How's your Christian walk?"

In the faith communities of my youth, that was churchy language for, "Are you living up to the standards? Are you keeping the rules and regulations? Are you checking all the things on the checklist?"

But at some point in those early years of trying to follow Jesus, I realized that my "walk" had become more of a "trudge." I was trudging along after what I thought was a Jesus path but found I was barely able to pick up my feet.

Oswald Chambers once wrote:

> It's difficult to get into stride with God, because as soon as we start walking with
> Him we find that His pace has surpassed us before we have taken three steps.

It took many years and more than one crisis of faith, but I finally came to understand something so revolutionary, so amazing, that it forever transformed my relationship with Jesus and my journey of following after him.

I realized that I wasn't walking *with* Jesus. I wasn't even walking *behind* Jesus. In fact, none of us is. But I did realize I was stumbling after Jesus.

And sometimes, in my stumbling after Jesus, I take a spill and fall flat on my face. Sometimes, I feel like I am running but with two left feet.

But it always feels like stumbling.

At this point in my life, if I am asked, "How's your Christian walk?" I answer, "I'm stumbling after Jesus, and I hope beyond hope I am stumbling in the right direction."

May you give up the dehumanizing and demoralizing belief that you can somehow match Jesus stride for stride, and may you stumble after Jesus with all the fierce, desperate, wild abandon you can muster.

And when you inevitably fall flat on your face in the road, know that it will be Jesus's hand reaching back to bring you to your feet once again.

When You Feel Stuck

I'm on day thirteen of the Whole30 diet, which is designed to eliminate sugar, gluten, dairy, and alcohol from your diet. In other words, all of the things that are enjoyable and awesome.

I know I may have mentioned this in a previous devo, but I'm suffering and need to share.

The instruction manual for this diet states the following about the phase of the diet I happen to be inhabiting at the moment: "This is the part of the program where our brains are desperate to drive us back to the comfort of the foods we used to reward ourselves with."

I know this is true because I was watching a Taco Bell commercial last night, and I had this vision of sitting down with a twelve-pack of those tacos with the Doritos shell and eating every single one.

At this point, I am doing this diet because I have to make some changes in my life. I am not feeling joy about it. There is no happiness here. I am told that it gets better, but right this second, I am putting one foot in front of the other on this one.

This morning, I started reflecting on how often we apply that same kind of template to our spiritual lives and our relationship with God. The results are no better than my current feelings of drudgery about my diet.

You see, when our lives of faith become motivated by guilt, obligation, or a resigned sense of duty, it's easy to lose any sense of joy in them.

Fredrick Buechner once wrote that a Christian who slips into this way of living and being in the world is the kind of person whose "goodness has become cheerless and finicky, a technique for working on his own guilts, a gift with no love in it which neither deceives nor benefits any for long."

If you are feeling like you're stuck in a bit of a rut when it comes to your faith, I want you to receive this blessing:

May you find ways to experience the joy of your salvation today and every day. May you discover a new sense of purpose, when it comes to your life of faith, that isn't grounded in a deflating sense of obligation.

You Are Beloved

Several years ago, my wife, Merideth, and I visited Rome and spent some time at the Vatican.

At the time, I was feeling a bit dusty and dry, spiritually. I figured that if there was anywhere on earth that I might experience a sign from God, it would be in Saint Peter's Basilica in the center of Vatican Square.

As we waited for mass to start, Merideth and I went into a gift shop. Merideth hates to shop, but I love it. Merideth got tired of shopping and went outside, while I stayed inside, poking around for gifts.

Suddenly, I heard a commotion outside and went to investigate. Merideth said, "You're not going to believe this! A perfect white dove just flew down into this square, hovered over everyone who was here, and then flew away! It was amazing!"

I was dumbfounded. I'd been searching for a sign, and I had missed the one that God had sent.

We went inside to attend mass. I was beating myself up and wondering what was wrong with me—why I always seemed to miss out on feeling God's presence; so spiritually dry.

Then I looked up. Above the ornate main altar in Saint Peter's Basilica is a beautiful stained-glass image of a white dove—the sign of the Holy Spirit. The words from Matthew's Gospel surrounded it: "This is my Beloved Son in whom I am well pleased" (Matthew 3:17 NIV).

These words are from the moment of Jesus's baptism in the Jordan River. As he comes out of the water after being baptized by John the Baptist, the Spirit of God descends upon Jesus "like a dove," and a voice from heaven declares those words: "Beloved …"

I began to weep uncontrollably. It's like I could hear the voice of God in my head, saying over and over again—"Beloved. You are my beloved. You are always my beloved."

If you've been struggling to feel the presence of God; if you're seeking purpose and direction for your life; if you are searching for a sign, remember that you are God's beloved. Know that the Holy Spirit is upon you. Know that the Son stands with you. Know that God is well pleased with you.

Sadness Doesn't Get the Last Word

I'm having a difficult time writing today.

We've been going through a sad season in my family's life.

Sadness can weigh heavily on you. It can cover you like a heavy gray shroud that keeps you from feeling the warmth of the sun or seeing the bright colors all around you.

It can also permeate the nooks and crannies of your home like a fog, touching everyone who lives there and making it difficult to see one another clearly.

Sadness is an unwelcome but familiar guest for many of us.

When sadness makes its way into your life, you find yourself wavering between holding on to it in a desperate embrace and violently shoving it out the door.

Some days, you wish you could banish it forever from your life.

Other days, you wonder if you'll ever be able to live without it.

One of the most important verses in the Bible is also one of the shortest. It's just two words: "Jesus wept" (John 11:35 NIV). Jesus was at a funeral for Lazarus, one of his closest friends. He was surrounded by grief and feeling the deep sadness that comes with loss.

Even though he knew that, in moments, he would raise Lazarus from the dead, Jesus wept.

He let himself feel that sadness; he embraced it. Because sadness is part of what it means to be human.

And then, after he wept, Jesus called Lazarus out of the grave.

Sadness isn't something to be feared because it doesn't last forever. It doesn't get the last word. Jesus does.

All of It Is Connected

At the end of a long day yesterday, I sat outside for a bit, staring at the clouds moving overhead in the dark sky. It had been a day full of contrasts. I'd experienced the wonderful highs of worshipping and preaching with my church, and I'd also felt the lows that come after expending so much energy and finally slowing down.

I found myself a bit lost and weary, yet somehow strangely blissful.

As I sat there staring at the clouds, I thought about all of the contrasts of the day and the way they were so disparate, yet so connected, intertwined, and interrelated. Together, they made things complete.

This is what I have come to understand about us. When we focus so much on ourselves, when we fight against the interconnected ways that all of our experiences relate, when we lose sight of the "One-ness" that God is constantly revealing to us, we lose ourselves.

And when we do this, we move through life half awake, half aware, and disconnected from all that would make us whole.

I read a poem the other day by the thirteenth-century poet Rumi, and the following lines stood out for me:

> Humankind is being led along an evolving course,
> through this migration of intelligences,
> and though we seem to be sleeping,
> there is an inner wakefulness that directs the dream.
> It will eventually startle us back
> to the truth of who we are.

So many of us have believed the lies that have been told about us. We believe that we are not good enough. We believe that we are not worthy. We believe that we are born broken. And so, armed with this belief, we move in the world like sleepwalkers. Despite this, however, there is Something (One) within us, guiding us, moving us, and leading us.

Then, there are moments when we do lift our heads and open our eyes—when we gaze up at the shifting clouds in the night sky and begin to see more clearly that somehow, in spite of ourselves, God is connecting all of it, making all of it whole.

And us along with it.

May you wake to the truth about who you are today. May you see the intricate ways that God has woven the stories of your life together, and may this bring you closer to wholeness and to One-ness.

Hold On to Hope

The last few weeks have been pretty lousy.

The world around us seems to be falling apart.

My mom died.

A pipe broke under our house, which will cost a zillion dollars to fix.

Our car is in need of repair.

My oldest son's college tuition is due.

Our dog had a weird accident, dislocated his kneecap, and needs surgery.

And on top of everything else that has been happening in my life, I caught a nasty cold.

I should not have been surprised at this, considering that my two youngest kids were deathly ill last week, but I thought I'd escaped unscathed.

Someone told me yesterday, "That sounds like a bad country song." I couldn't agree more.

Last week, during the class I am teaching on the book of Romans, I read out loud the following verse:

> We also glory in our sufferings, because we know that suffering produces perseverance; perseverance, character; and character, hope. And hope does not put us to shame, because God's love has been poured out into our hearts through the Holy Spirit, who has been given to us. (Romans 5:3–5 NIV)

I love the fact that the last thing in Paul's list after "character" is "hope."

You would think that he would say that "character produces success," or "victory," or something like that. But it goes right to hope—the kind of hope that "does not put us to shame."

In other words, when you put your faith in God, you can hold on to hope, no matter what is going on in your life, and that hope will not let you down.

May you hold on to hope today and every day, even when you are suffering and struggling to persevere. May you be confident that the hope you have from the love of God that has been poured into your heart will never fail you.

Love That Banishes Fear

I decided this morning to tune in to one of the cable news channels to get a bit caught up on the news of the day. I almost immediately wished I hadn't.

I have been shying away from the twenty-four-hour news channels for some time, mostly because they end up depressing me, and I don't need any more negativity in my life.

This morning, on the cable news channel I was watching, the news host was arguing with a United States congressman, and the two men essentially were talking over one another, raising their voices, and making their respective arguments unintelligible.

Both of these people claimed that all they wanted was the truth. The thought occurred to me, as I listened to them shouting at one another, that getting at the "truth" was pretty far down on their to-do lists.

What they really seemed to want to do was fire up the viewership and generate some outrage. They were going for the lowest common denominator—playing on people's fears.

Fear seems to be at the core of all of our public controversies, our recent tragedies and acts of violence that keep us on edge. Fear keeps us segregated. Fear fuels our outrage. Fear keeps us from truly searching for the truth.

For those of us who call ourselves Jesus-followers, however, there is another way to live. In 1 John 4, we hear these words:

> God is love. Whoever lives in love lives in God, and God in them. This is how love is made complete among us so that we will have confidence on the day of judgment: In this world we are like Jesus. There is no fear in love. But perfect love drives out fear, because fear has to do with punishment. The one who fears is not made perfect in love. (1 John 4:16–18 NIV)

If you and I are going to truly follow Jesus's example, we will allow the perfect love of God through Jesus to guide us in all that we do. God's love, as evidenced through Jesus, is the kind of love that is self-giving, unconditional, and unafraid.

God's perfect love banishes fear. Let this perfect love be your conversation partner. Let it permeate your thoughts and opinions. Let it enter into ever interaction you have with others. And let it order your life in generative and creative ways.

A Gift of Grace

The other day my dad took his car in for service at his local Toyota dealer. As he sat in the waiting area, he struck up a conversation with a young woman who was there having her car serviced as well.

They had a warm, friendly conversation, nothing in-depth, just passing the time.

Her car was ready before my dad's, and so she bid him farewell and went out to pay her bill and pick it up. A few moments later, a customer service representative came out to let my dad know his car was finished.

"I've got some good news," he told my dad.

My dad joking replied, "Let me guess—it's all free."

The man looked at my dad quizzically. "How did you know?" He went on to tell my dad that the young woman had paid my dad's entire bill. My dad was floored.

We could only guess that the young woman might have been moved to her act of kindness because he was wearing a hat that identified him as a Vietnam veteran.

She had no idea what kind of month he'd just had—how my mom had gotten so very ill and passed away.

She had no idea what a gift of grace she had given to him.

I want to live like that young woman. I want to be that generous. I want to be so in tune with the Holy Spirit that I am sensitive to people's needs, even when I have no idea what they might be.

If we would be followers of Jesus, we should learn to hold our money, our time, and our lives so loosely that God can use any one or all of them to be a blessing to the world.

May you always be ready to bear witness to the grace that you have been given so freely, by giving it without reservation to a hurting world.

Turn Your When into Now

Recently, I read a thirty-two-year-old quote from Apple cofounder Steve Jobs. In 1985, he was being interviewed and delivered the following intensely personal revelation:

> My favorite things in life don't cost any money. It's really clear that the most precious resource we all have is time. As it is, I pay a price by not having much of a personal life.

Jobs was notoriously driven to succeed. He was known for working hopelessly long hours and relentlessly pursuing perfection. Jobs turned Apple into one of the most powerful companies in the world.

But after all was said and done, I wonder if those words he spoke over thirty years ago came back to him when he was diagnosed with the terminal cancer that would eventually take his life.

So many of us constantly pour ourselves into what we believe is preparation for a day when we'll finally be able to enjoy the fruit of our labors, and all the while, we gloss over or ignore the things and the people that matter most, right here and now.

Jesus once said, "Who of you by worrying add a single hour to your life?" (Matthew 6:27 NIV).

Those of us who follow Jesus are called to a new way of living and being that emphasizes eternal life that begins now, not some time in the future. Jesus wants us to be bearers of the kingdom of God—now. Jesus calls to abundance, joy, fulfillment, Sabbath rest, and generosity—now.

Stop saying, "When I have enough money, then …," or "When I get my life sorted out, then …," or "When I get my career in order, then …"

Turn your *when* into *now*.

The Kingdom Is within You

In the Gospel of Luke 17, Jesus is questioned by a group of overly religious people:

> Jesus, grilled by the Pharisees on when the kingdom of God would come, answered, "The kingdom of God doesn't come by counting the days on the calendar. Nor when someone says, 'Look here!' or, 'There it is!' And why? Because God's kingdom is already among you." (Luke 17:20–21 MSG)

Another way to translate that last line is, "Because God's kingdom is within you."

Two things occur to me this morning: (1) It's important to understand what Jesus means by "God's kingdom", and (2) it's also important to understand why he wanted his followers to know that God's kingdom was "within" them.

Frederick Buechner described God's kingdom like this:

> The Kingdom of God is where our best dreams come from and our truest prayers. We glimpse it at those moments when we find ourselves being better than we are and wiser than we know.

Another way of describing God's kingdom is with a single word: shalom. This Hebrew word essentially reflects the hope of God's peace over all the world. Shalom is when God ultimately gets what God wants for all of creation, including us.

But why did Jesus want his followers to know that this peace, this kingdom, was within them?

Because no matter what was happening around them—war, struggle, persecution, trials, tribulation, hatred, violence, bigotry, inequity, poverty, doubts, fears—Jesus wanted them to know that none of those things could touch the peace, the *shalom*, that was within them.

And wherever they went, that's where the kingdom of God was evident. Wherever they were being their best selves, better than they imagined they could be, wiser than they knew, the kingdom of God broke through and was visible.

Carry God's kingdom, God's shalom, with you today. No matter what whirlwinds might be swirling around you, be at peace because the kingdom is within you. Let the world see it.

The Best Response Is Gratitude

Consider this: the universe is expanding and is beyond our comprehension The earth is shifting, spinning, turning, rotating, slipping, sliding. There is no universal up, no universal down, no objective stationary place of rest, no absolute viewpoint, only views from a point. And the sun, which is one of those stars that we gaze so longingly at in the evening, is made of matter but is also energy at the same time.

And then there's you—a combination of water, carbon and a few other things that stumble around in the dark, looking for a flashlight for about eighty years (if you're lucky) before you go back to being dust for other things.

> What is man, O God, that you are mindful of him? (Psalm 8:4 NIV)

You are small. You are dust. You are only here for a breath of time. And all it takes is a glance into the sky at night to be reminded of just how amazing all of creation is and how tiny, insignificant, and not-that-awesome you seem to be.

Except you aren't tiny and insignificant—to God.

> For you have made human beings just a little lower than the angels, and crowned them with glory and honor. (Psalm 8:5 NIV)

To God, you are amazing. To God, you are his best creation. To God, you are the very thing that God—the Creator and Sustainer of all of that awesomeness that I related to you a moment ago—has decided to imbed with his very DNA. You are a cocreator, a shining composition of stardust and spirit that was put in charge of reflecting God's glory to the world.

What do you have to say to that?

"Thank you" might be a place to start.

Because when you finally realize all that God has done for you, the best and purest response is simply gratitude.

May you be filled with gratitude today to the One who has given you life and showered with you immeasurable blessings.

Lift Your Ebenezer

Today, I've been reflecting on what it means to be filled with gratitude, which makes me feel like I also need to talk about remembering the "Ebenezers."

The Ebenezers aren't a New Wave '80s band that dressed like characters from a Charles Dickens story. Although that would be cool.

Ebenezers are literally "stones of hope." They are stacks of stones, monuments that were erected by the ancient Hebrew people to help them remember momentous occasions when God did something incredible in their lives.

We all have Ebenezers. They serve as memorials that we can look back on our lives and see scattered throughout our time line. I have some Ebenezers of my own.

My wife and I were apart for five years before we got married. I was recently divorced, which she didn't know. She was about to be married, which I didn't know. Because of a chance meeting of an old school friend on a random night in the middle of an arena full of people, we found each other again.

I think about every job I've ever had, every class I ever took, all of the ministries, churches I served—all of those things that were leading me to this moment, to this place, one building on another, nothing wasted.

My life is filled with these standing stones of hope-filled divine intervention.

You have Ebenezers of your own. Even if things aren't going very well for you right now, you can recall times in your life when a coincidence was too perfect to be just a coincidence—moments when you *knew* that God had intervened.

Remember the Ebenezers, and be filled with courage as you recall the presence of God in your life.

God's Love Never Ends

All good things must come to an end—or so we have been taught to believe. But what if I told you that there was one thing that didn't come to an end? And that this one thing assured that all of the really good things don't have to come to an end either. What would you say to that?

Check out this verse from the book of Lamentations in the Bible:

> Because of the Lord's great love we are not consumed,
> for his compassions never fail.
> They are new every morning;
> great is your faithfulness. (Lamentations 3:22–23 NIV)

Another way to translate that verse is "his mercies—his loving-kindnesses—never come to an end; they are renewed every morning."

What if Lamentations read something like this: "The wrath of God never comes to an end; it is renewed every morning"? That doesn't sound all that awesome, does it?

If you listen to the sermons that are preached across America today in countless churches, you would think that God is angry, that God is vengeful, and that God's wrath is renewed against us each and every morning. But nothing could be further from the truth.

Psalm 36 is an amazing prayer. For thousands of years, this psalm has been sung, recited, or prayed by the people of God in gratitude to all that God has done and continues to do for the people of God.

This psalm is called the Great Hallel or the *Hallel al Gadol*, and it is recited communally in the Jewish tradition at the high holy days but most importantly at Passover.

There is one line that gets read over and over again throughout the twenty-six verses of Psalm 136: "His love endures forever" (NIV).

This psalm reminds us that no matter what good things have come to an end, we don't have to be afraid. God's mercy, his loving kindness, will never run out.

And because of this knowledge, we also have hope that even the good things that seem to always be ending have a different kind of shelf life in the kingdom of God.

May you embrace this life-giving and restorative truth, and may it fill you with thanksgiving on this day and every day forward.

Being More Open to Possibilities

Yesterday was my birthday, and I got to spend it doing some of the things I love the most. I was blessed to be able to preach and spend the morning with my church family and to be reminded once again how amazing it is to serve as their pastor.

I also got to go on a bit of an adventure with friends and family as we continued our quest to find the very best barbecue in this part of Texas. But mostly, I just relaxed, laughed, and rested, which is kind of the best way to spend your birthday, I'm thinking.

I've learned a lot in this past year. I would have just as soon not learned some of those lessons, especially the ones that had to do with loss and grief. Still, it's all part of this journey I've undertaken to keep stumbling after Jesus.

The older I've become, the more I've come to understand that possessing the willingness to be transformed by God is probably at the top of the list of requirements to follow Jesus more fully.

But so many of us grow comfortable with the status quo when it comes to our faith. We don't want to be challenged. We assume that God only has big things in mind for people with more qualifications than us, and we are content to stay exactly the same as we've always been.

Writer John Pavlovitz addressed this very thing: "We discourage so much of the work that God is doing in each of us by never allowing it to reach the surface."

As I continue to grow older, I want to become more flexible, more open to possibilities. I want to be stretched in my faith and to realize that God is never finished with shaping and molding me to become the person I ought to be and to fulfill the destiny God has in mind for me.

May you embrace a faith that is easily molded and shaped by the Almighty. May you resist a cold, brittle, fixed kind of faith that really isn't faith at all. May you push back against religiosity in favor of a relationship with Jesus that keeps you stumbling, changing, and transforming.

When We Limit Our Reality

Our poor little dog had knee replacement surgery a little over a week ago. The veterinarian told us that he most likely fell on it in just the wrong way to make it happen.

So now, he has to be carried up and down the stairs and can't run or jump for six weeks. And, to add insult to injury, he has to wear one of those big plastic cones around his head to keep him from worrying at his stitches.

When he has his cone on, he can't see what's happening to his left and right and has to constantly keep shifting his head back and forth as he walks in order to see where he's going.

As I was watching our little dog navigating his restricted environment this morning, I started thinking about how limited my own perceptions are, especially when it comes to experiencing God around me.

I think most of walk around in life as if we're wearing spiritual cones that limit our perception and keep us focused mostly on the six inches in front of our faces.

And then, we begin to believe that the limited reality that we are experiencing is all there is to know. We lose sight of the Divine all around us because we grow complacent and comfortable with our narrowed, limited focus.

Philip Yancey once wrote that when it comes to our perceptions, there are no "walled-off areas." We can trust God with all of our reality, even the reality we can't fully comprehend.

May you have the courage to remove whatever is limiting your sight and experience of God today. Open your vision to a wider view that takes in all of the Divine all around you.

May you be filled with fierce and intractable joy as you discover a wider, more colorful, and verdant world—a world ready for your gifts of God-given ministry and mission.

Yearnings That Sustain Us

In December 2016, Merideth and I drove into Austin, Texas, with our two little boys, our dog, and our two cats.

It had been a long journey to our new town. We were moving into a house neither one of us had seen in person, enrolling our kids in schools we knew next to nothing about, and launching a ministry with a new congregation.

We had no idea what to expect, but between us there was a surge of joy at the adventure we'd begun. And we knew that what had started us on our journey was a yearning to go where God would have us to go and do what God would have us to do.

That yearning for God and us in God's will has carried us through some of the most trying times of our lives. Even in dark moments, when we've very nearly felt our faith slipping away, that yearning has sustained us and lifted us up.

I recently read a quote from author Josh Larsen that spoke to me profoundly:

> Yearning is perhaps our truest testimony, a constant reminder to myself that even if my faith is not something I can blindly accept, neither is it something I can blithely discard.

Maybe you have been struggling lately to hold on to your faith. You might even be wondering where God is in the midst of your suffering or the suffering of the world.

But deep inside, you have this feeling that you can't shake—a yearning, a longing for peace, hope, love, and joy. You yearn to know your place in the world. You long for something more.

Hold on to that feeling with all your might. That yearning will sustain you and keep you holding on, even when it feels like it's only by your fingertips.

And as you hold on with your yearnings, may the grace and peace of our Lord Jesus Christ be with you, now and always.

When Doors Are Closed for a Reason

I was talking to an acquaintance some time ago about an opportunity that I thought was a sure thing—until it wasn't. I was bemoaning the loss of this opportunity, when my friend offered this bit of advice: "Hey, brother, when God closes one door, he opens another."

First, I need to let everyone know that even though it sounds kind of biblical, "When God closes one door, he opens another" is a phrase that appears a total of *zero* times in the Bible.

I did some research, and it is actually more closely attributed to Alexander Graham Bell, who said, "When one closes, another opens," and Helen Keller, who said, "When one door of happiness closes, another opens."

But I did discover a verse that talks about God and doors in the book of Revelation in my own daily Bible reading today:

> When [God] opens a door, no one can close it. And when [God] closes it, no one can open it I have put an open door before you which no one can close. (Revelation 3:7–8 MSG)

So many times in my life, I have found myself pounding at the closed doors before me. I've railed against the ways that my plans have been thwarted at times. I've also had regrets over missed opportunities on more than one occasion.

And then, there have been the opportunities that opened up before me when I had the mistaken notion that I had something to do with their swinging wide. I've nearly broken my arm in patting myself on the back in some of those instances.

But in the end, Revelation 3:7–8 reminds us that all of our closed and opened doors are part of God's great big love story for you and me.

God's plans might be challenging to decipher at times. We might wonder why one door is closed and another is open, but the one thing we can hold on to with certainty is that God is in control of all of it. We may not be able to know what the future holds, but we can (to use a well-used phrase) cling to the One who holds our future.

When God Moves You

Unless you move, the place where you are is the place where you will always be.
—Ashleigh Brilliant

I calculated the once that my wife, Merideth, and I moved twenty-two times in the first twenty-five years of our marriage. Within the last year, we moved three times, including one that took us across the country.

One particular move was actually across the street. Literally, the house I live in is right across the street and one house down from the one we were renting. It's a miracle how we got that house—the house where our entire family, including my parents, were able to live.

I swore at the time that move would be the last move I would make for a *very* long time. I also thought then that I needed to rent a huge dumpster and get rid of a bunch of stuff.

All this moving caused me to recall a book by Reggie Joiner that I read some time ago. In his book, Joiner talked about how, even though we make lots of moves in our lifetimes, we were created to make one primary move: a move toward God.

Joiner writes, "When you move toward God, it has a ripple effect on every other aspect of your life."

I have known this to be so true for me. Every single time I have sought God's will and God's way, every time I have first moved toward God before all else, it's made an incredible difference in every aspect of my life, particularly in my relationships with the people around me.

This is why Jesus declared that the "first and greatest" commandment was to "Love the Lord your God with all your heart and with all your soul and with all your strength" (Luke 10:27 NIV).

This first move toward God opens your life to the second part of the commandment, which is a move (Joiner's ripple effect) toward others.

Jesus outlined this by saying, "The second is like it. Love your neighbor as yourself" (Luke 10:27 NIV).

May you move toward God today before you make any other moves. Dedicate yourself to pursuing God, first and foremost, in your life, and then prepare yourself for the incredible ripple effects that will happen next and the people you'll be moving toward as well.

Lessons from the Lobster

One of the most often-asked questions I get asked as a pastor has to do with pain and suffering. In my experience, people who are going through difficult seasons almost always want to ascribe some kind of meaning to what is happening to them.

But sometimes, there doesn't seem to be any meaning to ascribe.

"It seems so pointless sometimes," a church member, who was going through a very rough patch of life, told me once. "I am fine with accepting God's will, and I get that sometimes stuff just happens, but this just feels meaningless to me. It's like God's cruel joke."

In the past, I have been guilty of answering these kinds of questions with platitudes. "If God brought you to it, then God will get you through it" comes to mind.

There's truth in platitudes—don't get me wrong—but it seems to me that what we need most in our valley-of-the-shadow seasons is to be able reframe our suffering and hardships in a way that leads us to a deeper connection to God.

I read recently that in the first year of its life, a lobster will shed its shell up to fourteen times. Shedding its shell takes the lobster about ten days, and during that time when it's naked, vulnerable, and without any armor, it will grow 7 percent.

When we go through seasons of loss, hardship, tough times, pain, and suffering, we often find that the "armor" we've constructed on our own (a false sense of safety; security coupled with our own strength) falls apart. I know that feeling all too well.

But almost every moment of spiritual growth in my life came after a season of shadow. After I've experienced hardship and suffering, I have discovered a deeper sense of God's presence. I've drawn closer to God and stronger in my faith after I've known vulnerability and seen my self-constructed armor disintegrate.

May you find, in the midst of your hard times, a sense of God's real presence in your life. May you find that the meaning you seek within the season of shadow is the strength you gain through your full and complete reliance on God in the midst of it.

The Power of Words

Words are powerful. Words have the power to give life or to take it away. Words have the power to heal or destroy.

Consider this: "Death and life are in the power of the tongue" (Proverbs 18:21 NIV), or this: "Whoever keeps his mouth and his tongue, keeps himself out of trouble" (Proverbs 21:23 NIV).

I am ashamed to admit that there have been times in my life when I have used my words to hurt or destroy others.

Sometimes, I've done it unintentionally, but there have been more than a few times when I've used hurtful and killing words out of malice and anger. And most of the time, the person I've said those words about never heard them.

We have this mistaken notion that the things we say are somehow harmless if the person we're referring to can't hear us say them.

What I've learned about the power of words is that even though the person about whom I am speaking my angry, hurtful words isn't within earshot, they are hurt by them all the same.

You see, we are all connected through the power of the Holy Spirit of God. When we speak killing words out into the universe, they do more than just grieve the Spirit; they take their toll on the people we're directing them toward.

Jesus holds his followers to a higher standard. We hear his teaching on how anger (and our words) can be akin to murder:

> "You have heard that it was said to the people long ago, 'You shall not murder, and anyone who murders will be subject to judgment.' But I tell you that anyone who is angry with a brother or sister will be subject to judgment." (Matthew 5:21–22 NIV)

Jesus takes the seventh commandment and turns it on its ear. It's not just "Don't kill"; it's "Don't become so angry at another person that you think or say hurtful or killing things about them."

We need to guard our words more carefully and speak grace and peace out into the world. Each of us should follow the ancient advice of the great Roman orator Cato, who once said, "I begin to speak only when I'm certain what I'll say isn't better left unsaid."

May you speak life into the world today. May you find words that are full of beauty and truth, and let words filled with ugliness, hate, and anger fall away to be forgotten.

Discovering Peace in Hard Circumstances

It's easy to get mad at your adverse circumstances. Chances are, they deserve it.

That trying situation you are going through? It probably needs to be called out and vilified for being so awful. And that bad thing that happened to you? You have my permission to let off some steam by calling it every name in the book.

But you need to realize something as you are railing away at the unwanted circumstances, situations, and awful things that have happened to you: they could not care less.

I read this amazing quote from the ancient Roman playwright Euripides today. He wrote, "You shouldn't give circumstances the power to rouse anger, for they don't care at all."

It doesn't matter how mad you get, frustrated, or full of despair, circumstances aren't concerned about your feelings. They are not people who can respond to your frustration, and no amount of anger is going to change that fact. I struggle with this something fierce.

When I am running late and stuck behind a slow-moving truck on a two-line road where I can't pass, no amount of steaming and fuming behind the wheel is going to make it better. But nine times out of ten, I find myself doing it anyway.

When I find myself dealing with situations that cause me stress but are quite beyond my control, it's easy for me to start whining and complaining. But no matter how big my pity party might get, it's not going to fix it.

What I need in those moments is not to rail at my circumstances but to turn to Jesus and to find in him the strength to be at peace.

The apostle Paul once wrote:

> I know what it is to be in need, and I know what it is to have plenty. I have learned the secret of being content in any and every situation, whether well fed or hungry, whether living in plenty or in want. I can do all this through him who gives me strength. (Philippians 4:12–13 NIV)

Chances are, when I am facing hard situations and circumstances, I got into them because I lacked the peace and contentment of Jesus in the first place.

May you discover, in the midst of your circumstances, situations, and challenges, new depths of peace and connections with Christ. May you find in this peace and connection a renewed sense of contentment, no matter what you face.

Sabbath Sanctuary

The kitchen was the first room in our new house to get completely set up and live-in ready. Considering it's the one place where everyone tends to gather, it was a good choice to be finished first.

When you are moving, it's important to get at least one room completely finished and looking the way it should. It becomes your island in the middle of the chaos, the one place you can go to sit down and breathe for a while before wading back into it.

You might say that such a place acts as a sanctuary.

I looked up the formal definition of the word *sanctuary* and discovered that it means "a place of refuge or safety." I would also add, as part of my own definition, "a place of refuge or safety where you find peace."

When I was in seventh grade, I used to ride my bike to a small Lutheran church that was not far from my house. I was always careful to go there when I was sure not to find a soul around. There was something about that place that spoke to me. I felt peace when I sat on the steps leading into the church.

At the time, my parents were considering selling our house and moving to another town. There was so much up in the air, and I felt a certain amount of chaos swirling around me. Those trips to that Lutheran church always seemed to make me feel better.

I hadn't thought about that church in years, until this morning.

It occurred to me that so much of what we need when we are searching for sanctuary, rest, and peace is simply a way of keeping Sabbath. In the busyness of our culture, we have lost so much of what it means to understand and keep the Sabbath.

The fourth commandment simply states, "Remember the Sabbath and keep it holy" (Exodus 20:8 NIV). But what it means, if we dig deeper into it, is that we are to live a Sabbath lifestyle. There has to be set-aside time for us to enjoy Sabbath and special places (sanctuaries) where we best keep it.

Where is your sanctuary? Where is your place of refuge in the eye of life's storm? If you can't identify such a place, then you should. And once you do, use it to practice leading a Sabbath lifestyle—pushing back against the world's demands, breathing, pausing to worship and simply be.

Don't Be Right; Be Jesus

I recently read about a psychological test in which people were placed in a room with buttons to push and told that they had to figure out a sequence of pushing those buttons that would cause a light to flash. They then would be awarded a point.

The object was to get as many points as they could in a thirty-minute period.

So the participants would start pushing buttons, and eventually the light flashed. Then they would try to repeat the sequence, but it wouldn't work (because the light had nothing to do with the buttons).

As a result, the participants would start doing other things—jumping up and down and then pushing the buttons, tapping their feet, standing on one foot. Each person came up with their own unique sets of beliefs about how to get the light to flash.

And they were convinced they were right.

I've noticed something sad in common Christian culture over the past several years. There seems to be a near obsession with being right. As a result, common Christian culture has become steeped in an arrogance that troubles me.

Far too many of us Christians are approaching Jesus as a problem to be solved, rather than a Way to be followed. And nine times out of ten, we settle on solutions that fit our own needs.

The longer I follow Jesus, the more I realize just how little I know. In fact, I've learned far more from being wrong than I have from the few occasions I came close to getting things right. And I've also realized that sometimes, I need to "slow my roll," keep my mouth shut, and simply follow Jesus, without trying to figure everything out.

To borrow a bit from Frederick Buechner, when Jesus said, "I am the way and the truth and the life. No one comes to the Father except through me" (John 14:6 NIV), he wasn't saying that any particular ethic, doctrine, denomination, church, or theological or political bent was the way, the truth, and the life

What Jesus said was that *he* was the way, the truth, and the life.

May you find the strength today to simply follow Jesus and let him lead you. May you give up your need to be right or to have all of your questions resolved and simply stumble after him.

Test God's Goodness

The LORD had said to Abram, "Go from your country, your people
and your father's household to the land I will show you.
—Genesis 12:1 (NIV)

I had to go back to our "old house" (as we are calling it now) to work this morning because I don't yet have internet service in the "new house."

We had all of the furniture moved yesterday from the old house to the new house, but we left the desks standing, in anticipation of this particular moment.

It's odd to look up and see that the familiar landmarks in our rented house are now gone. We only lived there for three months, but it didn't take long for it to feel like home. Even in the short time we lived here, we made memories together.

At the end of a very long day yesterday, we finally gathered in our jumbled living room, ate pizza, and began to laugh a bit, which we needed to do. Moving is no fun, especially across the street.

I didn't think about it in the moment, but I wish now that I had said something important as we ate, considering it was the first of what will be many family meals in our new home. I think I would have said something like this:

"We dreamed of this place, long before we knew it was here. The fact that it was across the street from us all along was just God's way of showing off. We are all here together under one roof, just like we imagined it. When we started this journey across the country, we just stepped out in faith. We weren't sure where it would lead us or how it would all work out. And now we are home. God is so good. We'll tell the story of how good God is our whole lives."

I am a living, walking testimony of the goodness of God. Pursuing God's call for our lives has made us uncomfortable. It hasn't been easy, but it's in moments like the one we shared last night that I am reminded of how amazing the adventure of following Christ truly is.

May you find ways to step out in faith and be amazed at the goodness of God today. Test that goodness. Go where you feel led to go by God, without fear or trepidation. The road ahead might not be clear, but trust that it leads exactly where you need to be.

Wear the Colors of Christ

Football season has begun, and I feel like I can watch ESPN again. No more boring stories about basketball, hockey, and (yawn) soccer. I am still hanging with baseball because the Cubs are winning, and it's almost October. But it's football season, which brings a tremendous amount of joy to the people in my house, and it also means I can wear my team gear as much as possible.

I sent my six-year-old to school today in his Peyton Manning football jersey. My middle son, Jackson, has about three or four jerseys for both the Broncos and Seminoles, and my oldest boy has a few here and there that he wears to anger his friends who are Carolina Panther fans.

The other day I was all decked out in my Florida State Seminoles gear when I went to the store. I was wearing it proudly because the 'Noles had a big comeback win on national television just a few days before. Every other person I encountered nodded at me when I went by and said, "Go 'Noles!"

I didn't know these people. I had no idea what they did for a living or whether they were mean and nasty or not. I had no clue if we had anything else in common except our mutual admiration for the Seminoles. But in those moments, we were connected. We knew we were part of the same tribe.

I have often thought about how easily we don the colors of our respective tribes—our favorite teams or our alma maters, for example. But when it comes to identifying ourselves as followers of Jesus, we have a more difficult time figuring out how to do that well. It's a lot easier to know what we don't want to look like, isn't it?

We all know the people who plaster their car with corny religious bumper stickers, or who seemingly wear nothing but "Christian" T-shirts and hats, or incessantly post Christian-y posts on Facebook. And so, in order to avoid being lumped in with the "overly Christian" folk, we do our best to just "act natural."

Jesus told his disciples something profound that speaks right into this: "Let your light so shine before others that they will see your good deeds and glorify your Father who is in heaven" (Matthew 5:16 NIV).

In other words, you don't need a shirt or a bumper sticker to let everyone know you are a Christian. According to Jesus, you will demonstrate you are part of the tribe when you shine your light, when you show Jesus to the world in such a way that people will encounter you and say, "I want what he [or she] has."

May you demonstrate your allegiance to Jesus today by your words and your deeds. May your light shine in the darkness, giving hope to all who gather around it for illumination. May you show Jesus to the world without having to say a word.

Believe, Then See

In his international bestseller *The God Delusion*, renowned atheist Richard Dawkins writes, "We are all atheists about most of the gods that humanity has ever believed in. Some of us just go one god further."

Over the years, I've had the opportunity to read some of Dawkins's works, as well as the works of other popular contemporary atheist authors, like Sam Harris, Stephen Hawking, and the late Christopher Hitchens.

I have to say that I don't disagree with them completely when the offer severe critiques of the ways religion has caused so many problems in our world. They also raise serious questions about a God who condemns, rages, espouses violence, and directs his followers to judge others, act with intolerance, and generally walk around angry and combative.

And here's where I am about to say something shocking. I don't disagree with their assertions that people need to give up their belief in *that* kind of God. To be completely 100 percent honest, I don't believe in that God either. In fact, when I hear someone say they are an atheist, I think, *I probably have more in common with you than you would like to admit.*

By contrast, we have a description of God from 1 John 4:9–11 that paints an entirely different portrait:

> This is how God showed his love for us: God sent his only Son into the world so we might live through him. This is the kind of love we are talking about—not that we once upon a time loved God, but that he loved us and sent his Son as a sacrifice to clear away our sins and the damage they've done to our relationship with God.
>
> My dear, dear friends, if God loved us like this, we certainly ought to love each other. No one has seen God, ever. But if we love one another, God dwells deeply within us, and his love becomes complete in us—perfect love! (1 John 4:9–11 MSG)

Imagine if Christians began showing the world what it looks like to believe in the God of 1 John 4:9–11 and to embrace a life lived in the example of Jesus, God's anointed. The writer of 1 John admitted, "No one has seen God, ever." But in an inverse of the old saying, "seeing is believing," the author infers that through our love for other people, people can begin to believe in God and then to see.

May you demonstrate your belief in the God whose love never fails, whose mercy never runs out, who is still in the Resurrection and restoration business. May you show the world what it looks like to believe and then to see.

The Backside of God

I have these moments when I long for the presence of God in my life so deeply that it's hard to breathe. I know that sounds kind of odd, but it's true. I want to know more, to feel more, to understand more of God—more and more all of the time.

I catch myself wishing that there was a rift between whatever dimension we happen to be living in at the moment and the one where God exists in God's fullness. I just want a glimpse—just a glimpse—of what it must be like there.

Heaven, at least in my humble opinion, isn't somewhere *up there*. Heaven is just on the other side of here. God is all around us, in us, and through us, but we struggle to experience God because of the limitations of our sight. But just because I can't see heaven doesn't mean it isn't there.

I wonder sometimes if God shields us from whatever is on the other side of here because we can't handle its awesomeness. There's a story in the Bible that describes this kind of thing. In the book of Exodus, Moses is on top of Mount Sinai, receiving the Law, when he asks God, "Show me your glory."

So God shields Moses from the fullness of his glory by putting him in a cave, of sorts, and only letting Moses see his "back parts." And even that little bit of God's glory made Moses glow like he had walked through Chernobyl or Three-Mile Island. He was glowing so fiercely when he came down the mountain that he had to put something over his face, not to scare the people of Israel.

Wouldn't it be amazing to experience God so intensely that you couldn't stop glowing afterward? Would people stop you on the street to take selfies with you because you were radiating warm and incredible light? I bet they would.

I believe—I am convinced—that when we draw close to those moments, those burning bushes in our midst, the light created from them shines on us and makes us brighter. And isn't that the point? Didn't Jesus call his followers "the light of the world"?

May you be illuminated by the evidence of the Divine all around you today and every day of your life. May you seek beauty and truth and justice, and find the rifts between here and there in the midst of them. May you glimpse glory and let it brighten you like a torch that burns solely to shine the way to Christ.

Be a Place Where People Can Land

Positive reinforcement is much more effective in changing behavior than negative reinforcement. And by *much more*, I mean so much more that it's not even funny.

When I was serving as a youth director in Chicago, we took our junior high students on a mission trip to urban Nashville, Tennessee. Unbeknownst to me, the organization that ran our mission trip was the kind of "mission" organization that was much more interested in aggressive evangelism than mission.

As part of our training, we were asked to divide into groups and go to the local mall for "cold witnessing." The basic idea was that we were to walk around to find people in the mall to talk to about Jesus. Let's just say that I was not only way out of my comfort zone but suddenly reintroduced to a ton of the baggage I thought I'd left behind when I fled the Fundamentalist Baptist churches of my youth.

The young adults who led our witnessing expedition essentially taught my kids how to strike up conversations with perfect strangers for the sole purpose of asking them this question: "Where would you like to spend eternity? In heaven or in an eternal, burning, torturous hell?"

For the record, we had no converts to the cause that day. When it was all over and we sat down to recap the day, I quietly asked the college students who had shepherded our group in the mall, "So how effective do you think your methods of evangelism are, really?"

They weren't too happy with my resistance to their negative-reinforcement techniques, but it needed to be said.

Jesus had this habit of being present with people, meeting them where they were. He had infinite patience and grace for anyone who just wanted to have a relationship with God and very little patience for those who chose to embrace religion over relationship.

Jesus didn't condemn people or treat them as objects either. He just loved them. His heart broke for them. He put himself in harm's way to be with people no one wanted to be with—to eat with them, laugh with them, and lift them up.

He used positive reinforcement to show them the kind of life that God had always dreamed for them to live. I believe Jesus wants his followers to do the very same.

May you have your eyes opened to new ways to share your faith—ways that highlight the positive, abundant, and hopeful aspects of what it means to follow Jesus. May you be a safe place to land for those who struggle with their faith and who desperately need hope and peace.

A Simple Focus for Faith

Years ago, when I arrived at a church where I had been called to serve as pastor, I discovered that church leaders had created a "mission statement" some years before I got there. It was a paragraph long, at least, filled with all kinds of ideas.

At one of our elder meetings, I asked if anyone could recite the mission statement of the church. No one could tell me anything about it. At last, one elder (who had served on the team that had created it) managed to come up with one part of one sentence.

The point was made. Our mission statement was too long, too convoluted. Hardly anyone knew what it said, and no one was really connected to it. We needed to simplify things, and so we began working on doing just that. In the end, we settled on a simply vision statement: "Our vision is to know Jesus and show Jesus to the world."

This simple vision has carried the church forward for the past seven years—to unprecedented growth, life, and vibrancy. When we started focusing on what really mattered, we began to see changes in the way we functioned, welcomed, and conducted mission and ministry.

I've discovered, over time, that when I apply the same kind of practice to my own life—when I simplify my focus when it comes to my faith journey; when I keep my focus on Jesus and living according to his example—my attitude toward others changes too. I also find the courage to leave the heavy lifting of life to God and to simply surrender the outcomes.

The psalmist who wrote Psalm 131 declared, "I have stilled and quieted my soul like a weaned child is my soul within me" (Psalm 131:2 NIV). If you've ever weaned a baby off breast milk or a bottle, you know it's not fun. There's a lot of turmoil, crying, and drama.

But the psalmist declares the opposite is true about his spirit. Because he focused on God—because he surrendered the outcomes—he is simply able to be at peace.

May you experience the peace that, according to the Bible, "passes understanding." May you be blown away at the level of calm you can have when you simply focus on God, when you simply turn your life over to God, when you simply make God the center of your life.

Sometimes You Need a Pause

Many of us have heard that old aphorism, "It's not the destination; it's the journey." How many of us, however, really know what it means? On the surface, it speaks vaguely of the importance of being present in the moment, rather than focusing solely on what comes next.

But there's a deeper meaning to the aforementioned phrase, one that I believe eludes most of us. I think this phrase speaks directly into the frail and finite ways that most of approach our goals in life. We find ourselves longing for *someday*.

"Someday," we tell ourselves, "I'll finally figure out my purpose in life."

"Someday, I'll have enough money to do what I want."

"Someday, I'll get that promotion; reach that milestone; find my dream job."

"Someday, I'll get healthy; get moving; do that thing I've always wanted to do."

Our longings for someday all too often become the very thing that keeps us from recognizing the importance of now. I preached a sermon recently where I challenged people to turn their *when* into *now*. It's a simple shift in your mindset, really.

All that is required to begin focusing on the journey is to pause and take a look at where you are. In that pause, you can begin to recognize the importance of the journey and that the path you "chose" was not entirely your doing. That pause gives you the opportunity to be still for a moment and to recognize that there is a God, and you are not him.

Proverbs 19:21 offers this wisdom: "Many are the plans in a human heart, but it is the Lord's purpose that prevails" (NIV).

One of the easiest ways to simplify your life is to surrender your desires for the future. This doesn't mean that we shouldn't dream. We should dream. We should dream big, audacious, out-of-reach dreams. This doesn't mean that we shouldn't make plans. We need to consider the cost of decisions and think and pray about decisions before making them.

But when you relinquish your desires for the future in favor of God's desires; when you decide to be present in the journey, opening your eyes to see God at work around you, opening your ears to hear God's still, small voice in your ear; when you trust God with the future and embrace the present, your life gets simpler. Your way becomes clearer. Your focus is narrowed. You enjoy the journey.

May you discover the joy of your journey as you simply surrender the future to the One who holds it. May you simplify your life by embracing the present and seek to align your desires with God's own.

Getting Rid of the Clutter

Recently, my wife and I went on a bit of cleaning spree and decided to declutter some of our counters, shelves, the back patio, the outside patio, the kitchen, our closet, our bathroom, the kids' rooms—OK, so we started decluttering and just couldn't stop.

What we discovered in the midst of all that decluttering was that we didn't really need all of the things that we thought we needed when we moved into our house several months ago. And here's the kicker: we actually thought we had decluttered from our old house when we moved into the new one.

It felt better to have less stuff. It felt better to walk in the house and see the simplicity of minimalism. And it also felt better, knowing that, in the end, we don't need stuff to make us happy; in fact, having more stuff actually contributes to stress and anxiety. What Merideth and I were striving for was contentment with less. Clearing the clutter actually helped us take a step closer to achieving it.

In 1 Timothy 6:7–8, we hear these words of wisdom from the apostle Paul about contentment:

> For we have brought nothing into the world, so we cannot take anything out of it either. If we have food and covering, with these we shall be content. (NIV)

I know, I know—you're thinking that just having food and "covering" isn't really going to cut it in this day and age. But if you take "food and covering" to mean all of the ways that we care for the basic needs of ourselves and our families, then it can take on new meaning for us as we try to simplify our lives in order to achieve more for the kingdom.

I believe when we are less focused on the things of this world, we are able to be more focused on the kingdom of God.

When our counters and shelves, rooms, and closets became less cluttered, less filled with stuff, I found myself able to concentrate better on the things that matter most. I found more joy to share with my children, more attention to give to my wife, and a host of new ideas for how I could impact the world for the sake of God's kingdom.

I know that it sounds strange, but it actually happens. When you minimize the distractions and get rid of the material things that occupy space in your head (as well as the desire for more that always seems to accompany them), you find yourself much more able to remain focused on what is good, pure, lovely, and true.

May you find ways to simplify your life by decluttering it, clearing space for new ways to see the world through God's eyes. May you discover new capacity to be shaped by a more minimalist way of life, where your focus is on the kingdom of God and not on the things of this world.

A New Way to Define Success

More often than not, when I am reading through my various devotional books and daily Bible readings, I find connections between them—recurring themes, if you will—that speak to me in the moment.

Today was one of those days. For some reason, four of the five readings I had today all centered around what it means to pursue things that matter, the things in life that will last.

I read from the book of Ecclesiastes, where the teacher wrote: "I have seen all the things that are done under the sun; all of them are meaningless, a chasing after the wind" (Ecclesiastes 1:14 NIV).

Then there was this passage from the Gospel of Luke, where Jesus tells his followers what it takes to truly follow him and embrace eternal life, here and now:

> If people want to follow me, they must give up the things they want. They must be willing to give up their lives daily to follow me. Those who want to save their lives will give up true life. But those who give up their lives for me will have true life. It is worth nothing for them to have the whole world if they themselves are destroyed and lost. (Luke 9:23–25 NIV)

I read a quote from Oscar Wilde recently that kind of stuck with me. He wrote, "In this world there are only two tragedies. One is not getting what one wants, and the other is getting it."

Jesus's teaching to his followers was counterintuitive. Give up what you value most in order to attain what you need the most. Be willing to sacrifice your dreams in order to discover God's dream for you. Be willing to lose your life in order to find it. In the abstract, these things don't make sense, do they?

But when you place Jesus's teachings in juxtaposition with the words of the teacher in Ecclesiastes or the life of Solomon, things get just a little clearer. The path to success, according to our culture, is not to give up, lose, or sacrifice. Jesus basically taught his followers that if they wanted to be "first," they needed to race each other to the bottom.

Because, in the words of Jesus, it isn't worth a thing to gain the whole world if it simply destroys you. Another translation of that verse is, "What does it profit a man if he gains the whole world, and forfeit his soul?" (Mark 8:36 NIV).

May you discover a new way to define success today and every day. May you find your worth in God's economy and not the economy of so-called success in our current cultural climate. May you find everything you need by giving up all that you think you want.

When the Inciting Incident Happens

I read a quote the other day about "being ready" from Tim Fargo, a writer and blogger. He wrote, "Opportunity doesn't make appointments, you have to be ready when it arrives."

I like that quote, even though it's one of those quotes you usually see on a placard somewhere at a leadership conference or as a motivational poster on someone's office wall. It's simple and true.

The fact of the matter is, most of us don't live our lives poised to take advantage of opportunities. We don't live our lives ready to step boldly into the future. If we are being honest, most of us live our lives pretty much the same way every single day—the same patterns, the same roads, the same activities.

But on occasion, we experience what storytellers call an "inciting incident"—something that shocks us, moves us, jars us loose. Maybe it's a good thing, like a promotion or a new love interest, or perhaps it's something not so good, like a bad diagnosis or a tragedy.

The question that most of us never really have to answer is, "What do I do when that moment arrives?" I see this as a spiritual issue, honestly. It's a problem that takes place between the head and the heart.

When those inciting incidents arrive, we might think we would act a certain way, exhibit a particularly strong faith, give glory to God, etc., but until it happens, we don't truly know what we'll do.

In Luke 9:61, a man says to Jesus, "I will follow, Lord, but first let me go and say goodbye to my family." Then Jesus offers this cryptic and challenging reply to the man: "Anyone who begins to plow a field but keeps looking back is of no use in the kingdom of God" (Luke 9:61 NIV).

Jesus was using a very practical illustration to point out the real problem that most people have when it comes to selling out for God. If you're plowing a field and keep looking back to see what you've done, you'll get off course and start plowing crooked. But if you fix your eyes on one spot and unwaveringly move toward that spot, you'll stay straight.

So, how ready are you to follow Jesus, wherever Jesus might be leading you? How ready are you to put your hand to the plow and fix your eyes on him as you step forward?

May you discover readiness you never knew you had. May you be filled with boldness and courage to follow Jesus and to never look back. May you be willing to step out of what is comfortable and safe toward what is uncomfortable and life-giving.

A Long Obedience

In his fantastic book *A Long Obedience in the Same Direction*, pastor and author Eugene Peterson writes about the idea of faithfulness and discipline when it comes to living the Christian life.

In a very eloquent way, he offers an alternative to the stereotype that so many people have about Christians and the way we often are so "heavenly minded" that we aren't any "earthly good." Peterson writes:

> Hoping does not mean doing nothing. It is not fatalistic resignation. It means going about our assigned tasks, confident that God will provide the meaning and the conclusions.

What Peterson captures here is too good to miss. Christian hope is grounded in action. Its very foundation is exemplified by the words of Jesus, who said, "I have not come here to do my own will, but the will/work of the Father, who sent me" (John 6:38 NIV).

You and I have work to do. We are called to take the gifts, talents, time, and treasure we've been given and put them to good use for the sake of the kingdom of God.

And here's a secret: when it comes to living the Christian life, there's no such thing as retirement. In fact, the word *retirement* can't be found anywhere in the Bible, but that's another devotion for another day. The fact of the matter is that you and I are never done discipling. Never.

Pablo Casals was one of the greatest cellists whoever lived. At age ninety-six, he was still practicing three hours a day. When someone asked him once why he did this, he replied, "I'm beginning to notice some improvement."

Come on. That's so good, isn't it? How many of us approach our life with Christ like that? How many of us devote ourselves to studying, praying, giving, serving, loving, and living our lives in such a way that we are utterly devoted to Christ? Most of us devote all of our time to furthering our own careers, strengthening our portfolios, fulfilling our own desires.

May you begin to see all of the aspects of your life as a means to grow in your faith and show the love of Christ to the world. May you use all the things God has given you to glorify God and enjoy God, each and every day.

A Constant Conversation

I heard a story many years ago—a prominent televangelist would tell his viewers to send a prayer request in with a donation and then someone on his team (maybe even the televangelist himself) would pray for that request. An undercover news team sneaked a camera into the mailroom of said televangelist and filmed workers opening envelopes, taking out the cash and checks, and then throwing away the requests.

Those are the kinds of things that make you cynical, if you are inclined to that kind of thing, and sometimes I find myself trending that way when it comes to some of the nonsense that goes on in the name of Jesus.

So, in the interest of not being cynical, I have to ask myself a question: Just because the televangelist was a charlatan and a conman, does it mean that the prayer requests those people wrote down on those sheets of paper and mailed in with their money didn't get heard by God?

Jesus had a weird interaction with his disciples about prayer. He said:

> "Suppose one of you went to your friend's house at midnight and said to him, 'Friend loan me three loaves of bread. A friend of mine has come into town to visit me, but I have nothing for him to eat.' Your friend inside inside the house answers, 'Don't bother me! The door is already locked, and my children and I are in bed. I cannot get up and give you anything.' I tell you, if friendship is not enough to make him get up to give you the bread, your boldness will make him get up and give you whatever you need. So I tell you, ask, and God will give to you. Search and you will find. Knock and the door will open for you." (Luke 11:5–9 NIV)

What Jesus seems to be saying here is, "God loves it when we keep talking, keeping asking, keep praying." The visual image of a man banging on his neighbor's door until he opens up and shares his bread is an amazing way to describe our own relationship with God and with prayer.

I think that no matter what form your prayers take, the important thing is to pray—consistently, often, fervently, specifically, and with great persistence. Our constant communication with God keeps us connected to God and with God's will for us.

I believe that when we stay in constant contact with God, when we keep bringing our petitions—boldly, persistently—something amazing happens: We discover new ways to see what we need, to refine our understanding of God's will, and to align our desires with God's desires. We find a new peace with waiting on God, a peace grounded in trust.

We also sometimes find that what we were looking for wasn't what we needed. Or we discover that by constantly being in communication and relationship with God, everything we need is simply God himself.

How Do You Look at the World?

I was born with congenital glaucoma, which affects 1 in 100,000 or so people and now is easily detected and treated. In 1969, however, there were only two people in the entire country who were able to perform the necessary surgery to reverse the effects.

Because it was caught in time, the damage caused by the glaucoma was able to be minimized in my left eye, but my right eye was not so lucky. I've been legally blind in my right eye for my whole life—able to make out shapes, colors, and some peripheral vision but not much else.

From time to time, I run into things because I'm looking a bit too far to the left. It happened the other day, in fact. I face-planted into a pole while I was walking on the street, trying to figure out which way I was going. Luckily, no one was there to see it.

It's interesting to have sight in one eye and almost none in the other. I am constantly reminded of what it would be like to lose my sight altogether—a thought that I don't care to entertain.

I was reading today from the Gospel of Luke and came across this teaching of Jesus:

> Your eye is the lamp of your body. When your eyes are healthy, your whole body also is full of light. But when they are unhealthy, your body also is full of darkness. See to it, then, that the light within you is not darkness. Therefore, if your whole body is full of light, and no part of it dark, it will be just as full of light as when a lamp shines its light on you. (Luke 11:34–36 NIV)

What Jesus is essentially teaching here is a way of looking at the world that is "full of light." In other words, when the way you look at the world is healthy, then the way you respond to the world will be healthy. But if your vision is unhealthy, the way you respond will be as well.

How many of us look out into the world with a jaundiced, diseased view? How many of us see the world as a dark, dirty, ugly place? How many of us view people negatively rather than positively, always looking for the ways others are not us, are different? How many of us find ourselves viewing world events, circumstances, news, or politics with lenses of fear, anxiety, or straight-up anger?

Jesus's teaching here is clear. If you want to have a light-filled life, you have to start seeing the world through light-filled eyes. You have to see the world as God sees it—full of potential for beauty and goodness, and worthy of redemption and reconciliation.

May you find ways to see the world differently today. May you look through God-shaped lenses at the people around you, seeing them as children of God, made in God's image. May you see the events and news happening around you as opportunities to share and show grace and peace.

Seeking God in Good Times and Bad

There was a fatal car accident in our town over the weekend. A lady and her nine-year-old granddaughter were sitting at a stop light when a car driving from the opposite direction lost control and struck them. The grandmother was killed instantly, and the little girl died later in the hospital.

My wife texted me this morning with these words. "[She was] just sitting there minding her own business. That quick, one of us could be gone." I've been thinking about her words all morning and about a conversation I had with one of our church's elders yesterday. "Where is God when bad things happen?"

I've written about this pretty extensively over the past year, but it bears repeating that I believe God is in the midst of our suffering—with us in the moments of pain, tragedy, and heartache—just as I believe God is with us in our moments of triumph, joy, happiness, and success.

In Isaiah 57:15, the prophet speaks the words of God to God's people:

> For thus says the high and exalted One Who lives forever, whose name is Holy, "I dwell on a high and holy place, And also with the contrite and lowly of spirit In order to revive the spirit of the lowly And to revive the heart of the contrite. (NIV)

We are surrounded, enveloped, and overwhelmed by the grace of God, but like fish swimming in the ocean, with no real concept of the water around them, we spend most of our lives unaware of God's presence.

I think that we also spend most of our lives unaware of the fragility of our lives. We plan, and work, and spend our time as though we have an infinite supply of it in this life. And when bad things happen—when change occurs suddenly, we get bad news, a tragedy takes place—we are forced to confront our lack of control.

And that's when so many of us start wondering where God is in the middle of our bad things. I think the most daring, difficult, and challenging thing we can do, as followers of Jesus, is to constantly seek God, in good times as well as bad and even in the worst, most terrible moments.

Jeremiah 29:13 has these incredible words of hope imbedded in a not-so-subtle challenge:

> "You will seek Me and find Me when you search for Me with all your heart." If, even in moments of crisis or tragedy, we seek God with all of our heart, God promises that we will find God. (NIV)

May you seek the Lord today with all of your heart. May you earnestly desire to see God, experience God, and feel God in all of the moments of your day—the triumphant moments, the mundane moments, and even the terrible moments.

God Is on Your Side

I call on you, my God, for you will answer me; turn your ear to me and
hear my prayer. Show me the wonders of your great love.
—Psalm 17:6–7 (NIV)

Many years ago, when my wife, Merideth, and I lived in South Florida, I would accompany my father-in-law (who was a season-ticket holder) to all of the Miami Dolphins home games. I would always cheer for the Dolphins, even though my heart belonged to my beloved Denver Broncos. I even owned a Dolphins T-shirt or two and a couple of caps that I would wear to the games.

One Monday night, however, the Dolphins played my Broncos at home. It was the first time I had ever had a chance to see my team play in person, and I wanted to represent my true loyalty. I arrived at the game all decked out in my Broncos gear—jersey and hat.

People booed me when I came to sit down. My father-in-law spent much of the game kind of leaning away from me. The Broncos lost the game that night (even though they would go on to win the Super Bowl), and I took a lot of abuse afterward. Some of it was pretty hostile, to be honest. I kind of felt uncomfortable and uneasy, hearing some of the horrible things that people were saying to me.

There have been more than a few times in my life when I have felt like I was surrounded. Maybe you have too. When you feel like you are surrounded, when you feel like there's no one who has your back or your best interests at heart, it's easy to withdraw, to give up, to shrink back from the moment.

Maybe it's a boss who doesn't believe in you and is constantly antagonistic. Maybe it's a group of "friends" who are pressuring you to do or to say things that you know are wrong. Maybe it's the hundreds of voices in your head that have told you that you are not good enough. Maybe it's a bunch of Christians who make you feel like you aren't loved by God at all.

Pray the psalm above if you are feeling this way. Pray these words: "I call on you God, for you will answer me" (Psalm 17:6 NIV). Pause and let that sink in for a moment. If you call on God, God will answer. Then pray the rest of it—Psalm 17:8. Read the words out loud so you can hear your voice say them. "Keep me as the apple of your eye [because you are]. Hide me in the shadow of your wing." (God is on your side, my friend.)

May you be filled with the grace and great strength of the God who made the universe, the God who sustains the cosmos, the God who breathed life into you and who loves you beyond all love. May you know that even when it feels like you are surrounded, this same God stands before you, behind you, and all around you.

How Jesus Found Common Ground

I was scrolling through my Facebook feed yesterday and came across a post from an old seminary classmate. He declared that he was angry and that in the coming days, he was going to be posting things that some people might find offensive, but he didn't care if they did.

He went on to say something like, "If you no longer want to be my friend because of what I am going to say, so be it."

Lately, lots of people seem to have adopted that attitude. I was watching a cable news channel the other day, and the host of the program had two people on his show who had differing viewpoints on the recent election.

Neither one would allow the other to speak. They shouted over each other as they tried to make their own particular point be heard, which resulted in no one being able to understand anything they were saying.

Our culture is full of people who seem to only care about their own stories and have little interest in listening to the stories of others. Curiosity has given way to boorish self-importance. We aren't listening to one another. Far too many people want to tell the world why they feel the way they do, and far too few people are willing to do what it takes to actually feel what others are feeling.

In Matthew 9:36, Jesus looked out over the crowds of people who were pressing upon him to hear him teach. He was tired, but he looked upon them with compassion in all of their need. He didn't complain that they weren't attentive to his ideas, opinions, and feelings. The only agenda he had was the Father's.

The scripture reads: "When he saw the crowds, he had compassion on them, because they were harassed and helpless, like sheep without a shepherd" (Matthew 9:36 NIV).

If we are ever going to find common ground in our very divided society, we are going to have to start looking upon one another with the kind of open-hearted, open-minded, loving empathy that Jesus showed to everyone.

"All people are alive to God," Jesus said once (Luke 20:38 NIV). Think about how adjusting our attitudes about others, according to Jesus's example, might change the way we interact with one another. Instead of brusquely declaring our own thoughts and opinions with little care where they land, perhaps we would find the love to simply listen.

May you exercise loving, attentive listening today and every day. May you listen to the stories of others and discover within them connections to your own. May you see the world as full of people who are alive to God.

A Better Way to Share Your Faith

The churches I went to when I was a kid encouraged (strongly) door-to-door evangelism. In fact, by the time I was in high school, I was a veteran of door-to-door evangelism. I was also a veteran of getting doors slammed in my face.

Our technique for witnessing to people when we went door-to-door was almost completely lacking in any kind of tact whatsoever. The opening spiel went something like this: "Hello, my name is Leon from _____Church. I'd like to ask you an important question. If you died right now, would you spend eternity in heaven or hell?"

As you can imagine, our success rate on winning souls was somewhere between nothing and zero.

I think there are a lot of Christians who so desperately don't want to seem like door-to-door evangelists that they never really develop healthy ways to share their faith. In fact, I talk to a lot of Christians who confess that even when they have opportunities to talk about their faith with other people, they more often than not will choose to remain silent.

So where is the happy medium between pounding on doors and being obnoxious and saying nothing? I think, like a lot of things, it lies in our surrendering our will to God's and in being open to the leading of the Holy Spirit.

Jesus told his followers not to worry about what they would say when they had an opportunity to share their faith. "I will give you the wisdom," he told them (Luke 21:14 NIV). Jesus's promise to his followers was a faith that was alive to the Spirit and the Spirit's leading.

As followers of Jesus, we've been given a command by the Savior himself: "Go into all the world and preach the Gospel" (Mark 16:15 NIV). But we need to know a couple of things first.

To begin with, we can't pound on the doors of people's hearts and expect to be allowed inside. There are places only the Spirit can go, and maybe they need to have their hearts unlocked from the inside.

Second, we can't be afraid to tell our stories and share what following Jesus means to us. When we let our fear go and simply speak our truth, the Spirit will do the rest. And when we go out into the world with this in mind, we suddenly discover more and more opportunities to connect and share.

May you find ways to share the story of your faith today and every day. May you discover courage and words you never thought you had as you rely on the Spirit of God to guide you.

When Was the Last Time You Were Quiet?

Last night, Merideth and I spent about ten minutes scrolling through all of our possible TV-watching choices on Netflix. We couldn't seem to find anything that we both wanted to watch, so we just kept searching.

There are thousands of choices on Netflix, between television shows and movies. It's overwhelming at times to try to pick something. Finally, we just gave up, shut the TV off, and went to sleep in short order, which we should have done in the first place.

I did a quick search today to find out if other people had the same issue with the vast number of choices on Netflix. I discovered there are actually entire websites and web applications that exist, just to help people navigate Netflix and find something to watch.

Not only do we have an overwhelming number of choices at our fingertips, but we also have an overwhelming number of ways to help us make those choices. It's all kind of overwhelming. We're living in strange times, my friends.

When was the last time you simply sat still and rested without checking your phone or playing on your iPad? When was the last time you enjoyed a quiet talk with a friend over coffee that wasn't interrupted by a thousand texts, emails, or some kind of busyness that crept its way into your conversation?

When was the last time you simply found a quiet spot to pray, to journal, or to be still and know that God is God and you are not? If you are like me, those moments are few and precious.

This morning, I read this verse and it spoke to me intently: "Very early in the morning, while it was still dark, Jesus got up, left the house and went off to a solitary place, where he prayed" (Mark 1:35 NIV).

Jesus was often overwhelmed by the sheer need of the people to whom he was ministering. He was often interrupted by people wanting to argue with him, people needing to be healed, even his own disciples with questions about which of them would be greatest in the kingdom of God. He had a lot of choices to make.

But what we see in this verse is that Jesus made time to push back against the busyness, the endless choices, and the interruptions. He dedicated a particular time of the day and found a solitary place on the hillsides surrounding the Sea of Galilee, where he could simply be still with God.

May you resist the overwhelming number of choices today that lead you to disquiet, disunity, and a lack of peace. May you create space in your life today for solitude with the Creator, and in so doing, find solidarity with the Son, who did the same.

We Need to Hear the Truth about Us

I had a pastor friend many years ago who asked me if we could work together to improve our preaching. He offered to listen to my sermons and offer critique if I would do the same with him.

I soon discovered, however, that my friend had no real desire to hear anything negative about his preaching but was pretty keen on critiquing mine. After a few weeks, I pointed this out, and after that, it didn't take long for my friend to stop asking to meet altogether.

In Shakespeare's *Pericles*, the title character decides not to reveal what he knows about King Antiochus of Antioch because what he knows would prove embarrassing to the king.

When asked to explain why he prefers to keep silent, Pericles says, "Few love to hear the sins they love to act."

We all love to offer constructive criticism, but we rarely love to receive it.

I think everyone needs to have someone prophetic in their life—that one person who is unafraid to tell us like it is, even if it means risking the relationship. If you have someone in your life who is willing to risk it all to tell you the truth, that's a relationship to cherish.

In 2 Samuel 12:7, the prophet Nathan confronts the great king David with the truth about himself. He was an adulterer and a murderer. David had an affair with Bathsheba, the wife of one of his most capable military leaders, Uriah. When Bathsheba becomes pregnant, David eventually has Uriah killed so he could marry her and cover it all up.

At the risk of his own life, Nathan proclaims the truth to David—the truth that so many people undoubtedly already knew but were afraid to share. As a result, David was forced to come face-to-face with the darkness within himself and to repent. It cost him, but his relationship with God was restored as a result.

It's widely believed that David wrote Psalm 51 after his encounter with Nathan. When you read these lines, you'll see why he has been referred to as "a man after [God's] own heart" (Acts 13:22 NIV):

> Create in me a pure heart, O God, and renew a steadfast spirit within me. Do not cast me from your presence or take your Holy Spirit from me. Restore to me the joy of your salvation and grant me a willing spirit, to sustain me. (Psalm 51:10–12 NIV)

May you have a willing and open heart toward those who speak truth into your life. May you be guided by their prophetic wisdom. May you repent where you need to repent, forgive where you need to forgive, and may you discover a renewed spirit of joy within you as a result.

The Church Isn't Ours

Yesterday was a bittersweet day.

It was my last official day as the pastor of the church I've been serving for the past eight years and the end of a long week of "lasts" and goodbyes. I have been overwhelmed by the touching things that people shared with my wife and me about how our ministry had a positive impact on their lives.

One of the things that made parting yesterday bittersweet was the way so many people in our new congregation have expressed their prayers and well wishes to the congregation we are leaving.

In return, my now-former church is sending a letter of greeting and well-wishes from her members and friends to the members and friends of my new church.

It's these kinds of things that have made this whole process so amazing. It gives me such hope at how beautiful church can be and how humbling it is to serve *the* church in all her infinite variety.

Over the past two weeks, I baptized four people (including one adult and a middle schooler), had seven people join the church I'm leaving (even though they knew I was leaving), and ordained and installed three new elders.

As I gave the announcements yesterday at one of the worship services, I was sharing news on events and programs I'd attended for years that are now going to happen without me. At the end of the service, I asked the congregation, "Hey, guess what's happening next week?"

They looked at me expectantly.

"Church," I told them.

As I write this, I am humbled by the thought that in less than two weeks, I'll be standing before a new congregation, in a new city, delivering my first sermon.

We already have events on our family calendar that we'll be attending in just a little over a week. I've been getting emails about meetings I plan to attend, a leadership retreat after the first of the year, and much more.

It's pretty exciting to take on new challenges, embrace a new family of faith, explore a new city, hear new stories, and begin a new journey.

But it's also very humbling and comforting to know that I am just one small part of the whole story that is being written by the One who knows how the story ends. It's a privilege to be of service and an honor to serve the church, the body of Christ, wherever I happen to be called.

And to be constantly reminded that the church is God's, not mine.

God Blows Your Mind with Faithfulness

In May 2002, and my wife, Merideth, and I were in a strange situation and about to do something bonkers. We were leaving our beautiful home and a wonderful life in Tallahassee, Florida, to move to downtown Chicago so I could go to seminary. And on top of that, we had to sell our house and my car—by the end of June.

We, in fact, did find a buyer for our house—unexpectedly and right on time. The sale of the house closed right at the end of June, precisely when we needed it and on the very day that we drove away in our rented moving truck with all our worldly goods inside it.

And my car—wait until you read this. I had resigned myself to the fact that the sale of the car wasn't going to happen while I was still in Florida, and I'd made arrangements to leave it with a friend to keep it on the market.

One week to the day when we left, we were holding a garage sale, and a guy approached me about the car and asked if it was for sale. He ended up buying it on the spot. So I got to drive my car all the way up to the eleventh hour—right before we moved.

I'm writing today's devotion a bit later than usual because I am in a car dealership, selling my car. In a little less than a week, we'll be driving away to Austin, Texas, and I was thinking that my car wasn't going to sell before then—or at the very least, I was going to end up selling it at a tremendous loss.

I ended up getting the best price I've been offered by anyone and sold the car with less than one week to go.

Fourteen years after that epic move to Chicago, we find ourselves in a very familiar situation: praising God for God's timing and God's providence.

Merideth and I never ceased to be amazed at the many ways God just keeps reminding us that God is ordering our steps, going before us, telling us time and time again that we are God's, and as long as we keep stepping, God will keep blowing our minds with God's faithfulness.

The verse of the day in my YouVersion Bible app was from 1 Corinthians 15:57, which reads: "But thanks be to God! He gives us the victory through our Lord Jesus Christ" (NIV).

May your eyes be opened today to see all the ways God is guiding you, covering you in grace, and sustaining you, even in times of uncertainty. May your ears be opened to hear God's voice offering you encouragement, grace, and love. May your heart be ever softened to be moved to obedience that leads to abundant life.

I Was Just Coming to Work

Today's devotion is a bit more personal than usual. Earlier this week, my family had the unbelievable privilege of celebrating with my dad when he retired from Walt Disney World, after working there for nearly thirty-four years. For the past twenty years or so, he's worked in Guest Relations at the Magic Kingdom, and he became an institution—the patriarch of the department in more ways than one.

One after the other, his colleagues, supervisors, and friends spoke of all the ways my dad has impacted their lives—through his words of encouragement, admirable work ethic, kindness to everyone, a shoulder to cry on, a sympathetic ear, a hug when one was needed.

His coworkers and supervisors treated my dad like royalty and us along with him. He was honored like no other Disney World cast member, and that's saying something. We were told that things were done for him that never had been done for anyone—ever. People my dad has worked with over the years stood in line to hug him, to take a photo with him, and to shed a few tears with him.

One young woman, who was sobbing, came up to me and told me how much she would miss my dad. "You have no idea how much he means to me," she said.

I looked around at that moment and saw more than a few people wiping their eyes, trying to find ways to express what they were feeling.

It was overwhelming and beautiful to experience all of that gratitude. All those people gathered to give thanks for my dad and to show their gratitude for the way he'd lived his life among them, showed grace to them, demonstrated the love of Jesus in front of them.

As I was hugging him at the end of the day, I told him how very proud I was of him—and how proud I was to be his son.

My dad told me, "I had no idea I was doing so much. I was just coming to work." Those words have stuck with me for the past couple of days. *"I was just coming to work."*

There is a verse in Ecclesiastes that reads, "Whatever your hand finds to do, do it with all your might" (Ecclesiastes 9:10 NIV).

My dad never once dreamed that he one day would work in Guest Relations at Walt Disney World. He'd trained to be a teacher, after all, and to serve in ministry to the church. But God, in his wisdom, allowed him to work in a place where he taught so many people lasting lessons about goodness and grace and where he did incredible ministry in the name of Jesus.

Today, I am so grateful for my dad—for his faithful Christian witness, his genuine love of others, and his desire to do whatever God has given him to do with all of his might. I can only pray that I will have half as much of a lasting effect on the people God has placed in my path.

We Are Known

A couple of years ago, I was wandering around a mall, holding my Starbucks Venti Skinny Cinnamon Dolce Latte. I wandered into a store, and one of the employees working there called out to me. "Leon!" he exclaimed. "How've you been, man? What's happening? So good to see you, Leon."

I was taken aback and started searching my memory banks for any clue that might tell me who the guy was. "I'm good, dude," I said slowly. "How have things been with you?"

"Leon," the guy replied, "things have been so good; I can't even complain."

I finally broke down. "Do I know you, dude? How do you know who I am?"

He laughed and pointed at my Starbucks cup. "It's on your cup, man."

Sure enough, there, on the top of my cup, was my name, printed in large black letters by the barista just a few moments before.

That guy taught me a valuable lesson, however. For a few brief moments, I thought of a bunch of ways that he would have known who I was. Here are just a few: (1) he bought my book; (2) we are friends on Facebook; (3) he follows my blog; (4) he has seen video of me preaching; (5) he's read stories in a newspaper where I was interviewed; (6) he saw a recent television news story about me and my church; (7) he's attended my church at some point.

The truth is, I wanted the guy to know me for those kinds of reasons. Those were the first things that went through my head, in fact. They represented many of the things I had done to make myself known to others. And when I realized the guy knew my name because of my silly cup, I felt a weird kind of sadness wash over me.

I believe, in the end, what each of us really wants is to be truly known. Further, I believe that each of us secretly hopes that if we are truly known, it might give us some concrete evidence that we are not alone in the universe.

Jesus often taught about the relentless love of God. In John 10:29, we hear him say in front of his followers, "My Father, who has given [my disciples] to me, is greater than all; no one can snatch them out of my Father's hand" (John 10:29 NIV).

Jesus's parting words to his followers were that he would never leave or forsake them—words that we can claim and hold on to as well.

May you realize, today and every day, that you are known and loved by God. May you be surrounded by the Creator's great love for you through his Son and by the power of the Spirit. May you know, deep in your very soul, that you are never, ever alone.

The Best Way to Know God

I recently watched several videos made by people who are currently trapped in the city of Aleppo, Syria. The government forces are, even now, moving closer to the rebel-held areas of the city; bombardments have been renewed; more destruction is imminent.

Many of the people making the videos declared that these probably would be the last ones they would make. "[Government forces] are executing people in the streets," one woman grimly declared. Behind her, you could make out the bombed-out, burned-out remains of what had once been a thriving city.

When the innocent are wounded and killed, when war rages, when disaster strikes, when in our own lives we experience loss, grief, and pain, the question that comes to our minds most often is, simply, "Where is God?"

I admit that sometimes it's harder for me to come up with comforting answers to that question—especially when I'm the one asking it. I do take some small comfort, however, in knowing that we're not alone when we wonder if God is taking a powder when bad things are happening.

In the Hebrew scriptures, Job acknowledges this conflict when he says, "And these are but the outer fringe of his works; how faint the whisper we hear of him! Who then can understand the thunder of his power?" (Job 26:14 NIV).

The best and purest way to understand what God is up to in the world is through Jesus—the fullest expression of God to us. Through Jesus, we find accessibility to the Almighty, knowledge of the unknowable, evidence of the beloved presence of the omnipresent.

In John 8:12, Jesus declares, "I am the light of the world. The person who follows me will never live in darkness, but will have the light that gives life" (NIV).

Jesus embodies God for us, enabling us to understand what God is saying, what God loves, what God abhors, and what God wants for us and for all of creation. And we also know, through Jesus's own experience, that sometimes when things are very, very bad, we wonder where God is in the midst of it.

After all, when Jesus was on the cross, he cried out "My God! My God! Why have you forsaken me?" (Matthew 27:46 NIV). This should give us all hope when we wonder, doubt, and struggle because, as we know, God never left Jesus alone. In fact, God raised Jesus from the dead to prove it.

May you find ways to look to Jesus today as you wrestle with knowing and experiencing God.

Live Every Day as if It's Your Last

I have a friend who has been living with cancer for a decade. He's in remission now, a brief respite from the dread disease that still lurks below the surface. The whole ordeal changed him, both inside and out.

I read his Facebook posts now with a sense of wonder. He reflects on the world with a wisdom that I long to obtain. His outlook on the world is one that is permeated with hope and gravitates toward truth, beauty, and goodness.

I wish so badly that I could be like him—to see the world with eyes filled with wonder, to speak honestly and plainly about what needs to be made right in society, to bear witness to Jesus without pretense. I want all these things, but without going through the trials and tribulations that shaped him, of course.

In his *Meditations*, Marcus Aurelius wrote,

> This is the mark of perfection of character—to spend each day as if it were your last, without frenzy, laziness or any pretending.

I got to thinking about those words, and it led me to reflect on my own struggles to be the person I know that God desires me to be.

I think one of the things that has helped my friend develop such a keen sense of where God is at work in the world is that he was forced to empty himself of himself. He faced his own frailty and mortality and surrendered it, and when his life was given back to him, he found it had been refined, reshaped, and restored by grace.

Most of the moments I've regretted in my life have been when I've thought I could become "like God" and live as though I have all the time in the world. It's interesting how that mistaken belief can cause you to live in frenzy, laziness, and falsehood.

The Prodigal Son's first words in the story Jesus told in Luke 15 were, "Father, give me" (Luke 15:12 NIV). He wanted what he felt he was due. His desire was to become the center of his own universe.

But when all was lost and he came to grips with his brokenness and frailty, the words he spoke to the father were, "Make me." When he emptied himself of himself, he desired only to be reformed, reshaped, and redeemed.

May you live today as it were your last day. Fill it with moments of truth and beauty. Empty yourself of yourself, and be filled with the all-encompassing Spirit of God.

Direction Determines Destination

Evangelist E. Stanley Jones once told the story of a traveler who asked for directions to a certain destination. He got his response from a local man: "If you go on the way you are headed, it will be about 25,000 miles. But if you turn around, it will be about three."

That story reminded me of Pastor Andy Stanley's "Principle of the Path," which essentially states, "It's your direction, not your intention that determines your destination." Regardless of your good intentions, if you are headed in the wrong direction, you won't get to where you want to go.

The difficult bit sometimes is figuring out which is the right path. There are times when it is clearer than others, to be sure.

When choosing between self-destructive behavior or life-giving habits, the right way is not that hard to figure out, even though we often choose poorly and find ourselves in need of repentance.

But what about those moments when it's hard to know what to do, which way to choose? What happens when we have multiple options before us, and it's hard to decide? How do you choose one career move over another? One treatment option over another? One relationship over another?

How do you figure out what God might be calling you to do in terms of your life's mission? How do you find your purpose?

In Psalm 142, the psalmist is crying out to God for help, protection, and guidance. He feels trapped, immobilized, and beset upon from all sides by difficult decisions and challenges. And then he prays, "When my spirit grows faint within me, it is you who watch over my way" (Psalm 142:3 NIV).

The question you need to ask yourself as you prayerfully consider your future is simply this: "Am I desiring God, first and foremost, in all of this?" And if the answer to that question is an emphatic *yes*, then you need to be ready to act.

At some point, we simply need to surrender the outcomes, step forward in faith, and trust that God will guide and order our steps.

May you turn your heart toward a desire for God today and every day. May you find in that desire the very peace and confidence you seek to step forward in faith, knowing that the One who loves you more than anyone is watching over your way.

You Are Not a Reservoir of Worry

I have known what it's like to feel perfect peace about a decision I've made, a problem that is before me, a crisis that I have to face. I know that feeling, and it's amazing. But sometimes in the midst of dealing with decisions, problems, and crises, I find myself having a hard time connecting with that feeling of peace.

And most of the time, the reason why I struggle to connect with that feeling of peace (one that should be familiar) is because I am trying too hard to control the outcomes.

Sometimes, I even start to work against God's purposes by doing dumb and self-destructive things. I remember when I was fighting God's calling to go into ministry. I walked around morose, miserable, angry, and worrying about everything. I was working on a master's degree in history and had to drag myself to class every day. Everything in my life became a chore.

I started seeing a therapist, who made me take a bunch of tests. He showed me the results and pointed to a graph with his pen. "See that line? That's the baseline that denotes depression."

I nodded.

"See this other squiggly line? That's you."

I noted that my squiggly line dipped below the baseline.

"Yep," he said to me, "you're depressed."

I'd like to tell you that my transformation was miraculous, but it took some time for me to figure out I wasn't in control and that worrying my self sick wasn't going to make my problems, decisions, or issues go away.

The apostle Paul wrote about this in his letter to the Philippians:

> Do not be anxious about everything, but in everything, by prayer and petition, with thanksgiving, present your requests to God. And the peace of God, which passes understanding will guard your hearts and your minds in Christ Jesus. (Philippians 4:6–7 NIV)

E. Stanley Jones once wrote, "We are not meant to be reservoirs of worry. We are instead channels, attached to infinite resources." I love that quote.

The feeling of peace that I long for when I am in the middle of worry is not far away. The "infinite resources" that Jones is talking about come from God, who is never far from me. And all I have to do to access these resources and the awesome peace that comes with them is to reach out my hand, so to speak.

You are not a reservoir of worry. You are attached to infinite resources of peace and hope. If you are worrying today, pray that God will cover your worry with his peace. If you are fretting over the future, ask God to give you the kind of peace that doesn't make any sense. And then simply be still and know that God is God, and you are not.

Believing without "Proof"

I once visited the island country of Malta, which is south of Italy and just north of Tunisia. Malta is a beautiful country with a rich history. Wherever we went, we encountered one of the over three hundred churches that were dotted throughout the island, many of them large, ornate buildings.

One of those churches, which I'd visited on a previous trip to Malta, is Shipwreck Cathedral—a church built on the traditional site where (as the book of Act relates) the apostle Paul washed ashore with the passengers and crew of a ship, which crashed into rocks just off Malta's coast.

Paul told everyone on board the ship to not be afraid, that God would not allow anyone to lose their life in the wreck, and his prediction came true, of course. The Maltese people welcomed the survivors and gave them food and supplies.

As Paul was gathering wood for a fire, a poisonous snake bit him on the hand and refused to let go. He had to shake the snake off into the fire. Everyone expected Paul to be dead by morning because the snake (an asp) was one of the deadliest in the region. But Paul didn't die of the snake bite, which caused no end of consternation and wonder among the people who saw the whole thing.

When I stand in a church that was founded nearly 1,800 years ago on what was believed to be the spot where Paul shook a poisonous snake off his hand, I get a funny feeling. Although I believe that these stories in the book of Acts happened, being in that spot leads me to say to myself, "This was real. It was actually real."

I admit that I am frail, and sometimes I need to see, I need to experience, I need some proof that I can feel deep down in my bones that God is real, Jesus is alive, the Bible is true, and all of this Christian stuff means something.

But the thing that's even more amazing is that there are scores and scores of people who believe and dedicate their lives to following Jesus with less proof and hardly any feelings like the one I've described.

Jesus responded to a statement of faith by Thomas, one of his disciples who saw Jesus risen from the dead, by saying, "Blessed are you that you have seen and believed." And then Jesus asked, "How much more blessed will those be who have not seen and still believe?" (John 20:29 NIV).

May you discover new ways to find your faith renewed that are based on trust and obedience. May you find your doubts and fears stilled inside your heart as you simply choose to experience God all around you.

Mary's Yes and What It Means

On the outer wall of the Our Lady of Assumption Church in the medieval town of Erice, Sicily, is a whole row of marble crosses that were embedded there in the early 1400s.

In the early medieval period, the main church of Erice was at the very highest point of the town, but because people were still practicing pagan rituals to Venus, the Roman goddess of fertility, in the early 1300s, the church was built on the site of the ancient temple to erase it from memory.

I got to thinking about the whole thing after I took a photo of one of the crosses. The church was dedicated to Mary, the mother of Jesus, and this church was built on the site of Venus, the goddess of fertility. I wondered if there was something deeper at work—even deeper than the intentions of those medieval builders.

The worship of Venus that took place in that ancient temple in Sicily would have been filled with a great deal of perversity and fleshly indulgence. Both male and female prostitutes would have worked at the temple, plying their trade and extracting both funds and favors from worshippers who desired fertility and health, both for themselves and for their land.

This kind of worship would have cost these ancient worshippers in more than just coin. The cult of Venus was demanding and degrading—financially, physically, sexually, and psychologically. Venus had to have her way, or you wouldn't get yours.

By contrast, the Church of Our Lady of Assumption was dedicated to a teenaged girl who found favor with God but was given incredible news. As we know, Mary was given the unenviable task of a miraculous conception that would have been impossible to explain to anyone else. She would be the mother of the Savior, the Messiah, but it would cost her more than she would know.

Mary could have said no, but instead, she submitted humbly to the will of God and took on a burden few would ever comprehend. Her humility, strength, submission, and sacrifice are worthy of our admiration and emulation.

Mary's example is in stark contrast to the demands of the pagan goddess that was worshipped on that ancient site in Erice. It is, in fact, in stark contrast to the many false gods that we have constructed in our own culture—materialism, consumerism, hedonism, and so on—that turn us into selfish and self-indulgent creatures.

May you seek the same humility and submission to God's will that Mary exhibited—dedicated to serving others and denying your own desires in favor of what is best and brightest for the kingdom of God. May you find purpose and meaning in service.

Share Your Story

Yesterday, I stood on the Areopagus in the center of Athens, Greece.

The Areopagus is the site where the apostle Paul addressed some of the leading intellectuals of the city, using Athenian cultural references and their own curiosity about religion and new ideas to preach the gospel to them.

The apostle Paul was astounded at the number of gods that were being worshipped in Athens, and he began sharing his "new ideas" with a twist:

> So Paul took his stand in the open space at the Areopagus and laid it out for them. "It is plain to see that you Athenians take your religion seriously. When I arrived here the other day, I was fascinated with all the shrines I came across. And then I found one inscribed, to the god nobody knows. I'm here to introduce you to this God so you can worship intelligently, know who you're dealing with. (Acts 17:22–23 MSG)

I can imagine that Paul looked over his shoulder at the temples high above him when he was witnessing to the Athenians. Then he referenced one of the great poets of Athens, Aratus, and said the following:

> [God] doesn't play hide-and-seek with us. He's not remote; he's near. We live and move in him, can't get away from him! One of your poets said it well: 'We're the God-created.' Well, if we are the God-created, it doesn't make a lot of sense to think we could hire a sculptor to chisel a god out of stone for us, does it? (Acts 17:27–29 MSG)

While we were standing on the Areopagus, we met a woman and her daughter from South Africa. She told us she had a "testimony" and then shared that twelve years ago, her husband had died, leaving her with two small girls. She told us that she believed God had "become her husband" and a father to her daughters. Her belief in God and her staunch faith as a Christian had sustained her through some terrible times.

It struck me how incredible it was that nearly two thousand years after the apostle Paul stood on that very spot, sharing the good news that God was redeeming all of creation through the Resurrection of Jesus Christ, our new friend from South Africa was doing the same thing. Paul had no idea of the impact that message would have. He just shared his testimony.

May you share your testimony with boldness and grace. May you tell the story of how God is redeeming all of creation but, more specifically, how God has and continues to redeem you. The culture around us longs for better news and a bigger story. You have that story. You are that story. Share your story. You never know how God will use it.

In the Cave of the Apocalypse

This past week, I got to do something that I have wanted to do for years—I visited the island of Patmos, the traditional site where the book of Revelation was born. In the first chapter of Revelation, we find these words from John the Revelator:

> I, John, with you all the way in the trial and the Kingdom and the passion of patience in Jesus, was on the island called Patmos because of God's Word, the witness of Jesus. It was Sunday and I was in the Spirit, praying. I heard a loud voice behind me, trumpet-clear and piercing: "Write what you see into a book. (Revelation 1:9–11 MSG)

Tradition teaches that it was John the Evangelist, the youngest of the disciples of Jesus, who received the revelation while he was in exile on Patmos. These traditions teach that he would climb the highest hill on the island to pray inside a cave. It was in that cave that he saw the vision that would become the Apocalypse, or the book of Revelation.

We visited the Cave of the Apocalypse while we were on Patmos. The Greek Orthodox Church established a monastery on the site of the sacred cave over one thousand years ago. The site had been a place of worship for almost a millennium before.

The sanctuary built around the cave was dimly lit by candles and a couple of weak electric chandeliers. The walls were completely covered by paintings, elaborate gold and silver icons, and other adornments. The smell of incense was overpowering.

The guide told us that we would see two niches in the cave—one where Saint John would rest his head while he prayed and another where he would sit. As I walked by them, I felt something stir inside of me. My usual skepticism was replaced by the power of reverence—the kind of reverence that comes when you realize that you are just one small part of a much bigger thing.

For nearly two thousand years, faithful Christians have worshiped on that site—a site where even the most jaded person would have to admit that *something* happened. When that realization hits you, it isn't easy to shake. I gazed on the walls of the cave in awe, with my eyes misting over.

I was overwhelmed by the glorious weight of the "great cloud of witnesses" who had gone before me in the Christian faith and who, I believe, are still cheering us all on as we take up the mantle of knowing and showing Jesus in our own lifetimes.

May you take great comfort in knowing that you are part of something incredible—the church, the body of Christ, the visible hands and feet of Jesus in the world. May you find encouragement and joy in the knowledge that those who paved the way are lifting you up even now.

God Is All Around You and In You

In his book *Finding God in Unexpected Places*, Philip Yancey writes about encountering a remarkable woman in South Africa, who started a ministry in one of the most violent prisons in the country.

In one year, the prison went from 279 reported acts of violence down to two. Yancey asked her how she was able to accomplish such an incredible task. She told him that God was already present in the prison; she just needed to help reveal his presence to the inmates.

I think the dominant understanding of God in Christian culture needs some work. The fact of the matter is that God *is* present in all things, in all spaces, in all times. I have come to believe that God is the very "ground of our being," as some theologians have offered.

But most of us struggle to experience God because we've been taught that God is high in his holy temple, removed from us by some imaginary gulf between heaven and earth. So many people still see God as a slightly grumpy old man with a white beard, peering through the clouds, watching to make sure we don't mess things up too badly.

It's difficult to talk about God without imposing some of our own desires and ideas upon God, which, in turn, serves to limit our understanding of God. I know. It sounds kind of messed up, but here's a way to understand this better, by way of a couple of questions.

What if God was so much more than merely a being, like we are beings? What if we were able to imagine God (as those theologians I mentioned believed) as the very source of all things? And what if God, in God's infinite wisdom, decided to impart some of God's DNA to human beings?

Consider this: when that woman Philip Yancey met in South Africa walked into that awful prison, she carried with her some innate knowledge that propelled her into a vibrant and powerful ministry of restoration and redemption.

Here's what she knew: every one of those inmates was created in God's image with the same God-given ability to create beauty, fulfill their destiny, and embrace eternal life with God through Jesus. They just didn't know it.

In the story of the Feeding of the Five Thousand in the Gospel of John, the five loaves and two fish were completely insufficient in the hands of the young boy who brought them, but when they were turned over to Jesus, they became something much more.

May we live our lives today filled with the realization of God's presence in the world and in everyone we meet. May we fulfill our purpose as followers of Jesus to be lights that enable others to see God and to see themselves as God sees them.

Living Life with Wild Abandon

My late mom went through some of her keepsakes a few years ago and found my very first driver's license among them. She brought it over to my house to give to me, and I've had it sitting on my desk the past day or so—a glaring reminder of how old I've become in the past thirty-one years since it was issued.

That kid in the photo had a defined chin and a nice thin neck. He had a full head of hair, to boot.

Funny, isn't it? I can't recall much of what was happening in my life when I turned sixteen, but I remember that feeling of freedom when I drove slowly around my neighborhood, looking for some girls to impress.

I've often heard it lamented that (to paraphrase the great playwright George Bernard Shaw) youth seems to be wasted on the young. I suppose there's some truth in that. Then again, freedom, hope, and the prospect of limitless possibility are feelings that shouldn't be stifled, especially for those of us who believe in the Resurrection of Jesus.

Because of the Resurrection of Jesus, we have the hope of unbounded freedom from anything and everything that would enslave us or keep us down. Because of the Resurrection of Jesus, there are no limits on what is possible from a God who is still in the business of doing impossible things.

"If the Son sets you free," Jesus told his followers, "you will be free indeed" (John 8:36 NIV).

So why is it that we live our lives by looking backward instead of forward? Why, when we have been set free and given limitless possibilities through Jesus, do we choose to live in less-than ways? Why do we too often make the road of life a lifeless commute, rather than a top-down, radio-blaring, wind-in-our-faces joyride?

The thirteenth-century poet Rumi wondered the same thing. He wrote, "When a bird gets free, it does not go back for remnants left on the bottom of the cage."

I believe that Jesus means for us to live our lives with wild abandon—full of hope, giddy with the limitless possibility of the road before us.

"For freedom," the apostle Paul wrote, "Christ has set us free stand firm therefore and don't go back to the enslaved life you used to live" (Galatians 5:1 NIV).

May you discover newfound freedom today and every day forward. May you see the road before you as a path to new adventures, undreamed possibilities, and abundant life. May you be known as a sold-out, hope-filled follower of Christ who lives in joy.

Trust Leads to Joy

Yesterday, I officiated at a communion service at one of our local assisted-living communities. As part of the service, I offered a short homily. *Homily*, in case you were wondering, is a Latin word that means "short sermon." I can't really back up that last claim, honestly, but at any rate, it was a short sermon, of sorts.

I'd intended my homily to be about joy, but as I stood up to speak, I was struck by a feeling that the words I'd prepared were woefully inadequate for that particular moment. I think I had planned to say something or another about having joy in your heart all of the time and how having joy would change the world around you. Great sentiments, to be sure.

But as I looked out over the small crowd of older adults who had gathered, I realized that my cheery sentiments weren't going to cut it.

Every person there was struggling with physical issues. One was confined to a wheelchair, and the others were using walkers to get around. In a rush, a question came into my head: "How do you find joy in your life when your life has been diminished by age, illness, circumstances, tragedy, or a host of other things?"

And in a flash, the word came to me: trust.

I paused before I spoke, and then I shared what God had placed on my heart, not what I had prepared. You see, the basic element that is required for true joy—the joy of the Lord—is trust.

When we live our lives in fear of tomorrow, in bitterness over our present circumstances, or regretting the past, we are demonstrating our lack of trust in a God who loves us and who gave himself for us in the person of Jesus Christ.

But if we trust that God is good and that through Jesus Christ, God has already defeated sin and death for our sake, we should have no problem at all feeling joy in any circumstance. The apostle Paul declared that he had learned "to be content in any situation, no matter the circumstances" (Philippians 4:12 NIV). This was a guy who wrote those very words while he was chained to a guard in prison. If you truly trust God with all of your heart, then you will find deep reservoirs of joy to draw from, no matter what is going on around you.

You will find these reservoirs of joy because your trust in God has removed all of the fear, anxiety, bitterness, regret, and anger that has kept you from finding them.

May you know what it is to truly trust God and to give him your whole life. May you be released from all of the things that would inhibit your trust and keep your from feeling the joy of the Lord.

Being on the Way

I was reading one of the daily devotional books that I read nearly every day, and a passage of scripture quoted in the reading caught my eye. In this passage from Genesis 24, the servant of Abraham is speaking, and he says the most incredible thing about his journey to find a suitable wife for Abraham's son, Isaac.

In the middle of the story, the servant of Abraham says, "As for me, being on the way, the Lord led me" (Genesis 24:27 NKJV).

You might be wondering why this verse is remarkable. Think about what the servant *doesn't* say. He doesn't say, "I waited to start my journey until I had clear directions from God." He doesn't say, "I wanted to be careful about which way I went, so I waited until I knew for sure where God wanted me to go." He says, "Being on the way, the Lord led me."

In other words, the servant stepped out in faith, believing that God would guide him. He didn't wait for confirmation on when or where he should take the first steps of his journey, he just started walking and trusted that God would lead him.

I was having a conversation with my wife the other day about a time in our life when we began a new journey together, even though the way forward wasn't clear. What we knew then, beyond a shadow of a doubt, was that if we didn't take those first steps, we wouldn't get very far.

And there was something about those first steps that just felt right. As we prayed fervently for God's will to be revealed, what came to both of us was an overwhelming desire to step out in faith and trust God to do the rest.

We also knew instinctively that somewhere along the way, God would meet us on the road and reveal the way. I told Merideth, "You know, every time we've stepped out in faith like that, God has never let us down." We reminisced then on the miraculous ways God has provided for us, showed us incredible signs, and kept leading us forward.

Author, preacher, and evangelist E. Stanley Jones once wrote, "Don't ask for the whole way; ask for the next step."

If you are struggling today with a decision you need to make, a change in your life that needs to happen, or a journey you need to take, step out in faith. Don't be afraid where your feet will land; God will guide them. Surrender yourself to this knowledge, and allow it to grant you peace.

When You Wonder Where God Is

Some years ago, someone asked me if I thought their family was cursed. The person related a litany of horrible things that had happened to family members over the course of the previous year. It was one awful thing after another.

My instinct was to say, "It sure seems like it." There was no good explanation for why so many bad things had come their way. But I sure understood their need to find a reason for the bad things—to discover some kind of meaning in their suffering. I simply told them that sometimes things happened; it didn't have to do with a curse.

I remember reading something about this in Philip Yancey's great book *Where Is God When It Hurts?* Yancey addressed the way that so many of us seek answers from the scripture to help us understand why we are suffering, but we don't always get the answers we're looking for.

Yancey wrote,

> The Bible consistently changes the questions we bring to the problem of pain. It rarely, or ambiguously, answers the backward-looking question "Why?" Instead, it raises the forward-looking question, "To what end?"

In my devotions today, I read from Psalm 109:30–31, which states, "With my mouth I will greatly extol the Lord, in the great throng of worshipers I will praise him. For he stands at the right hand of the needy, to save their lives from those who would condemn them" (NIV).

In ancient Hebrew law courts, the accuser would stand at the right hand of the accused in order to prosecute the case against them. The psalmist turns this image around, placing God in the right-hand role, ready to defend the one who is needy, not to accuse them.

If that person who asked me whether their family was cursed was standing in front of me today, I think I would have a better answer than the one I gave then. I would still tell them that sometimes things just happen and that I don't believe for a minute that God causes all things. I do believe, however, that God is present in the midst of all things.

Which means God suffers with us, mourns with us, and laments with us. God is not far away from us when we are going through suffering. Instead, like Psalm 130 indicates, he is standing at our right hand, defending us against whatever evil might be working to bring us down. And this enables us to actively and boldly seek to discover what we might gain from the experience.

May you feel the loving, protective presence of God with you today and every day. May you come to know the kind of hope that comes from trusting your future to a God who is continually establishing a hopeful future.

I'd Rather Be a Doorkeeper

Years ago, when I was in seminary, I served as the youth director of a large suburban Chicago church. Because the church was located in a very high crime area, it had a pretty stringent security process, which required someone to staff the front entrance and screen whoever was trying to enter.

During the day, a paid staffer monitored the entrance, but in the evenings, it was zealously guarded by a particular volunteer. This volunteer—I'll call him Bob—was an older man with a not-so-convincing gruff demeanor. Bob was a big guy, and even though he'd stooped some with age, he still set an imposing figure, albeit one that was pretty soft around the edges.

Bob's eyesight wasn't the best. It took a couple of years before he could recognize me through the glass door well enough to let me in on those rare nights when I didn't have my keys with me. He read his devotional books and his Bible every evening, using a huge magnifying glass to see the words.

I know what you're thinking. "Seriously? A half-blind dude watching the door to the church? That's pretty safe." There's some truth in that, I suppose.

But all in all, Bob was very good at his job. He didn't have a lot of money and couldn't even walk all that well. He took the bus or a cab to the church every day (even when there was two feet of snow on the ground), and there were more than a few nights when I had to give him a ride home.

Yet he was always there at the door, serving, greeting people, connecting with my youth-group kids, and being a calm, caring presence of hospitality.

This morning, I was reading my own devotional book, and I came across this verse in Psalm 84:

> Better is one day in your courts than a thousand elsewhere; I would rather be a doorkeeper in the house of the my God than dwell in the tents of the wicked. (Psalm 84:10 NIV)

Every day when Bob would show up at the church, he would bring along a little sign to place at the desk where he sat. On that plaque was the last part of Psalm 84:10: "I would rather be a doorkeeper in the house of my God."

As I read that verse today, I thought of Bob sitting at that desk, reading his Bible with that huge magnifying glass, faithfully filling his post, night after night. There were no accolades for Bob. Not many people saw him doing what he did. But every night, he shuffled to that front desk, put up his sign, and served the Lord. I will never forget him.

May you find the humility and strength to serve God with whatever gifts you have, in whatever way you can, and with the most joy and diligence you can muster.

Creation Is an Ongoing Process

In just a little while, I will be boarding an airplane for a six-hour flight from Orlando to Portland, Oregon—from the East Coast to the West Coast of these United States in just a matter of hours.

It's amazing when you think about it. I'll get inside what is essentially a long metal tube with wings and fly across the country, just like hundreds of thousands, if not millions, of other people today.

Just a little over one hundred years ago, when the Wright Brothers made that first flight at Kitty Hawk, North Carolina, no one could have fully imagined what we are able to do today.

But here's the interesting bit: they did imagine something like it. It would take great imagination, grit, and determination to make that first flight happen. But after that first flight—that's where the real creativity—the otherworldly kinds of dreams and visions—was born, when people began asking, what if?

I think far too many of us Christians have lost our sense of wonder when it comes to our faith. We assume that everything that needs to be said about the Bible, our faith, God, Jesus, Christianity, the church—everything that needs to be said—has already been said.

We start thinking that we have defined everything we could define when it comes to our theology. We start believing that we have the answers at last. We fall back on our certainty with a sense of pride, perhaps.

Jesus said something very interesting to his disciples once:

> Very truly I tell you, whoever believes in me will do the works I have been doing, and they will do even greater things than these, because I am going to the Father. (John 14:12 NIV)

Jesus gave something to his disciples that was truly amazing. He gave them potential—potential through the power of the Holy Spirit of God. He wanted them to dream, to imagine, to act with boldness, to heal, to practice resurrection, and spread the gospel to the whole world.

He taught us that God is still speaking—that creation is still in progress, that resurrection is springing up all around us. And that we can be a part of sharing this glorious news with anyone who will listen.

May you be filled with wonder and holy imagination today and every day. May you dare to dream of a world made right, of lives restored, of brokenness mended. May you share the good news of resurrection life every moment, every day, all of the time.

Maybe It's Time for New Rhythms

As human beings, we know that we have rhythms of wakefulness and rest. Our bodies become accustomed to these rhythms, even when our particular rhythms might be pushing the limits of what we should be experiencing.

For example, I went to bed last night, exhausted after a long day of meetings. I figured I would sleep until my alarm went off, but I was mistaken. A full thirty minutes before my alarm sounded, I awoke and could not go back to sleep, regardless of how tired I felt.

I started thinking about all of the nights I stay up too late, working, watching TV, answering emails, and the like. I also started thinking about all of the stressors, busyness, deadlines, and such that are always on my mind, sometimes causing me to wake long before my alarm—and I often lie there in bed, working through problems and thinking about my schedule and a host of other things.

There is a passage in the book of Hebrews that talks about what it really means to keep the Sabbath—that it's not just one day of not working. Sabbath, as it was intended, was a way of orienting your life, of living in a rhythm that was life-giving and God-honoring.

> There remains, then, a Sabbath-rest for the people of God; for those who enter God's rest also rest from their own work, just as God did from his. Let us, therefore, make every effort to enter that rest, so that no one will perish by following [the ancient Israelites] example of disobedience. (Hebrews 4:9–11 NIV)

The writer of Hebrews is affirming the Jewish belief that a lack of Sabbath-keeping leads to death. In other words, if you keep pushing the limits, if you keep working like you are enslaved, if you don't take the time to do life-giving things, to rest, and to find peace, you will end up killing yourself, physically and spiritually.

Maybe it's time for some new rhythms. If you are living your life from one crisis to the next, one stressor after another, perhaps it's time for a change. Sabbath is more than just taking a day off; it's a way of thinking and being. When you have a Sabbath mindset, you discover time for rest that complements your time for work. You also find an inner peace that defies busyness and the frantic lifestyle that so many of us are tempted to lead.

May you find Sabbath rest today and every day. May you keep the Sabbath with your whole life, finding rhythms of rest, work, and play that give you eternal life, both now and forever.

God Is OK with Bragging

Did you know that God is totally fine with bragging? Don't get me wrong; God is never cool with you bragging about *yourself*. For example, in Jeremiah 9:23, the prophet declares the following:

> This is what the Lord says; The wise must not brag about their wisdom. The strong must not brag about their strength. The rich must not brag about their money. (Jeremiah 9:23 MSG)

I met a pastor recently who, within the first hour or so of our meeting, made sure that I knew he had an IQ of 140. I heard later that he also shared this information with his congregation in a sermon not long after he arrived at the church as a new pastor. Additionally, he made sure to bring it up in conversations with church members, staff, etc.

When I heard this, I shook my head in disbelief. "Who does that?" I asked the person who was sharing the information. "I would never do something like that with my congregation. I know better! I guess that's one of the reasons why my church has over 500 people in worship, and his barely has 150!"

And just like that, I went from being righteously indignant over that other pastor's bragging—to bragging in my own right. It's easy to do, isn't it? It's easy to fall back on our own strengths, our own ideas about how we're superior to other people.

The rest of that passage in Jeremiah gives us something to brag about, however, that doesn't land us outside of the will of God.

> But if someone wants to brag, let him brag that he understands and knows me. Let him brag that I am the Lord, and that I am kind and fair, and that I do things that are right on earth. This kind of bragging pleases me. (Jeremiah 9:24 MSG)

This subtle (and very Hebrew) way of reframing what it means to "brag" is so powerful. It means that we aren't pushing our way forward to take credit for all of the good things in our lives; we are acknowledging the sovereign and amazing grace of God that we are able to do and accomplish whatever it is that we accomplish.

But even further, it means that we are also giving glory to the One who makes all good things possible and that a relationship with this One is worth celebrating, sharing, gushing over, and—yes—even bragging about.

May you count all of your blessings, abilities, possessions, successes, and affirmations today as gifts from almighty God, who should get the glory for all of them. May you find ways to celebrate your relationship with God, to share it with others, and to brag on God's grace and mercy.

God Will Never Let You Down

Most of the deep disappointments we have in life happen because of the actions of other people. People let us down. There's not a single person reading this today who hasn't been hurt by another human being. I know that I have to raise my hand, acknowledging this to be true in my own life.

People have betrayed me, and people have stabbed me in the back. People have let me down and shattered my confidence in them. I've vouched for people who have then made me look like a fool for doing so. People have voted against things that mattered to me, sometimes in spite of my efforts to prevent it.

And try as I might, I struggle sometimes to keep my focus on God and not human beings when it comes to seeking affirmation, purpose, and meaning.

There's a pretty hard-core verse from the prophet Jeremiah that speaks some truth about what happens to us when we place all of our trust in people and not God:

This is what the Lord says:

> Cursed are those who put their trust in mere humans, who rely on human strength and turn their hearts away from the Lord. They are like stunted shrubs in the desert, with no hope for the future. They will live in the barren wilderness, in an uninhabited salty land. (Jeremiah 17:5–6 NIV)

The thing about Jewish prophecy is that it's not actually predictive. In other words, what the prophet is saying here is that if you turn your heart from God and rely on human beings for your affirmation, purpose, and meaning, you will find yourself in a very dry place and constantly disappointed.

He is painting a picture of what might be if you take your eyes off God and cast them continually upon others. But God doesn't punish you for your lack of trust; you simply find yourself living a less-than life, continually seeking the approval of others, opening yourself up again and again to heartbreak.

On the other hand, God desires the very best for you. God will never leave or forsake you, despite what others might do or not do to disappoint you. When our faith and trust is in God, we are not immune to disappointment when others let us down, but we simply have God's strength to deal with it and put it in perspective.

May you find your approval, affirmation, purpose, and meaning in the One who created you, loves you, and desires abundant life for you. May you look upon those who let you down with grace and mercy, forgiving them, even as you have been forgiven by God.

Acknowledgments

None of this would have been possible without the relentless encouragement that I received from my wife, Merideth, over the past five years. She has always been my biggest supporter in the creation of these devotions and in everything else in my ministry as well. And she gave up lots of morning time with me—drinking coffee and chatting—in order for me to hole up in my office to read and write. Thanks, honey!

Before she passed away, my mom would faithfully read the "Daily Devos," and after she died in 2017, I found copies of some of the ones that meant a lot to her, printed off her basic printer and stored with her photo albums and keepsakes. I miss her every day. I made a decision not to include the many devotions I wrote before and after her passing—I'll include them in another volume some day.

To my dad, thanks for putting up with me when I have been grumpy, cross, or otherwise a pain in the keister to deal with in the mornings when I was working on all of these. I know it wasn't always easy, but I appreciate it.

To my kids, who sometimes find themselves inserted into these devotions, you continue to teach me more about grace, forgiveness, love, and joy than I ever learned in seminary! I hope that one day, when I'm long gone, you'll pick up this volume and remember some of the things I felt and thought, and that it will bring me close to you.

I also want to thank the many "early adopters" from my former congregation—the First Presbyterian Church of Eustis in Eustis, Florida. For two years, you all were my main audience, and I can't thank you enough for the ways you supported and encouraged me to keep writing. Many of you have hung in there all this time and also kept asking, "When are you going to turn those into a book?"

To my current congregation—Shepherd of the Hills Presbyterian Church—I don't even know where to begin to thank you all for the many ways you have supported the "Daily Devo." You have shared them, commented on them, engaged me in conversations, challenged me, and helped me grow. You have been more than an audience, though. I think of you every time I sit down to write. Thank you from the bottom of my heart.

And to all of my subscribers and avid readers, I don't know what I would do without your engagement and enthusiasm. So many of you encouraged me to write this book. So many of you share these with family and friends. So many of you reach out to me, just when I need to be lifted up, and you do just that. Every single day, I get up and think about you all, wondering if you will find inspiration and hope, challenge and exhortation, and maybe something new to think about.

Let's keep stumbling after Jesus together, shall we? We've got miles to go yet.

Printed in the United States
by Baker & Taylor Publisher Services